A Soldier of Life

A SOLDIER OF LIFE

THE MACMILLAN COMPANY
NEW YORK · BOSTON · CHICAGO · DALLAS
ATLANTA · SAN FRANCISCO

MACMILLAN & CO., LIMITED
LONDON · BOMBAY · CALCUTTA
MELBOURNE

THE MACMILLAN CO. OF CANADA, LTD.
TORONTO

A
SOLDIER OF LIFE

BY

HUGH DE SÉLINCOURT

"For truth needs doing; beauty seems
A dream till we awake from dreams;
A fading wraith, a fugitive
From life until we bid her live."
HENRY BRYAN BINNS.

COPYRIGHT, 1917,
By THE MACMILLAN COMPANY

———

Set up and electrotyped. Published, January, 1917.
Reprinted April, 1917.

To JANET

January, 1916.

A SOLDIER OF LIFE

I

My name is James Wood, and my story is so extra-ordinary that though I have small hope that it will be believed, I feel it is my duty to put it as faithfully as possible on record.

Duty is the right word. To write about myself is contrary to my inclination and contrary to my intention. The business is a nuisance. I am not a hero, not a fine fellow in any guise: simply an ordinary young man with some aptitude for the quiet enjoyment of things, who, after serving in the war and being wounded in the war, quite honestly and gladly felt that he had done with duty for the rest of his life. There is nothing heroic in my make-up.

In one way I am completely ordinary, distressingly and painfully ordinary. My difficulty will be that of the sheep who tried to distinguish himself from his woolly brethren by bleating. His cries were elo-quent, but failed to convince the passer-by, who hardly got so far as realising which sheep was bleat-ing. I might help you to believe what follows if I confessed to punching the housemaid in the eye at the age of eight, or to some other precocious enor-mity, but I regret to say I did not do so. My mis-demeanours were trivial and infrequent, and common

to every other little boy.   I zealously cribbed with
the French master, and was zealously honest with
the form master.   I did as others did.   Perhaps I
was slightly less gregarious; but I never found any
difficulty in getting as much privacy as I wanted.   I
was never bullied by my fellows; never felt wronged
or unjustly treated by my parents or masters.   I
only hope that this confession to the most complete
and uneventful usualness may help to win conviction
for my story; for I have noticed a tendency among
men to like, at times at any rate, to be considered
unusual, below or above the average in some way.
At times, too, I have shared that liking, which plants
me more firmly than ever on the average level—
the level of my flock, you understand—whose brand
signifies public school and 'Varsity—and a very good
brand, too, as brands go.

The war found me unattached.   I had just failed
to obtain a fellowship at one of the minor colleges
at Oxford, and was on the lookout for a youth of
means whom I could escort round the world as a
tutor.   In fact, such a youth had actually been discovered, the route had been mapped out, I was to
start in the spring, ship the following winter—oh,
two years at least, or even three, were arranged to
enchant a far less exacting person than I have ever
been, when war was declared and my life was
changed, like the lives of half the other inhabitants
of Europe.

At first I was appalled by the idea of war, by the
awfulness of the destruction which modern contrivances meant, by the horror at the thought of the

suffering that would come. I was angry at the frightful senselessness, like every one else, and was certain that, but for some bungling or stupidity somewhere, war could quite certainly have been avoided. However, general ideas soon passed before their personal and particular application. What must I do? There was really no question. I had been a member of the O.U.O.T.C., and possessed a certificate that I was adequately trained. I applied for a commission, which I instantly got.

I never felt heroic, however; or only for a brief moment when I donned my uniform for the first time. My chief thought was not patriotic, of laying down my life for my country. My chief dread was not of German bullets, but of the extreme unpleasantness of living gregariously in quarters with other young patriots, for I had come to value privacy more than ever, to become more swiftly tired of company that was not of my choosing. All high thoughts of war and patriotism and so forth went after I had joined the colours. One thing and one only obsessed my mind; one enemy alone I fought hour by hour, minute by minute; and that was the unheroic, unromantic, commonplace fact of boredom. No words of mine can describe it — this active, fierce, insistent boredom. Fresh air and exercise kept you well alive to the full torture of it. It was bad enough at home; but at the front, after the first few days . . . boredom is a cumulative force.

And please do not think I am peculiar in this; companies used to sing, as they trudged about in the mud:

"Nobody knows how bored we are,
Bored we are, bored we are.
Nobody knows how bored we are,
And nobody seems to care."

You awoke from boredom to sights of hell — sordid filth and beastliness — sank back into blacker deeps of boredom; mud for our minds blacker than the mud in which our bodies floundered.

Fortunately I was wounded. I say fortunately with entire seriousness. Badly wounded, yet the pain I suffered in my body from the wounds was nothing to the pain I suffered elsewhere from boredom. I am disabled, and still I regard the wound as fortunate, preferable to the disablement that boredom was working on my spirit. Dirt and horror bore a man more than anything in the world.

You may think that I exaggerate this state of torture. I do not. Imagine being obliged to play hour by hour, day in day out, often too during the night, a game which you thought tedious and silly. That would be bad enough. Our game was worse than that. Our game, played under conditions of filthiness and discomfort — the stench of putrefying corpses made you retch; my body often was lousy as an old cheese — was tedious and silly; and also it was mischievous and destructive. It couldn't even do its own stupid business of destruction — for you can't destroy a nation. Yet we were forced into it. No way at all out of it. The temptation was, not to run away, but to put your head up so that a kindly sniper might give you a final change of experience. Young —— succumbed to that temptation — such a nice chap. He said to me, "I can't stand any more. Good-bye." And before I realised what he meant he exposed his head, and he was in my arms, shot through the eye. Have you seen the hole a bullet makes in a man's head?

There were other instances that I might cite. I will not do so. The war is outside my subject. Only it is necessary that you should understand this boredom — there is no other word; it was something more than the mere weight of shame at being a man at all; a shame that no one mentioned; a shame that stared out of many an eye.

Well — I was wounded. I was taken out of the dull, dirty business. A foot and a hand were smashed. I was stone-deaf. For about a month, I suppose, I was blotted out by pain. Then there came moments of ecstasy when I was without pain. They spread. I felt weak and stiff, but clean and comfortable. Spring was coming. I thought of the lambs in the fields at home. Oh, to see the old sheep cropping, the lambs skip up and waggle their tails in glee as they pulled and pulled at the udder, while the old sheep so calmly surveyed the horizon! The days passed, I was transferred. I could hobble with a crutch, one arm in a sling, the very picture of a wounded hero. I smiled idiotically, like most deaf men.

That journey of delight I must not dwell on. The white cliffs of England, the jolly smell of the land, the feel of the old place, the absurd waiting-room, the hedges, the sheep, the lambs, all touched me with a rapture. In sheer delight, I simply cried

like a pig. I could not help it. And while I cried
there came a sudden roar, like another explosion, in
my head, and the roaring went on until the train
stopped at a wayside halt, my roaring with it. I
heard voices; I seized the man's hand who lay next
to me, and I cried, " I can hear, I can hear, I can
hear!" He said, " Congratters, old man!" and I
subsided. The word was passed through the train.
They were all glad. Looking up I saw a brown
speck in the sky and heard the lark singing what
was the song in my heart.

This incident of my deafness and its sudden re-
moval is important. It put me in a mood to appreciate miracles. It was a link between me and the
greater marvel which was soon to happen. I was
not likely to be blinded with surprise at anything,
because it was outside the range of my experience.
I was not on the lookout for miracles, I was not
credulous or superstitious; but I was humble. My
attitude towards the common facts of nature had
changed. The wind blew, the sun shone, the lambs
played, the birds sang, life burst out in green luxuri-
ance through the hedges and trees — all was quite
in order as usual; I saw them all with new eyes.
You see, I was still very weak, not at all myself. A
passing cloud dropped rain while the sun shone —
sparkling drops; an arch of colour was built across
the sky. My hand shook with sheer excitement.
The shadows that swept over the fields — they
thrilled me so that I knew my nerves were shattered,
and that I needed a long rest, before I should become my normal self, or as far my normal self as I

ever should be without a right foot and a left hand.
Mind you, I did not realise then what I realise now.
I was only prepared for marvels that might meet my
vision in nature; I did not think of my own personality as a part of nature. The unusual excitement was at the time sufficiently explained by my unusual, overwrought state of mind. I did not pay .
much attention to my sensitiveness. I accepted it as
a part of my general condition, but not without a
touch of resentment. I explained it as a natural
reaction, and that in a little while I should regain my
balance.

My mother and sister met me at Victoria and took
me to a nursing home, where I lay in luxury. They
came to see me every day, and under their kindly
influence I felt certain that I should become my
normal self much sooner than I had expected.
They were deliciously the same. I caught their exquisite normality, and entered cheerfully into their
gentle plans for living quietly together for the future — in the country of course; somewhere, anywhere, a quiet, clean, comfortable existence.

The prospect was fair. It slid, as it happens,
pleasantly into the prospect which had from time to
time opened out to me alone. For I had thought
of settling down to write stories. The idea had
come to me when I realised the immense market
there must be in the countless magazines which I
had assiduously read during convalescence. To
catch the little trick of how the tales were put together added interest and helped to pass the time.
I felt sure I could make a good detective story; in-

deed, I had planned one or two adventures. I had no high aim, nothing to say. My wish was to pass the time and earn some money, nothing more.

I throve at the nursing home. On two occasions, however, what I might, much to my chagrin, almost call this other self came into being, the shattered self which set me trembling at the sight of a shower of rain and at the sight of a rainbow.

Once it happened in the nursing home, while I was looking at some primroses which a friend, quite an unromantic friend, had brought me. I was alone, soon after tea, lounging in a long chair, waiting for my nurse to put me to bed. I was looking at the primroses, thinking how nice and pretty they were; lazily trying to remember Wordsworth's lines, which I have always thought moral to absurdity, and getting no nearer than

> " A primrose by a river's brim
>   A simple primrose seemed to him —
> Just that and nothing more."

I was wondering what it ought to have seemed to him if not a primrose — whether a mutton-chop would have been better, or a mustard-pot — when it happened again more definitely than ever. Really it was as sudden and pronounced as the restoration of my hearing. The simple primrose was enough for me. Too much. I saw primroses for the first time. They came to life before my eyes. I could not have been more moved if they had assumed little human faces, little human shapes, solemnly stepped out of the low vase in which they were standing, ranged themselves in a courtly row, and bowed

to me, like flowers in a children's fairy-tale. Their
effect on me was more uncanny because they did not
stir, did not assume any shape, but their own delicate
loveliness.

I stood in a wood carpeted with primroses; a
wood familiar to me from childhood. What was
the life that had pushed up from the black mould
of the solid earth, had taken on this colour? Where
did it get its colour from? What gave the primrose
the five curved leaves of its flower, its delicate circle
of darker yellow, the little cup in which the flower
stood, the glow of its stalk with the myriad tiny hairs,
and the thick green leaf with its shading of grey?
Each primrose was a marvel of exquisite workman-
ship; and they grew in millions; they grew in laughing profusion. And the countless other flowers . . .
the trees and the leaves on the trees. . . . The
same trembling took possession of me. Tears came
into my eyes. My breath came in shudders. I
stretched out my hand, and in a kind of holy rapture
gently pulled — gently between thumb and finger
that responded to the flower's light touch — gently
pulled one primrose from the low vase, and held it
to my face.

The door opened; my nurse came in briskly.
Like a child caught out in some naughtiness I put
the primrose into my buttonhole. I was myself
again.

"Primroses are jolly," I said, and put the whole
thing from my mind. But I could not forget it.
You know, if you've given your ankle a twist, how
carefully you tread for a time, dreading that any

minute it may give again.   Well, it was like that·
only less insistent the feeling, and more permane..

Of course I knew there were worthy people who
have raptures, saints who have ecstasies, poets and
lovers in a fine frenzy rolling, and so forth.   That
is all very well.   But I was not one of them.   I
disliked being taken out of myself in this way.   I
preferred to be myself.   The change was too swift
and disconcerting to be at all pleasant.   I felt that
some other power or Being entered and swamped my
personality, and my personality, such as it was, was
me, and I liked to run it, as it were, on my own lines.
The change and the consciousness of it was, I tell
you, frightening.   The bottom seemed knocked out
of my bucket.   The lunatic, the lover and the poet
— you know the rest.   I was not a poet, not a lover,
and had no sort of wish to become a lunatic.

For a week or two nothing of this queer kind
happened.   I got fat as butter, and went home, to
be spoiled by my mother and sister.   We live in
Surrey.   I practised with a mechanical forearm and
a mechanical foot, with which my uncle was proud,
so the old fellow said, to present me.   Then it happened again — this time worse than before, for this
time it actually happened with my mother and sister;
happened, too, with far more intensity and, owing to
the intimacy of the relationship, with far greater
discomfort.

Now I beg most emphatically to state that we
were an eminently sensible family.   I was fond of
my mother and she was fond of me.   She lived her
own life and was pleased for me to live mine.   We

did not get in each other's way at all, and I felt for
her a natural affection which I could have felt for
no other person.   As for my sister, she was a dear
and healthy girl, engaged to marry a nice and quite
uninteresting man.   Naturally, on my return there
was a good deal more mutual emotion between us
than was customary, but not more than the circumstances called for and not more than I could appreciate.   Naturally too, it broke out again when I got
home.   The wounded hero was shown off a little,
and I played up to the part and liked playing up to
it; but the business was not all overdone and we
had settled quietly down to a proper level, and I
had even begun to write out my detective story, when
I had what I considered my second attack.

What I considered — please note; for I am giving
you as far as I can my state of mind as it was then.
Since then, as you will see, it has very considerably
changed.   It is really this process of change, if that
is the right word for it, that forces me to write what
I am writing; forces me as unanswerably as my sense
of duty forced me to ask for a commission.

My second attack, then, happened in the afternoon.   I had been taking a slow shuffle round the
garden, and remember thinking, not without some
dry but not at all bitter amusement, how very little
trouble I had taken with my body when whole, and
what a lot of trouble I would gladly take to get back
even the decent semblance of a foot.   It was rather
a customary trend of my thought, for I liked to
read J. H. Fabre and to know the marvels of insect
instinct which he had noticed, and was inclined to the

opinion, quite vaguely held, that man had not explored a tithe of the power latent in his own machine. I brooded pleasantly during my shuffling stroll; no pique, no emotion, no excitement were stirring in me as I made my way into the hall and sat down with my mother and sister, who were winding wool by the hall fire.

They spoke to me cheerfully, saying that I was looking ever so much better. I cheerfully agreed, saying I also felt ever so much better. And then *It* took hold of me. And this time not swiftly, not abruptly; but slowly and deliberately, as though with conscious pleasure in its own irresistible power. At first there was a physical sensation of collapse, as at the beginning of a nervous seizure accompanied by the same tingling tremble that intense fear induces, and that spreads from the diaphragm to the extremities. My knees, if I had been standing, would probably not have supported the weight of my body. This lasted some twenty seconds, and was followed by a feeling of wild elation, as much beyond the reach of any control of mine as was the previous sinking. It was as though something in me cowered, something else in me was lifted, while I sat conscious of resentment at both, and unable to restrain either, merely thankful that neither my mother nor my sister were aware of any change in me. They continued to make their skein, my mother winding a loose ball, my sister moving her hands from side to side as the pull on the thread touched each guardian upturned thumb.

I looked at my mother, and was confronted by the

mystery of motherhood. The wonder of some Intelligence that realised the mystery for the first time
was mine. I was taken deep below the familiar surface of things, below the common crust of habit, to
the very heart of life, where love and life are one.
My mother was more than my mother: she was
woman. I saw each minute detail of her beauty —
her ordinary human face, common as a primrose;
her eyes, her fingers, her neck, her breast, to which
her dear arms had held me. I saw her, too, a baby
in her mother's arms; growing up till she met my
father and was drawn by some power to love him;
and their delight in each other brought me into existence. Part of that life which spread the primroses over the earth was in her; was in me. This
woman's love had made me, had made my sister,
who in her turn the power was using to make blossom into new life. I only saw these elemental facts.
The rind of custom with which these facts have
been carefully (and wisely perhaps) covered was
stripped off, like old bark from a tree. Oh, there
may have been many reasons for her marriage with
my father besides love — prospects of comfort, or
this or that or the other or these, may have induced
her feeling — but they did not matter, they did not
affect at that moment the primal fact, or touch the
marvel of human existence, or the scope of the possibilities that rose and rose before me as I looked.
The power of life streamed from her to me, as it
had streamed from the low bowl of primroses, and
I was dazed by its beauty. I felt like a man free
of his body's weight, who at last found that he could

ride upon the wind through the sunshine. How long I looked I do not know. Time had no meaning. I tried to close my eyes, and could not.

At last my sister waved her hands and clapped them; my mother gave the last turn to the loosely wound ball and eyed it critically. The spell was broken. I came to.

My mother said: "Are you coming with us into the garden, dear?"

My sister answered for me: "Oh, he's sleepy, darling; let him doze in his chair over the fire."

I smiled and said, "I think perhaps I will."

They went out.

Just as my second attack had been stronger and more vivid than my first, so was my resentment at its coming stronger and more vivid.

Now I had no objection whatever to a man's realising that motherhood is a very wonderful fact. I had thought so myself once or twice before, quite reasonably and intelligently, and had resolved to be as nice as I possibly could to my mother in consequence. But to have this realisation forced upon me to this staggering intensity, that I did most violently resent. I had had no say in the matter whatever. For some minutes after my mother and sister had left me I felt faint and light-headed, as you feel after taking gas. I hated it; it made me feel uncommonly uneasy. What might not happen next? My mind became active in its endeavour to guard against future assaults, and to wipe out the disturbing memory of those to which it had yielded.

Roger, our Airedale terrier, trotted into the hall

and sat himself down, leaning against my legs, lifting his head to be patted.   I patted it, and tried to
ease my mind by observing on my own account, as
it were, the wonder of Roger.   He was indubitably
wonderful, especially in his extreme devotion to me.
Common sense tried hard to belittle my experience.
I laughed at myself.   " Will you be swooping me off
into an ecstasy, old fellow? " I said.   " If you do
I'll smack your silly old head hard.   So I warn you."
And I was delighted when he twisted himself to
search for a flea which he must have picked up in the
chicken-run.

   " There's food for rapture," I thought.   " Life
within life: parasite on parasite."

   But it was no good.   I knew that something in
me was somehow changed, and that that something
was beyond the reach of my mind or my reason or
my common sense, or anything over which I had any
control.   Also in spite of my resentment, which did
not pass, I was shyly but definitely ashamed at my
resentment.

   I lifted myself upstairs — I was an adept at that
by then — to think the matter out in my study which
has a view into trees and over tree-tops.   That view
has always appealed to me as peculiarly restful
and remote.   The trees were putting out fat buds.
I pushed open the window and leaned on the
sill.

   " Now then," I said, " come on.   If anything
should give me this heady rapture, it should surely
be the sight of these black twigs bursting out into
new life."

I tried to hypnotise myself into the mood of rapture, staring into the network of branches, staring at the thick trunks. I can't tell you how much I wanted to be able to summon this power, to have it at my bidding. I wanted to rid myself of its mystery, you understand. I wanted really, I suppose, to convince myself that I was not afraid. But afraid I was; and exactly what I was afraid of I could not tell, and this ignorance made it worse.

I ought to be glad, I argued. The only experience that at all tallied with it was the experience of mediæval saints. They were glad. They regarded it as attainment, as the earthly crown of all their striving, as communion with God. Why was it that I could not feel glad? Why should I be annoyed?

The question was easily answered — *then*, though I should not answer it in the same way now. Saintly strivings had been wholly absent from my life; saintly attainments never even touched the dimmest horizon of my desire. They brought it on themselves, as it were: mine was brought on me. They did all in their power to stimulate and excite their emotion; I disliked unregulated emotion of every kind. I felt superior — not very unpleasantly, I think — but undoubtedly superior to them. I preferred my way to theirs. And then the story of Paul came into my mind, and though I smiled at myself for seeing any analogy between my story and his, and though Paul was one of the characters in history that I most disliked, the thought of his experience — how the heavens opened, and he heard a great Voice saying, " Saul, Saul, why persecutest thou me?"—troubled me with an uneasiness that no smile of mine could still.

"Well, I may be going to church next Sunday. Who knows?" I said to myself. Common sense bade me not forebode evil; to wait and see what happened.

Now you must not think that I had strong views about church-going, that I was a zealous free-thinker who thought it wrong to go to church. No such thing. I liked going to church, though I never made a habit of it; at times very much, especially to our little church in the country. It was pretty, and stood in a wood, and in summer-time the porch was covered with roses. I liked the service too. It reminded me of school and college chapel, and many other pleasant associations. And to come out quietly into a summer evening among all the villagers in their best clothes and to walk quietly home was an experience the peacefulness of which I treasured.

Yes; but that was one thing. To burn with religious ardour was another. I cordially disliked fanatics. And a queer dread lurked in my heart lest the last trick to be played on my personality was to turn me into a fanatic.

Conversion seemed somehow to be the logical and likely outcome. I couldn't quite see what I should be converted from or what I should be converted to, but conversion loomed over me; and not even the most careful visualisation of our gentle, song-voiced, amiable curate — surely the gentlest, most amiable curate that ever took mild pride in intoning — could disperse for me the cloud that was still small as a man's hand, yet was fated, I had no sort of doubt, to fill my sky and burst above my diminished head.

I filled my favourite pipe and lighted it while there was yet time. I saw the humour of the situation, but it did not cease on that account to be disturbing and, let me assure you, very deeply disturbing.

The certainty as to what must be the outcome of my experience increased as Sunday drew nearer. I could no more have spoken to my mother or to my sister or to any living soul about what I was dreading than I could have thrust my one sound foot into the fire. I was curious and fearful as a man might be before his wedding day. Yet as my fear and curiosity grew, so did my amusement at my own distress. There was something intensely ludicrous about it which never ceased to tickle me. Explain it how you may, explain it I cannot; I merely state the fact, and for the truth of it I can vouch.

Common sense helped me a great deal, for it was a trying time, and I needed help. Common sense said: " More has happened to you by the bursting of that shell than the loss of a foot and a hand, than the loss and recovery of your hearing. You will be able to bear it as you have been able to bear, without making much fuss, your disablement."

I had my share of British pluck and British doggedness. But I was relieved when Sunday morning came to observe that neither my mother nor my sister showed any sign of going to church. I preferred to go alone. Whatever might happen to me I preferred that it should happen in comparative privacy, and not in the family presence. A man may have his little modesties.

A path led from the bottom of the garden through a wood over a field to the wood in which the little church stood — eight minutes walk for an able body. I allowed half an hour to be on the safe side of casuality, and I stole out of the house to avoid escort. In the first wood I stopped.

"After all," I said to myself, " there's nothing driving me there. I can quietly go home again." And to prove the truth of my words I went back some ten yards. But, believe me or not, I could not go any farther than those ten yards. At that my discomfort became acute. Any shred of doubt that remained as to what was in store for me was removed. I set my jaw and put my best foot foremost.

" What must be, must be," I said. " Whatever it is it's best to get it over." The spire of the little church pointed up through the black twigs from the wood in which it was ensconced. The country was peaceful and delicious. One of those days in spring which touch the heart. The earth smiled. All the powers of life and beauty were in the ascendant. Why should I resist?

It was in a quiet solemn mood, untouched except by awe and curiosity, that I reached the porch over which the rose tree was sending new long green shoots. I stood outside the porch, waiting; wondering why no one was about, and why no bell rang. I supposed I was early and waited, yielding wholly to my mood of solemnity, idly thinking of all the churches scattered throughout the land, of all the worshippers assembling. The birds were singing. A field mouse rustled in a bunch of dead grass and peeped out. A wood-pigeon clattered out of a fir tree behind the church. A blackbird escaped with his noisy startled laugh. Two rooks flew high on some distant business.

" I'll wait inside," I thought, and hobbled up to the church door, which was shut and also, I discovered, locked. Even then I only thought that my watch was very much faster than usual; but the notice-board caught my eye, and the notice told me what I had forgotten, namely, that service was held every other Sunday in the morning and every other Sunday in the evening, and that this was a Sunday for evensong.

I cannot possibly describe my discomfiture or my subsequent sense of relief. It was as though a sponge had been applied to the writings on my troubled mind and all superstitious dread wiped out.

" It's all a hoax," I cried out to myself, " a silly hoax played upon me by my nerves. There's nothing in it." And I stretched myself luxuriously in the sunshine, like a man freed from a weight he has been carrying.

You see, the impulse drawing me to the church for that morning service was so strong and so authentic that as that had proved a delusion, I was certain that the whole experience — the attacks and the memory of them and so forth — was a delusion also; that it was accidental, due, as I had thought originally, merely to a passing weakness of the nervous system; that there had been and would be no serious tampering with my personality. I was so certain of this that I actually felt conscious of a twinge of disappointment, though I assure you I was honestly and deeply relieved.

I did not see then, as I see now, that just the intensity of this relief and the swiftness of its coming proved perhaps more surely than anything else could have done the reality of my past experience. Even then I knew, without definitely stating it to myself, that I should not give any living being the least hint of what I had experienced, or of what I imagined that I had escaped.

Anyhow, for the time being my misgivings ceased, or if any came were instantly quieted by the thought that a man, after having lived through things such as I had lived through, could not expect to resume his previous state of being immediately or without perhaps a conscious struggle.

II

DURING the next few days my feelings resembled those of a small boy who fully expects to be caned or kept in, and who is let off with a reprimand. The affair was not forgotten, but it had lost its poignancy of importance. Moreover an incident took place on my normal plane which was so unusual that it wholly occupied my attention.

For a long time the bosom friend of my sister Doris had been a girl named Amy Stone. They had been friends at school, and Amy used to spend half her holidays with us. Her coming was so recognised as a rule that our plans were made to facilitate her visit. She was an institution. The girls in the first flush of their friendship had decided that their dearest wish was that each should marry the other's brother. This was broken to me in a moment of confidence by Doris on a moonlight evening one summer holiday, after I had been at Charterhouse three years — that is to say, about eight years before the war, when I was sixteen in fact. I took the proposal very seriously at the time, but on the whole it had a pleasant effect on my relations with Amy; I remember begging Doris to be careful not to let her love of Amy lead her into an engagement which she might afterwards regret. I was not more solemn than boys are wont to be about their sisters' affairs, and

I was pleased with some points on which I insisted: that a girl might be good and delightful, but it did not follow that her brother must necessarily be equally good and delightful; that marriage was a very serious affair, and so on. I worked in a little Mendel, too, I forget quite how. Doris was duly impressed, and we both felt very queer and friendly and grown up to be discussing together a matter of such stirring importance.

In spite of its importance, however, which we at that moment deliciously tasted, the matter did not unduly weigh upon our spirits. It made me a little self-conscious at my next meeting with Amy. That was all. We had many matters to which to attend of less weight but of more immediate urgency, and so though it lent, for a year or two, a spice to our doings, it dropped little by little from our consciousness, and was never mentioned by any of us again. So much so that when Doris became engaged it was so remote that I never thought even to tease her about her early plan.

I was still very fond of Doris, but we had few interests in common as we grew up, and with Amy I had none at all. Since my disablement I realised what an " awfully good little sort " Doris was, and realised it not without a qualm of conscience. Everything she did for me she did without any fuss. Her kindness was never heavy, never insistent. And when I tried to express gratitude she seemed almost hurt.

I said once: " I'm a most infernal nuisance, I'm afraid."

She said, frowning angrily, " It's mean of you to say that." I looked at her in surprise, not following her line of thought. She threw back her head to ask, " Have I ever made you feel a nuisance? "

" Oh, I see," I grunted.

At which she, sharing my dislike of emotion, snapped her fingers and exclaimed:

> " O Woman, in our hours of ease
> Uncertain coy, and hard to please,'
> When tears of anguish wring the brow
> A ministering angel thou,"

and, laughing, left the room.

The lines are true enough to be trite. My sister is a nice ordinary girl; her compassion was sublime. Never again, I decided, would I blame a woman for being slightly stupid. What was a mere lack of intelligence placed against this rarer, richer quality? Of course if a man were always fit and strong. . . . I suppressed the conclusion as unworthy, the trend of thought as graceless.

I do not think that I slipped into complacency on the tack of woman's sublime compassion because I remained sensitive to it; but when Amy came I was not wholly unprepared to witness another demonstration of this fine quality in action.

At first, however, she seemed hardly friendly. Not knowing what trouble might not be at her heart — her brother, I knew, was somewhere at the front in the Army Service Corps; not dangerous his position, but not safe; and Heaven only knew for whom she might not be caring dumbly, patiently — I wondered which was worse for a girl — for the man to go to the fighting who had declared his love before he went or for the man to go whom she hoped might declare his love. And was either worse than the position of the war bride, or, for that matter, the position of the mother of a small family? Of course it was no use being sentimental about it, but I would rather a thousand times go through what I had gone through than sit at home and wait, wait, wait for news. Looked at coolly I suppose war is the most senseless cruelty, and there is something hideous in the slow deliberation of the huge machine's working. Easy to start as the hangman's drop; and who can stop it? And what power in heaven or earth can ever repair the damage? Such was the train of thought that Amy's unusual aloofness started in my mind. She seemed to be suffering. And the dullest imagination could find a thousand reasons for a girl's suffering during a war.

I spoke to Doris about it, and she assured me that Amy had nothing personal on her mind; but I could not take her assurance, until one day Amy said, *à propos* of some paragraph in the paper about the continued inaction of the German navy: " Oh, won't it be a terrible thing if they don't come out, and we can't put another battle like Trafalgar into our history! "

The little outburst surprised but reassured me. She obviously visualised glory more vividly than loss of life. I own I was a little shocked. I can understand a naval man who has been pottering about in the North Sea all the winter longing for a final smash at the enemy, for his ship's sake and for other reasons, but somehow to find this spirit in an amiable girl did shock me. Still, there it was, and its presence in Amy reassured me, as I say, though her manner to me did not alter.

I teased her about this manner of hers, and said she ought not to be so cold and distant to me, even though I was not a naval man; and, relieved about her, I forgot about her. Always she so quickly became one of the family that I hardly noticed her presence. That was Amy's chief charm to me, what might be called her gentle insignificance.

Also the worst fit of depression got hold of me that had come since my convalescence. I wanted to run about. I wanted my left hand. Dislike to the sight of myself became an obsession. One morning in bed — I mention it with shame — I cried like a kid. All that happened was that I forgot, and reached out my stump for something. But it did for me. The crying brought me to my senses. Anyhow, there was no tampering with me this time, I cheered myself up to think; it was me, like it I might or not, and nothing but me. That I knew, and I wondered how I could have been foolish enough to have been drawn to the church on Sunday morning. Oh, that was all moonshine and foolishness. And I used it to pull myself finally out of the swamp. It was sillier even than these tears.

Rain freshens the landscape, and I tried to be a little nicer than I probably had been. It is natural that one should try tentatively to make amends, and naturally, too, I tried to pay what little attentions I could to Amy, as my musings about her must have

leaked out into my conduct.   It is always unfair to
sentimentalise about people and then to be angry because they do not expand to your ideal.

The rain didn't disturb you in the night? "

" Oh, no."

" Would you, if you are going out, pick me some
bits of pussy-palm? "

" Oh, yes."

" Big bits, to put in a tall vase in my room."

" As big as I can cut."

And I tried to make her talk to me about a cousin
of hers who was a lieutenant on a battleship.   My
efforts were not, however, at all successful.   Nothing I said led her to talk in her usual way; nothing
set her on her usual jolly prattle.   She remained ill
at ease and abrupt.

When she was going out with Doris for the morning walk, and I offered to lend her my pen-knife, she
seemed really upset, and Doris said:

" Silly boy, don't you know it's unlucky to lend
knives; severs friendship."

" But not an old friendship like ours," I said.
" Besides, Amy isn't superstitious, are you? "

" Yes, I am in some things," she answered.

She brought the pussy-palm up into my study
alone.

" Hullo," I said, " that is jolly."

She put it in the big pot without speaking, and I
began to fill a pipe, which is not easy to do with one
hand.   The tip is to lean your forearm on the stem,
then your right hand is free to pack and press.   In
the same way you can hold a matchbox firm while

you strike your match.   I was explaining this to her
when she interrupted me.

"I should always like to do it for you," she announced.

"Now, that is dear of you," I answered, laughing.
"But I'm getting quite smart now.   Don't you think
so?"

"Oh, it's not only that.   I mean everything."

"Why, you've been horrid to me all the time
you've been here.   Not a bit the old Amy.   This is
the first time, you know, you've come up to have a
little chat with me."

"Oh, I know I've been horrid, but that's only because . . ."

I suddenly saw that she was in deadly earnest; I
suddenly saw an Amy I had never imagined.   I was
too embarrassed to speak.   She went stumbling on:

"Only because . . . can't you see?   You think
no girl could care now.   As you are.   Sort of done
for.   I've seen it all the while in your manner.   Oh
yes, I have.   And a girl could.   I could.   Oh, it
would be such a tremendous honour.   If you were
utterly crippled, which you aren't a bit.   She could
make you much happier.   I know I could.   In all
sorts of ways.   And Doris is going to be married.
What'll you do then?   Oh, I'm not clever and all
that, but I could be sweet to you.   Why, just to wait
on you!   The way you bear it and all.   And you
might have been blown to pieces, and I should never
have known."

I could have bitten my tongue off for saying,
"You'd have read it in the paper."

"Not that. Never have known. Never have known." She burst into tears.

I so much wanted to say, " Oh, you darling, you're all that I want in life," that you will never believe how nearly I said it. The words nearly forced themselves gasping out of me.

I thought she must realise and escape from the room. She stood where she was, crying. I was torn to pieces with anger and pity and admiration. The silence was dreadful.

I heard my detestable voice saying: " I'm not the kind of a man you think. Most hopelessly not a hero. I loathed going to fight. I was bored sick with fighting. I was thankful to get out of it as well as I have done."

I felt a worm, the image of weakness. Also rather a cad. There was something indescribably touching about her as she stood in front of me, crying like a little child, young, sweet, rosy-cheeked her hair dishevelled . . . how dared any man repulse such an exquisite offer? Yet while I saw all this and more, her denseness enraged me. And she sobbed out:

"That only makes you more won-wonderful. More sp-splendid."

And still she stood there in front of me. She must have known by then, but still she stood there.

"It's tremendously flattering. But I'm hardly used to living at all yet as I am, let alone changing my whole plan of life. Do be the dear little friend you used to be. You'll soon see I've hardly changed an atom. Never was a hero. I haven't decided

what to do, what work, you understand, and I'll always think of you as a dear little friend and — oh
yes! there is something I'd love you to do for me.
The *Fortnightly Review*. I left it on the hall-table.
Would you be ever so kind and fetch it for me? "

She actually brightened at that, gave a vigorous
sniff, dabbed at her eyes with her handkerchief and
ran off. She came back smiling, and as far as I
could see perfectly at her ease. She put her hand
on my shoulder and gave me a kiss on my forehead,
which she had never done before, and told me that
I was a stupid old dear to take myself so seriously;
and ask wasn't I a little ashamed of myself to have
been so frightened at her? One had little rushes
of feeling, hadn't one? They bubbled out and
away, and one felt better. Or couldn't I understand? She patted my head. She went away a
weeping child, whose heart I thought was broken;
she came back a grandmother, who seemed a little
amused at a small boy's thoughtless but forgivable
behaviour, and was kind enough to explain that he
wasn't really so bad as he seemed.

I thankfully took my cue from her, but I was
staggered. I longed to ask her bluntly, " Did you
or did you not ask me to marry you? " but not even
my intense curiosity gave me courage to do so.

I came back from France confident that I had
touched the depths of experience; that life held no
further secrets from me; that I had touched the bed-
rock bottom of reality. But wherever I hobbled it
seemed my fate simply to butt into one mystery after
another. I was then too much in the midst of it

all to be able to see properly what was happening. I did not notice, for example, that these mysteries lay in just the commonest, most everyday affairs of life; or rather perhaps just in those things — the lark, the primroses, my mother and sister, nice ordinary Amy, my very ordinary self — to which I was most accustomed. Some explanation I was of course obliged to find, and I invariably found the same, the easiest, most elastic explanation, namely, the overwrought state of my mind brought about by my wound. In other words, I put it all down to the fatal bomb. And as far as it went, the explanation was correct enough. There is no doubt the bomb was the cause of it all. But there were many little gaps and fissures over which my mind could only leap with its utmost agility. I clung to my accustomed view of life. I had no fear that I should not wholly recover from the effects of the bomb, except the nuisance of being minus a hand and a foot.

At the moment, however, the Amy incident usurped my attention. I rehearsed the scene and all that led up to it a hundred times, and I recount it as it happened, without in any way lessening the foolish part I played in it. My excuse, of course, was that I was not yet quite myself; and the excuse was valid at any rate in this, that it helped gently to eliminate the feeling that I had been somehow a little mean as well as weak and foolish.

" It's a commonplace of knowledge," I said to myself, " that women are inexplicable creatures." And the dictum sufficed to cover my ignorance.

But as I say, the Amy incident occupied my mind. The other experiences which had alarmed me lost their significance. I called them symptoms of nervous debility, and took to a plateful of porridge at breakfast to cure them, though I was already fatter than I liked. My normal self I would become at all cost; my normal self even if it meant a slightly fatter self. This became, without exaggeration, a point of honour with me.

And on the very evening on which I had definitely formulated it to myself as a point of honour, the first visible sign of the great event quietly occurred. Think of the coming of a thunderstorm. There are distant rumblings; black clouds gather; everywhere expectancy broods. Will it burst? Will it pass over? Then heavy drops begin to fall. Not that this event was like a thunderstorm. But its approach suggests a storm's approach to me now, as I look back on it, perhaps because there had been a thunderstorm in the afternoon, followed by a sudden hurricane of wind, which blew the dust from the fireplace in my bedroom right on to the broad window-sill, which I wiped clean with my pocket handkerchief when I went to bed.

I went to bed at ten. I was in bed by half-past ten, as I was skilful now at undressing with one hand. I heard our big grandfather's clock in the hall strike eleven, half asleep; and how very pleasant it is to hear a familiar clock slowly strike, when it is too distant and deep-voiced and slow to disturb; it seems to lull one off to sleep with quiet dignity. But what happens during sleep?

I awoke, or seemed to awake, quietly, without any start, without any fear. The moonlight was streaming into my room, for I never draw my curtains. At the time I thought that I was dreaming, and that the dream, as my dreams often do, was taking place in my own room. I have the power, which had never before failed me, of waking myself at the crucial moment of a nightmare when the axe is about to fall or after I have dropped over the precipice before the fatal bump. I say to myself this is only a dream, and wake up, angry and disturbed and in a sweat. But on this occasion I had no wish to wake up; it never occurred to me to do so. And the queerest thing of all, as it struck me next morning, was that I had no sensation of queerness whatever; that on the contrary it all seemed as natural and right as eating one's breakfast.

My bedroom is my favourite room in the house. It is large and low, with prominent huge wooden beams in the ceiling. The windows are latticed, and form an alcove. My bed stands along the wall, opposite the windows. A large fireplace is between them and me. The room has a pleasant irregular shape. Being an invalid, a fire was always lighted for me at half past eight. I generally threw on a log before I got into bed. I had done so that evening. It still glowed.

In the moonlight, about ten yards from the window and seven yards from my bed stood a distinct shape, the shape of a young man, not looking at me, but looking out of the window, up along a moonbeam towards the moon. I wondered how he managed to stand so very straight and so very still. I did not wonder what he was doing in my room, or whether he was a ghost or a spirit of good or evil, or what in this world or the next he might be. I only wondered calmly and without fear at his straightness and his stillness. I noticed that his heels were raised from the ground.

So far was I from fear that I was pleased, the same kind of sensation of pleasure as when the old clock lulled me to sleep with its slow striking of the hour. I lay and looked, and waited, expecting nothing, and I was not startled when the smouldering log stirred in the grate. I felt supernaturally at rest; that was all. Complete repose was mine, which was somehow radiated from the presence before me, like warmth from a fire. How long I lay in enjoyment and looked, I cannot tell — whether it was half a second or two hours. I had no sense of time and though I knew I was in bed in my own room, no sense of space. I should not have been surprised to have found myself lying on heather on a wide moor, with the bees humming round me and the grouse chuckling in the distance. Neither time nor space mattered. Only this repose mattered.

At last he turned to me, and said in a low, astonishingly clear voice: "So at last you can see me. I am glad you are not afraid. You must try and not be afraid to-morrow morning in the daylight. It has taken me a long time to make you see me, but now I shall often be able to come. I'll leave this feather — look — on the window-sill. It will help you not to forget. Now go to sleep."

His hand passed over my face; the lightest touch, like a breath of warm air.

The birds woke me in the morning. I listened without opening my eyes. I felt I had slept deliciously, and wanted to continue to sleep. No recollection whatever remained of my dream. I must have dropped asleep again, for the maid was bringing my tea long before I expected her.

I sat up and drank my tea, thinking idly, as one does, that I had had rather a jolly dream; trying to remember it and failing because my thoughts turned to the Amy incident, and I smiled at the thought of what I should be feeling like if I were actually engaged to marry her. Were other women like her? I decided that I was not a marrying man and lighted a cigarette.

As I was lighting it my dream came back to me like a flash with startling vividness. I looked at the place where it had stood. And as I looked his words returned as though they were repeated in my ear.

I lay straight back on my bed so that I could not see the window-sill. I dared not look at the sill. Supposing the feather were actually there! I was angry at even supposing it. Yet I dared not make sure that it was not. The memory of the dream was uncannily vivid, nor did the repose I had experienced in any way reassure me.

"Oh, rubbish, rubbish, rubbish!" I said aloud; and at last I could stand it no longer; mocking at myself, I got out of bed and hopped across the room.

There on the window-sill lay a feather, the breast

feather of a bird, about four inches long and two
inches broad, delicate, small and soft as down, in
colour brown and white and greyish.

There it was. I sat down on the window-sill and
brushed the feather against my cheek. Numb with
astonishment, I sat there, stroking my face with the
feather.

Aloud I said: " Oh, some one in the house must
have left it there, and I must have seen it without
taking notice of it, and then had a queer dream,"
and I laughed aloud.

I whistled and sang all the time I was getting up,
which did not prevent my remembering uneasily that
I had dusted the window-sill in the late afternoon
with my handkerchief.

I asked them casually at breakfast, " What sort of
a feather is this ? "   Doris and Amy thought it was
lovely; and my mother said that she thought it was a
heron's feather, and asked me where I had found it.

" Oh, I picked it up at the bottom of the garden,"
I said. Obviously they all saw it for the first time.

My mother took me on one side after breakfast
and asked me if anything were the matter. I looked
troubled, she said, and worried. I kissed her, and
told her I had not slept very well; and reminded her,
teasing her, that all fussing over wounded heroes
was strictly prohibited. But it braced me to know
that my looks were betraying me.

" I'll take it by the neck," I said to myself. " I'll
be interested and not afraid."

I went straight to my study to enter the words it
had spoken to me, while I remembered them, with

the date of appearance and one or two remarks, in a notebook. I sat pen in hand, thinking what else I should enter. When I came to, I saw that the words *" Try and not be afraid to-morrow morning in the daylight "* had been underlined!

"Well, I won't be," I said. But I was terribly restless, and it is a great nuisance to be restless when you have only one foot.

Suspense had always been my worst enemy; if a commonsense fellow like myself starts a day with something ahead of him more important than the matter in hand, he is thrown out of gear; the day is lost; he can settle to nothing; his mind jumps this way and that. Each minute of the day becomes a tyrant to be slain. It was my intimate knowledge of this that caused me fiercely to cling to my natural normal self, which I knew how to handle, and made me dread the recurrence of the primrose incident, and the other intensities. I knew they meant for me restlessness and discomfort. My manner of life was not made to include them. I saw myself a decent hack, shall we say, and had no wish whatever to race or hunt. Every one knows it is a mad, mysterious world; most of us prefer that the madness and mystery should be a becoming background to our plain sensible selves, and should not touch us.

I spent a long, miserable, fretful day, in which all my energy was expended in being ordinarily civil. I read F. W. H. Myers on " Human Personality," and the numerous authentic stories of sane healthy people who had had experiences beside which mine was insignificant were not consoling. One woman had two quite distinct personalities. Her character and memory and habits changed with them; everything about her changed apparently except her features and her body. The dispassionate coldness with which each case was stated was unpleasant; no loophole for doubt was allowed. Oh, the accounts were interesting enough in reference to other people; they had formerly added a value to my impregnable rock of common sense. My own experience, however, changed my attitude. My common sense belied itself, and cried out that such things ought not to be.

After dinner I was going through a motley heap of paper books in a cupboard to find a creepy little treatise on the materialisation of spirits when I saw a book called, in huge red type on the cover, with a great curling question mark, "What would Jesus do?"

Fretful and upset as I was, I could not help smiling at the instant help the bold question gave me. I glanced through the book, which was full of fine practical suggestions and burning enthusiasm, and I asked myself, "Well, and what would the nice sensible man you wish to be do in your place? Would he fret and worry and go all to pieces as you are doing? He would not. Would he induce of his own accord just the state of mind he most wishes to avoid? He would not. Then what would he do?"

It was a beautiful catechism, and pat came the answer.

"He would say to himself: Such and such a

thing has happened; I will quietly await further developments. Nothing can touch my sanity unless I allow it to do so."

And softly, like a reasonable man inspired, I put back the paper books, shut the cupboard door, took down Arnold Bennett's "The Human Machine" and gave myself over to his doughty writing. Never had my favourite living author proved doughtier or more reassuring. Each unfaltering sentence was a timely slap upon my back. This was the fellow. He walked through mysteries like a dog through cobwebs.

I went to bed encouraged by the confident gait of his writing, and able to remember that after all I was a man who had received the baptism of fire. That baptism at any rate should make a difference. I ventured to remember the Dane's bold accosting, and murmured: "Whence and what art thou, execrable shape? Art thou a spirit of health or goblin damned?" Ah! and therein lay my doughty writer's chief refreshment. He came in no questionable guise. He was almost as real and authoritative as a groom speaking of horse-flesh. He spoke, and nonsense was not.

I went to bed later and to sleep without difficulty. Reassured and restored I slept.

That night there was no moon. I woke to hear the clock strike two. The room was dark. A steady wind was blowing my curtains, swelling them out like sails, blacker shapes moving against the darkness. I closed my eyes again in relish of the warmth and comfort the windy night outside brought home to me, and I thought I slept again.   For the same dream came.

My eyes opened to see him standing poised as before, visible by his own brightness.

" Who are you? " I asked.

Without turning he answered in his low, very distinct voice:

" That is what I most want you to recognise."

" Then tell me, and I'll try."

" It would be no good yet."

" Why not? "

" Can you tell me who you are? "

" Certainly; a man named James Wood."

" That does not tell me much."

" But it's something to begin with."

" A label for the framework.   But if I told you my name it would mislead you far more than inform you."

" Mayn't I ask you questions? "

" Questions you could ask might satisfy your curiosity, but they would only obscure your understanding."

" They would help me to place you."

" I have no place."

" May I ask one question? "

" Yes."

" Do you mean me good or ill? "

He turned then and smiled.

" Good, in my sense of the word.   But men hardly know what good and evil are; man's ideas are so very relative and rough."

" We've a fair working idea."

"That is what makes the confusion. Your standards change to suit your circumstances."

"Were you a man once?"

"Not more than I am now, and not less."

"You want to mystify me."

"That must be the first stage, I fear," he answered, with the most delicate touch of apology in his voice. "But only your reason," he added, as though in comfort.

"Oh, come now, I'm a man and reason is man's safest guide."

Again he smiled, and there was no superiority in his smile; it resembled the smile of a child.

"There is something deeper; the two are rarely combined, or reason would be less fitful among you, and less often in abeyance."

"We may be sorry creatures," I declared, "but while I live on the earth, I wish to be a man, and in spite of everything I'm proud to be a man."

He literally glowed with approval at that, so that the room seemed actually lighter for his presence, but I would not give way.

"Our life may be cruel and detestable, but it is uncommonly interesting."

"Did you feel less a man when you saw the primroses, or your mother and sister?"

"Oh, that was you, was it?"

"Partly, perhaps."

"Well, then less myself, certainly."

"You know what that means, that 'myself'?"

"I have a rough idea. All men have."

He sighed.

"That is the great difficulty."

"Whose?"

"Theirs, if they only knew it.   Yours."

I grunted.

He became very dim.

"You must try and forgive my intrusion," he said, and his voice grew fainter and fainter.   "Believe me, I am not wholly responsible for it."

I lay in the darkness, listening to the wind, watching the dark shapes of the curtains swelling out in the wind.

I lighted my candle, put on my dressing-gown and hopped to the window, out of which I leaned.   The wind blew steadily.   Stars twinkled.   A cloud was moving away from the moon, sweeping across the sky.   Branches swayed in the wind.   New life was bursting from them.   I could not see the buds.   In a few hours the night would go; the day would come. Sunshine perhaps and a day of growth.

A shiver sent me back to the warmth of bed.

III

My state of mind after this second visit swung between dread and confidence. At times I remembered rumours that my grandfather had become odd to the verge of lunacy, and had been, on one or two sad occasions, secluded; and I remembered that insanity was sometimes induced by a sudden shock which split the personality. At other times — and they became more frequent — it comforted me to think that I never felt more balanced and more under my own control; and to remember that "my familiar," as I called him in these moods of confidence, whatever he was or whoever he was, was not formidable. He seemed, on the contrary, diffident and courteous, and most anxious not to disoblige me in any way. Moreover there were no ill effects of his visits. On both occasions I awoke refreshed in the morning, and unless I allowed myself to think of my grandfather's tendency, or of the myriad subtleties of lunacy, no inconvenience attended his coming. If he were a spirit he was a tame and mannerly spirit. His efforts to mystify me were provoking but nothing worse. If he found any satisfaction in appearing to me and conversing, there really was no objection. In fact I was becoming used to the idea of him as swiftly as I became used to the idea of being under fire.

43

And that suggested a very odd question. Why do men so quickly become used to terrible conditions of life who can never cease to be affected by trivialities? What control have we over our moods? What induces them? And why do we nearly always feel ill-used as a prelude to bad temper?

After all, my worst symptom, I concluded, was only a tendency to be unduly impressed by the commonplace, and if I kept my platitudes to myself, there would be little harm done.

I entered my last communing in the exercise book very carefully, and repeated the comment that I found not the slightest difficulty in remembering our conversation. Again I had the feeling of writing to dictation. This time there was no underlining.

My mood of confidence gained hold of me. The need was strong of taking a firm stand on my normal, much cherished self. I took it and threw up fortifications. I entrenched myself against the abnormal. It may have been this idea, though at the time I was hardly conscious of it, and even now I am not able to say with absolute certainty that it was so, that caused Amy to appear to me in a far more prepossessing light than she had ever appeared before. Not that I was in the least like the gentleman in one of de Maupassant's stories who took a wife because the dark held terrors for him which he could not face alone; but it crossed my mind that Amy would be a useful ally, would serve excellently as ballast, shall we say, or as a counterpoise. It crossed my mind, to be summarily dismissed; partly for the reason that it seemed somehow an unworthy attitude in which to approach a young lady, partly for the vaguer reason that the intention would be guessed, and perhaps thwarted, by my familiar if it entered too definitely into my mind.

But mingled with all these considerations was of course the very simple fact that Amy was a sweet and pretty girl; and her little outburst, from which she had removed with her own hand the prickles, gave clear proof that whatever she might lack, her taste in men was irreproachable.

On the morning after my familiar's second visit, my attitude to Amy underwent a change, subtler than anything that can be expressed in words. There was no hand clasp, no tone of voice, no look, no word that was in any way noticeable, and yet Amy was aware of the change, and knew that I knew that she was aware. There was some kind of understanding between us, though how it took place I am totally unable to say. It was noticeable in her bearing and demeanour; and again I could not say what made it noticeable. She was not visibly more upright or more sprightly or the reverse. Yet I sensed the difference, and was not in the least surprised that she came into my study during the morning.

She said: "I only looked in to see if you wanted any more pussy-palm." I disregarded the excuse, and said, holding out my hand: "I was the most awful prig the other morning."

"No more than any man would have been," she said.

"Do you know such a lot about men?"

"That's rather a funny thing to say, isn't it?"

"No; not as I meant it."

She was playing with my hand, bending and unbending the fingers.

"You're rather a nice boy," she said, and put my hand against her cheek for a moment. Then she opened it and smoothed her fingers along the lines in the palm; and sighed and laughed and said:

"No heart line."

"Why, it's a long deep furrow," was my stout assurance.

"So you're going to be friends with me, are you?"

"Haven't I always been friends with you?"

"Have you?"

She laid down my hand and picked up a flower. She stooped over me to put the flower in my buttonhole. Her hair touched my face. I kissed her, and said:

"Well, I am now."

"Shall I fetch you the *Fortnightly Review?*"

"No; sit here," I said, offering my knee, on which she demurely sat, keeping her balance by holding on to my coat.

"A girl can be nice without being horrid," she announced.

"You can. But I had no idea . . ."

"What?"

"I don't know."

"I know what you were going to say."

"Tell me."

"You had no idea that I could be."

Her hand on my mouth prevented any protestation.

"It's no good denying it."

"I never knew you."

"Whose fault is that?"

"Yours."

She pretended to box my ears, but only pressed her hands against both my cheeks, looking into my eyes as she held me, and said: "Oh, I like that."

"So do I," I managed to say, "immensely."

Without releasing me she said: "In some things you are a complete baby."

"I like you to think so."

She got up and sat on the table.

"Now, answer me three questions."

"'And that is enough,' said his fa——"

"Ssh! Be serious."

"That's just what I don't want to be."

"I know that well enough. But first: haven't I put you at your ease?"

"My knee was beginning to ache."

"Don't be silly: answer me."

"I held out my hand to you."

"Oh, you're impossible!" she cried, and walked away to the fire, where she stood with her back to me.

"That's unfair," I suggested, but she took no notice.

"What's the second question?" I threw out, but she took no notice.

"Do be friends again," I pleaded. "Don't be cross!"

" I'm not cross," she said, and turned round.   She began tiptoeing herself up and down on the fender.

" Think of me exactly as you like," she said.   " I don't care in the least."

" What should I think of you ? " I asked lightly.

" Oh, I know what you'll be thinking when you're alone — that I'm only a poor sort of . . ." She pulled a contemptuous face.   " I don't care an atom. Think what you like."

" Rotten of you to say that.   No, don't go," I called out as she went towards the door, and " Come back," I shouted as the door closed.

But she had gone without looking round.

And my very first thought was, " Of course she is just a minx," and the instant memory of her forecast made me furious.

Now if there is one thing more than another that a sensible man declines absolutely to bother about, it is the sex problem.   The very words conjure up row on row of the deplorable, fantastic faces of faddists of every description.   Mine were strong ideas on the subject.   For a decent man there was no problem at all.   Those folk invented problems and so forth who wanted to justify their own bad conduct. No will o' the wisp of a Miss Amy should dance me into that morass.   A little fun was all very well — but thank you! and I banged my fist on the table to declare :

" It's all that blasted intruder.   Why the deuce can't he stop in his own . . ."

Astonishment, not fear, stopped me; for there he stood in front of me in daylight, by the window on the other side of the table. The gentlest note of apology was in his voice as he said:

"I told you I was only partly responsible for my appearance."

"Well, I wish to goodness you'd clear out altogether," and I shut my eyes tightly, so as not to see him.

When I opened them again, he was gone.

His disappearance alarmed me more than any appearance of his had ever done. "He's sure to get even with me for that," I said to myself.

But I blustered myself out of alarm. If he's so easily dismissed, so much the better. And it suddenly occurred to me for no reason that he disapproved of Amy and instantly the determination seized me to go and find Amy. Looking round for my cap, which lay on the table, I caught sight of her in the garden. Resolutely I put on my cap, and as defiantly as I could made my way downstairs into the garden. To my extreme annoyance Amy was nowhere to be seen. I called "Amy!" but no answer came. I called again.

My mother leaned out of her window.

"Amy has just run down the drive, dear; she is taking some letters of mine to the post-office. Is it anything I can do?"

"No, it's not, thank you very much."

My mother's window was on the ground-floor. I went up to her.

She said: "She's a very dear girl — Amy —isn't she?"

"Very."

"Quite like a second daughter to me."

I shook my finger at her, smiling. "Mother, mother," I said, "don't you, now, be making plans."

She looked at me with delightful surprise.

"Plans, dear?" she questioned.

"Yes, plans. Or putting ideas into your poor little son's head. Both are against the rules, as you know very well."

"I was making no hints or plans, dear, I assure you. But I do think that Amy would make any man a very sweet little wife."

I could not help being amused. There was something deliciously matter-of-fact in her manner. I was much struck by its common sense in spite of my amusement. There was no doubt whatever that hers was the true way of looking at it. Amy would make any man a sweet little wife. It was a little unromantic perhaps to be thus disposed of. But the strong placid sense of it appealed to me. Here was firm, knowledgable ground in a world of mystery.

But I suddenly asked: "Do you know Amy?"

To which my mother instantly replied, "Oh, her airs and her graces. Perhaps not. But believe me, she is an extremely sensible young woman."

"Do you know, I always thought I was an extremely sensible young man."

"Yes, I should say you were as young men go," she gravely acquiesced. "Aren't you?"

"I'm not so sure that I am."

"Well, I can't stand gossiping here all the morning. Besides, I'm chilly."

She shut the window.   Distress passed over her face, as she saw me settle the crutch under my arm.

"There's more in it than I can find in Amy," I said to myself.   "If only this infernal spirit or whatever it is would let me alone.   He is entirely out of place among us.   Why does he come to me? Many fellows would go into raptures, and decide to lead a higher life and all that with him.   I'm not going to.   I'm going to be myself."

I thought in distinct emphatic words, and stopped to see him clearly standing by a tree and to hear him saying:

"Yes; do be yourself.   There is no need to be enraged with me."

"I shall marry Amy," I said with decision, " and live in comfort all the rest of my life."

He shook with silent laughter and disappeared. No mockery was in his laughter, only irrepressible amusement.

Was I under his power or was he under mine?   I tried to will him back under the tree.   He came, but very faintly visible.   Still he was there, and I was pleased at my power.   I spoke to him with authority:

"Will you always obey me?" I asked.

To my supreme discomfiture he quoted a book of my nursery days:

"'Oh, to be sure,' said the old cow."

"I don't in the least believe in you," I said.

"You are too cross to be treated seriously," was his retort.

"Jimmie! Jimmie!" came Amy's voice, and out of the bushes behind me she sprang. "What have you been staring at like that?"

"How long have you been hiding?"

"Hardly a minute. Oh, look at that tree; isn't there a queer light on it? Come here and look. From here it's quite like the shadow of a man."

She pointed out the tree under which my familiar had been standing.

I looked from where stood.

"So it is," I agreed. "Isn't that queer now?"

And certainly the sun caught the moss on the bark in an odd way which was very like the shadow of a man.

"Do you believe in ghosts?" I asked her.

"Yes, rather; I should love to see one if I weren't alone. Wouldn't you?"

"If a person saw that tree suddenly in certain moods, he might take it for some sort of a ghost, you know," I said sententiously.

"Oh, I mean real ghosts. Don't you believe in them?"

"One must, I suppose."

"How horrid your old crutch is! I can't take your arm."

"But look here. I can use you as a crutch if you'll let me. Like this." I put my arm on her shoulder. "Am I too heavy?"

"No."

I put my hand under her chin, lifted her face and kissed her.

"You are a darling," I said. "So real and re-

assuring.   Why did you go out of the study like that,
saying horrible things?"

"Weren't they true, then?"

"Of course not," I said.   "I mean . . ."

"Oh, well, why shouldn't you kiss me if you like?
I like it."

I could not imagine why I hated her to say that.
Common sense spoke loudly to me the nonsense of
minding about trifles.   What did it matter what a
pretty girl *said*, when she was in love with you
enough to be amusing?   Yet I wanted to take my
arm off her shoulder, my hand out of hers.

"Ass!" I said to myself, and kissed her again;
but I overbalanced, and held her for support more
tightly than I meant to do.

She pushed me away.

"You mustn't kiss me like that," she said, hurt
and angry, obviously and sincerely hurt and angry;
yet the next moment she was near me again, saying
in a coaxing voice.   "Never mind.   He can't help
being a bad boy sometimes, can he?"

"It's not that," I said.

"Not what?   And now he's angry with me."

"I overbalanced."

"Oh!   Listen to him, listen to him!" she cried,
doubling up in laughter.

"I didn't know you could be such a little . . .
such a little minx.   At one moment you make me
feel the most dreadful prig, and at the next, a cad."

"Oh, don't!" she burbled, and her laughter became more genuine.

"I'm serious," I said.   "Why do you do it?"

She shook her head, unable to speak. At last she stuttered out: " And he's serious now."

" If you were a small boy, I'd smack your head," I said, beginning to laugh too. " You're simply a cheeky little devil. That's all you are."

" Isn't it enough? " she asked, suddenly grave again.

I went on in silence. By the house I said: " Look here, Amy, I simply don't know in the least what you're playing at. I think it had better stop, do you see."

" Which do you feel now? " she asked me.

" Never mind that. Only it must stop."

" Then I did begin it? "

" It's not good for either of us."

" No; my sides still ache with laughing so much."

" I mean what I say. I may seem a prig, but I've had very queer experiences, and it's no good pretending I'm a kid — like I was. It's jolly of course, but . . ."

" Were you ever a kid? " she jested.

I don't know why, but a feeling of intense misery came over me.

She sidled up to me, looking innocently up into my face.

" May I ask one question? "

" Yes," I said.

" Don't you ever feel a donkey as well? " she asked me, and ran away shouting with laughter.

I went up into my study.

" Why in God's name didn't that blasted bomb finish me properly off? Whatever good am I on

earth like this?" And I drenched myself in pity.
What's the point of the whole absurd business?
Sights of horror came into my mind — men I had
seen blown to pieces. Men, born of women, born
of love between men and women, their coming longed
for; and having come, loved and cherished, worked
for, the unfolding of their natures watched, their
interests shared, their hopes of manhood. . . . And
then marched out into the mud to slaughter.
"There's no meaning in anything," I cried. "Why
mind? Why bother? All the while they're blowing themselves to pieces; using every device that
man's ingenuity can invent to blow each other to
pieces. What does anything matter? What does
anything matter when that's the end of everything?"
So I raved myself exhausted, and like a sensible
man in my regained composure I saw that I really
was quite anxious to go on living; that it was only an
attack of nerves; that the truth of the matter was
that I could not stand being made fun of by a silly
girl.
"I have always been an ordinary sensible man,"
I assured myself, "and that I intend to remain, with
or without help. And Amy would make a sweet
little wife for any sensible man. The mater was
absolutely right."
In much the same way perhaps a drunken man is
always assuring himself and others that he is perfectly sober.
"Amy is the answer," I said to myself. "She is
the ballast I need. It's only her airs and graces that
I'm up against. It's my fault for approaching her

in the wrong way.   She takes her cue instinctively
from me.   It's all as clear as day when one thinks
about it sensibly.   I need to go slow. ' I have to
recover from an illness.   I have to decide what work
to do; and I must meanwhile be amused.   There is
madness and misery in the world; there is mystery;
and it is the duty of a sensible man on that account
to be as sensible as he possibly can."

I decided to do an hour's work before lunch.
Medieval history was my special subject, in which I
had just failed to obtain a fellowship.   I resolved to
read for two hours and a half every morning.   I
attacked the second volume of the " Cambridge History " which I had bought a month before the war
broke out.

But it was no good.   In a little while, concentrate
as I would, my mind wandered back to what I had
seen in Flanders.   All history leads up to this, was
the thought that kept pricking me until at last I
could stand it no longer.   I slammed the book in
despair.

" All history needs to be rewritten," my heart
cried out, " when it ends in this, ends in the fact that
every able bodied citizen in Europe is busy helping to
blow men to pieces in the mud.   Never in the history
of the world has there been such a slaughtering as is
taking place now."

Proud headlines ran through my mind.   " Greatest battle in history.   Four million men engaged."

But I refused to give way to this preposterous
weakness.   I was not strong enough to work yet.
My brain needed rest and nourishment.   My com-

mon sense suggested more porridge, more milk, more fish — and above all Amy, with her sterling normal spirit that could long for another Trafalgar to be enrolled on the annals of the British Navy.

I thought of a brave man I knew whose mother had been terrified by a mouse before he was born, and who could never see a mouse without trembling. "That's my case," I reassured myself. "I've had a bad taste of the nasty side of war. My nerves are a bit unstrung. Things have got out of proportion. Plenty of porridge, milk, and fish, and I shall be right as a trivet. The war is my mouse. That's all. Or I should have been much more upset by this stupid spirit business."

A motor-car came up the drive. It reminded me that it was the doctor's day to call. He was a well-known doctor who motored down from London three times a week to a house near ours which had been turned into a hospital. He was a friend of mother's, came to see how I was getting on once a week, and nearly always took lunch with us. I liked him much and respected him more.

He interviewed me after lunch, a very thick man of medium height. The most remarkable thing about him was that he combined a gentle voice with an abrupt manner. He began as usual by prodding me, stroking me, tapping me, and holding open my eyelids and staring into my eyes with an intensity that was at first alarming.

"Any pain?"

"Nothing to speak of."

"Nerves?"

" Oh a bit rackety still."

" How do you know? "

" Ordinary things upset me, seem to be of immense importance."

He nodded. " And the mind? "

" All right. I have no headaches, but I can't work."

" Why not? Concentration weak? "

" Yes. It all comes round to. . . . For instance, I started reading this morning. History. I didn't think in the ordinary way. Of course it all leads up to August, 1914. And so on. The thought came and battered me. More like violent toothache than a passing thought. My whole body gets weak."

" The usual obsession. Tell me now. It's a thing that personally I'm extremely interested in. Have you ever had hallucinations of any kind? "

" Why do you ask that? "

He had dropped his professional manner.

" It is a most remarkable thing how many cases of hallucinations have come my way since the war. My colleagues have met them; are inclined to pooh-pooh them, as the men themselves do. But I have seen too many strange features in humanity to be able to dismiss any manifestation lightly."

" You mean cases of incipient lunacy," I said casually.

" By no means. Far stranger than that. Lunacy, roughly speaking, infers some form of decay. This manifestation seems to infer the opposite, a form of growth. Roughly speaking. That is why

I asked *you* the question, because you happen to be one of the sanest young men I know."

" Funnily enough I have had a sort of hallucination. Two vivid dreams of a youth with whom I conversed. Twice now I've imagined I saw him in daylight — this morning, as it happens. On both occasions there were natural explanations. A light thrown on a tree."

I went to the bell and rang it.

" I've noted down our conversations. Quite foolish and ordinary, but it might interest you to see them."

" It would immensely."

The maid answered the bell, and I asked her to fetch the notebook from my study.

He plied me with questions as to the youth's appearance and so forth. He read through my notes without a word.

" You'll go on with this? " he said in great excitement. " Yes; that is perhaps the strangest thing," he went on, pressing his thumbnail on the page — the dent is still visible. " The absence of alarm; and it's typical of many cases."

Rarely have I seen a man in such a state of restrained excitement.

" Heavens and earth! " he cried. " If ever we get this wonderful machine working in anything like decent order, at anything like full pitch. At present the best thing we can do with our energy is to bomb each other; what will happen when we — when we —" he subsided, hesitating —" don't." The word dropped like a round stone into a pond.

We both laughed.   But suddenly mistrust gripped me.

"I say, doctor, you're not playing tricks with me?"

"Tricks?"

"Taking a line, to ease my mind?"

"Oh, that!" he answered. "You know I'm not."

"There's lunacy in the family."

"You mean your grandfather. I knew him well. It was more like genius with no means of expressing itself. You can be proud to have his blood in your veins. No, no. I know your stock, young James Wood. It'll be the fault of your own self-satisfaction if you come to grief."

"Me self-satisfied?" I said, astonished.

He chuckled.

"Being more highly strung than most young men you need a thicker coating for your comfort. That's all."

"What do you mean by 'come to grief'?"

"Not develop all there is in you. Get covered with rust. Dry rot at ease till Judgment Day. Unused energy is the cause of most illness. Machinery has played the devil with our health."

He was looking attentively at his watch while he spoke. He put it thoughtfully to his ear and looked at it again. Then his manner changed. He put his hand on my shoulder.

"You are doing well," he said, "making far more rapid progress than I had hoped. You have stamina and a good level head. You will pull through finely.   No one could have tackled this hallucination more sensibly than you have done; and if you continue to note down these interviews, as you have been doing, and let me see them, you will be doing me a very great service indeed.   An inestimable service.   I have certain theories forming in my mind on the subject.   We may be on the track of great things."

"Won't you tell me about your theories?"

"Certainly I will.   But not now.   For one thing I have no time.   For another they are still too vague to be put into intelligent speech.   I cannot tell you how valuable your notes may be to me."

He took my hand, and was going.

I called him back.

"Oh, doctor, I've not mentioned it to any one. Not the mater even."

"Excellent!   Excellent!   You can rely on me. Good luck to you."

There was nothing formal in his farewell words. They were so compact with intention that I almost arched my back to them, like a cat to a caressing hand.   But how far was he treating me, I wondered, and how far was he sincere?

IV

THE knowledge that my experience had a recognised name, and could be inquired after by a doctor like any other homely symptom, was of course most reassuring, but it was also, owing to some odd little freak in my nature, most annoying. Perhaps my ordinariness was not quite the source of congratulation to myself that I liked to suppose; but the odd little twist (or really the usual little twist) was a fact, though I cannot explain it; and I went so far as to encourage the idea in my mind that the doctor was by his whole conduct astutely treating a strange mental case. The picture of myself at brave grips with a treacherous foe became dearer to my mind's eye in proportion to the distance to which the danger receded; and in this way I disposed of the doctor's astonishing statement that self-satisfaction would be the only cause of my discomfiture. He meant it to be a surprise to turn my mind from graver matters. The doctor was a judge of character. It was a clever stroke to hit on his patient's exact opposite to startle him from a dangerous line of thought, because self-satisfaction was as he used it only a polite term for the complacent conceit which is conceit's most odious form, and of which no one in his right senses could accuse me. His motive in doing so in such a dramatic way was clear.   Moreover it was certainly at the time successful.   Startled I was, and impressed.

That was one little circle round which my thoughts ran.   Another touched my attitude towards Amy, the war, and my familiar.   The doctor's commendation of my behaviour, his wish for me to continue my record, and his repeated expression of its importance, gave me very considerable satisfaction, and made me resolved to treat the whole affair coolly and scientifically.   That frame of mind induced me to look along my nose at my familiar, and I saw, or thought I saw, that extremes of feeling on my part led to his coming.   I traced a connection between the battering the thought of war had given me and the rapture at sight of a primrose.   All I had to do was to discover which was cause and which was effect; and the discovery seemed to offer no difficulty.

Always Amy came to my mind as the solution of the problem.   Only my approach to her must be more carefully made.   There must be no doubt as to whose was the leading spirit.   She must be kept in her place — oh, not a lowly place at all, but in her place.   A girl needed a play-fellow who was her master.   All her little airs and graces to me were due to her instinct, which set blindly to work to discover if I were capable of mastery.   And then I instantly saw — so clearly that I wondered that I could have been so long blind to it — the striking analogy between what my attitude should be to my familiar and what it should be to Amy.   They were both

irresponsible beings; both, uncontrolled, might play
the mischief with me. The more I thought of it,
the closer became the analogy, and the simpler. At
such moments I seemed to see myself without a blur,
and smiled at the thought of my familiar's attempt
to insinuate doubts of my personality into my mind.
I was sure of it as of the chair I sat in and of the
solid arm of the chair I patted in my pleasure.

A hundred situations with Amy occurred to me in
which I played the proper part, as I congratulated
myself I had done on the last occasion in spite of her
wanton and excited laughter, and my access of unaccountable misery. Both were due to nerves on
her part and on mine.

Yet I was unprepared for my next encounter with
Amy. It seemed almost too good to be true, so
precisely did it fit in with my sense of fitness. For
she came to me with a headache after tea, and was
soon nestling on my knee like a sick child anxious to
be petted. Even while I petted her, and while she
listened to all that I said, the uneasy feeling never
left me that she might jump up and point out de-
risively that here was another proof of her ability to
do as she liked with me. But as she did not, my
uneasiness served only by pointing to my natural
foresight, to confirm my sense of security, though I
could not have named the steps which led to her
nestling on my knee.

After dinner I wrote to a friend to inquire about
the duties of an underwriter, and whether it would be
possible for me to get work at Lloyd's: also I wrote
to my late tutor at Oxford asking if he would be

good enough to mention any ideas he might have of a possible future for me.

I never could get quotations correct in my mind; but I found much comfort in saying:

> " I am the captain of my boat,
> I am the master of my fate."

I summoned my familiar quietly, firmly, as I like to address men-servants; and as he did not come, I assured myself in the same mood of quiet firmness that both his appearances in daylight were delusions, one or two degrees deeper than his appearances at night.

Rain was steadily falling when I went to bed, and I was certain, without troubling to find any reason for my certainty, that the night would be undisturbed by my familiar.

I was mistaken. He came. At what time he came I am unable to say, as I heard the clock strike but forgot to count the hours. On this occasion I am less able than ever to say whether I was awake or asleep at the time of his coming, but I opened my eyes to see him standing poised before me, and looking at me with lowered eyes, his neck unbent.

He spoke at once without moving, in his low, very clear voice, in which I noted with pleasure a mingling of mild entreaty and reproach.

"Why must you resist me?" he asked.

Of the repose that came from him I was again conscious, and I turned it to the advantage of my assurance.

" Why do you who know everything bother to ask questions of a mere ignorant man like myself? "

" But I know very little about you."

" You speak my language; you lay down the law about reason; you laugh at my plan of marriage; you affect omniscience to mystify me, and yet you say you know very little about me."

" I realise my ignorance; you do not.   That is the difference between us.   You become confident and emphatic when you are most uncertain, and what you do know you pass over as commonplace and uninteresting."

" There you are," I declared, " laying down the law again.   If I told you the reason of my resentment at your intrusion, you would not believe me."

" I can only know through you," he said mournfully enough to encourage me; " I know when you are speaking the truth."

" Thank you," I said, " but I am not in the habit of lying."

" You do not even realise the difficulty of knowing what the truth is.   I did not think my work would be so arduous."

" What is your work? " I asked.

" Our work," he said.   " Yours and mine.   Reunion."   And he moved away towards the window.

" I can get on very well without you," I assured him cheerfully.

" But I cannot get on at all without you," he answered, not turning.

" I have power over you, then? "

" Not more than I have over you."

" Tell me who you are."

" That is the last thing you will be able to understand. You begin at the wrong end."

" You can't expect me to help you if you won't throw any light on who you are or what you are or what you want. It's an absurdity."

" I might have frightened you into submission," he said; " but I chose this way."

" That was very kind of you."

" No; it was daring. I risked failure."

His manner disturbed me.

" Now about Amy," I said with all the authority I could muster. " I intend to marry her whether the idea amuses you or whether it doesn't."

" There is nothing to prevent you, is there? "

" I'll stand no interference on your part in that direction."

" Oh no. I have no power to interfere with what you do. Only I want to know what a man's love is. You do not love Amy."

" Of course, if you say so, far be it from me to contradict you."

" But you do not. Surely you realise that you know that. You said as much to me when I looked at you out of your mother's eyes. She touches almost nothing of you, or I should feel her influence."

Discomfort took hold of me; and the feeling of repose, which had hitherto been invariable in his presence, lessened while he spoke. It was keen as a physical sensation, like an icy draught on the neck in a hot room. But I would not give way. Stubbornly I said:

" I intend to ask Amy to marry me. She would make any man a sweet little wife."

Anger and dismay were visible on his face. My discomfort became acute, and grew to consternation when the anger and dismay vanished and laughter shook him like a reed. Somehow it seemed indecorous that he should laugh like that. He appeared sensible of his mirth's discourtesy.

" You must excuse me," he said.

" Yes, but what makes you laugh? " I asked with genuine interest.

" Because I cannot see why you should be forcing yourself to do what you do not want to do. Won't you tell me? "

" Everything is complex," I explained, " in our life. No man can take an important step without hesitation. Marriage affects her happiness as well as mine. Marriage ——" I stopped. " It's all quite clear to me," I went on. " But when I talk to you about it all my thoughts change to nonsense. Not that they *are* nonsense in the least."

He glowed as he had done on his second visit, so that the room lightened in his vicinity.

" Good! " he cried. " Good! Now you must see why I cannot tell you who and what I am. At last we have taken the first step towards an understanding."

" It has been quite involuntary on my part."

" Of course it has. Why, when you feel the need of me ——"

" I shall continue to resist you with all my power. I will not have, if I can help it, any dealings whatever with what I cannot understand. I shall not even consider the possibility of not resisting you, unless you answer categorically questions I may put to you."

"Well, ask," he said with a sigh. "I will do my best."

"Who and what are you?"

"Partly your grandfather's wish, partly a dream of your own."

"Are you a spirit?"

"What else?"

"Are you my astral self?"

"I only assume this shape for convenience."

"Are you my astral self?"

"What is your earthly self? Believe me, you will only mystify yourself. I am all that I have said, but so much more. Cease, cease this questioning, or you will turn me into a torment — turn me against my will into a torment."

"Are you . . ." I began, heedless of his entreaty, but I stopped; for pain seized me — not physical pain, but anguish vague and intolerable.

I closed my eyes.

"Believe me! Believe me!" I heard his low voice, wailing. I kept my eyes tightly shut.

"Leave me alone," I cried. . . . And I must have spoken in my sleep, because I heard the maid's voice answer:

"Yes, sir; I've brought the tea."

I started up; and my first thought was that I must have been dreaming.

"Did I say anything, Rose?"

"Yes, sir, but I only heard the word 'alone.'"

Talking in your sleep, sir, I think; answering my knock at the door."

And yet I could not convince myself that I had been dreaming. At first I was deeply disturbed; but that gave way to a sense of relief that I had not yielded; that I had stood my ground until anguish that no man could withstand was used as a weapon against me. My resolution strengthened. I immediately set to work to copy out my interview into the exercise book, that fear might not encroach upon my will. As I wrote, I set no store by the meaning of the words. I refused to think, or to weaken in any way the firm stand I had taken.

There seemed several new points to be noted about this latest visit. (a) The benefits to be gained were mutual; (b) his susceptibility to the emotion of grief; (c) his growing dislike of being questioned, and so on. I made careful comments in as impersonal a style as I could command, feeling that at each cool comment the weight of influence was being lifted.

My thought was: "Here is something on which I can test and develop the vigour of my common sense." And I saw that the deadliest danger to which I was exposed was the cunning insinuation that I did not realise what "I myself" was: that mined personality. But forewarned is forearmed, and I countered by owning that all knowledge was comparative; a deeper knowledge than mine might be possible, but to obtain it I must cling all the closer to what knowledge I had.

But it was not sufficient to meet this intruder by

argument; I must meet him by action. Plain common sense must be the guiding principle of my life. There must be no wavering or hesitation in the face of the enemy. I must press well home the definite advantage which in this last interview I had without doubt gained. Common sense pointed a steady finger towards Amy, and steeled me to the great decision of asking her to be my wife. It was only necessary to still a vague fluttering towards some shadowy notion that I called romance. And that was easily done. For against this shadowy notion I could wield such solid facts as that we had been friends from childhood; that she cared for me; that my mother approved of her; that she had at least three hundred a year of her own. Not that I was mercenary, or that her money attracted me — not at all — but it is absurd to deny that three hundred pounds is three hundred pounds, and that man does not live on bread alone, and the man would be a hypocrite who would not prefer that his wife should have a little money, unless he were an old-fashioned fogey who thought it unsuitable for a woman to be in any way independent.

Of course I was fond of Amy. Why, otherwise, should I have wished to kiss her, and enjoyed kissing her? Why, otherwise, should I have liked her to nestle on my knee? Naturally in my sensitive condition little things jarred on my nerves, and remarks of hers offended me, even hurt me; but what of that? No girl is perfect, and it was an untold advantage to know beforehand her limitations, so that afterwards when we settled peaceably down to life there would be no bitterness, no disappointment. I congratulated myself on having no illusions about the girl with whom I was in love. Besides, no man marries a girl for congenial conversation, and Amy could be capital company.

Looked at from her point of view, there was even more to be said for the marriage. A woman's instinct in these matters was not to be taken lightly. Love was a woman's life, but a man's pastime. Her instinct was a sure guide for me to follow, and certainly, as I had never cared for a girl more than I had cared for Amy, it was my plain duty, even if it meant some slight sacrifice, which it didn't, to submit to her wishes. No man of course was born a good husband; but every decent man could, without too great a strain upon his nature, become one. I knew exactly what I meant by a good husband. The words conveyed no outrageous ideal, no boy's rather unpleasant dream of a perpetual honeymoon, but a sound sensible meaning. I should be kind and courteous and not in the least exacting.

I was on absolutely safe ground in vouching this to myself. I had to all intents and purposes proved it already. She had lived in the house for months at a time and never got on my nerves. She had the gift of fitting into the life of her surroundings. I knew it; I had experienced it. True, lately, she had annoyed me, pained me a little now and then; but the fault was not hers. It was mine, for approaching too flippantly an extremely serious matter. She had, woman-like, caught my flippancy, and used it with perfect justice against myself.

My common sense went on adding reason to reason to its complete satisfaction, and being satisfied opened the door ceremoniously and without hurry or alarm to the other image of her, to the delight and enchantment of her woman's self, which cannot be more delicately or more exactly expressed than in my mother's words that Amy would make any man a sweet little wife. Common sense had done its duty and retired, consenting, with no loss of honour or dignity, to leave me in the arms of this lovely vision. Common sense gave full approval, and allowed me to forget all inconveniencec, all little traits that had annoyed me. She became simply a pretty woman, and I became simply an eager young man.

Not in love with Amy? It was my turn to laugh at the question. Not in love with Amy? With all my power of will I summoned my familiar so that I might laugh in his face at the ridiculous question.

He did not come, however, to my unwavering satisfaction, for I knew that he was afraid of my resolution, even if he had the power, which I now doubted, of appearing in the daylight.

A feeling of triumph took hold of me. I offered incense before this image of woman which common sense had allowed Amy to become. In my mind the plunge was taken. I had earned a man's right to indulge in visions of delight. My wounds were the signs of duty done. My hesitations were the signs of an honourable man. I had faced them one by one, and who should deny me the reality of delight which I had, without boasting, doubly earned?

On the first occasion that was possible I would make my proposal to Amy; and I instantly decided, with a fresh wave of pleasure at the decision, that I would make it with all the warmth I could find, so that she should not have the least suspicion of a feeling that after due consideration I had agreed to accept what at its first offer I had refused. Every girl likes to be wooed, even though she may have the courage to falter out a declaration. I glowed with pleasure at thought of the joy which I now had it in my power to give; which was my privilege and even my duty to give.

Was I or was I not sincere, then, in thinking of her happiness? That is a question which others will probably find far easier to answer than I do now, though at the time no doubt of my sincerity touched me. Now I know that it is not so easy as I thought it once for any man to be sincere. But it is not part of my intention to make excuses myself. When the temptation touches a certain power of pressure, however, I yield; for its force, resisted, would only turn me into a prig. That I have detested in myself and others — especially, be it confessed, in others. The practice of any virtue must be perfect before it is tolerable.

Well, sincere or not, my resolution held and renewed my confidence, of which I was in far greater need than I dared own.

I decided to let a week pass, during which I would key my attitude to Amy up to a higher and more serious level, and after that week to take the first opportunity to make my proposal. This intention

I solemnly registered in my mind, and with equal
solemnity I broke it.

For Amy came into my room to mix me the Sanatogen I had begun to drink in milk at twelve every
morning. She sat on the table's edge without
speaking, stirring the spoon round and round the
tumbler. Two distinct thoughts passed, without
jostling each other, through my mind. What
started them on their way I do not know. They
came, as I watched the stirring. The first was: " I
fear no seriousness of mine will ever change these
airs and graces."

The second was: " Unless I speak now, I shall
never speak."

Why they should have acted as convincing reasons
for an instant declaration I can only guess; they have
since then appeared to me as, each by itself, sufficient
proof of the need for an everlasting silence; but I
mistrust now such solemnity as was mine at that
moment.

Well, there she sat on the edge of the table stirring
my Sanatogen in milk, and as she stirred the spoon
made a dull tinkle against the glass, and she was
thoughtful.

" Amy," I said deliberately, " I know I am an old
crock and an awful duffer in many ways; and I ought
not really to be asking you, but I can't help it. I do
wish you would marry me."

" Oh, James," she said, " how lovely! But I
nearly dropped the glass when you began, and this
stuff would never come out of a carpet."

She continued to stir the tumbler; and the dull

tinkle had the same thoughtful rhythm. Her head was slightly lowered, so that I could not see her eyes. I saw chiefly the parting in her hair, which told me little.

Most inopportunely I remembered the laughter of my familiar, and the reason he gave for laughing. Fury at this tampering interloper disposed of all tenderer feelings.

"I'm very much in earnest about this," I said fiercely. "I can't tell you how much I need you — not just to look after me, but loneliness gets on the nerves. I need companionship; something belonging to myself, to take me out of myself."

"What's changed your opinion?"

"My feelings have changed. You've changed them."

She was silent; the rhythm of the spoon's dull tinkle on the glass became more regular.

"This is one of the great moments of my life," I thought.

"I'm most tremendously honoured," she said.

"And pleased?" I suggested.

"And pleased," she agreed, and added with less solemnity, "And I'm most awfully surprised, too, you know. Most awfully surprised."

"Oh, come now, you aren't really. You must have known."

"Honour bright. I hadn't a notion."

"But you are pleased."

"Of course I adore being proposed to — by you. But . . ."

"But what?"

" I must have time to think it over."

" Yes, do. And tell me after lunch."

" I mean, properly think it over."

" All right. To-morrow after breakfast, then."

" No, at least three months."

The possibility of delay had never touched my speculations.

" Oh, that's absurd," I blurted out. " It's utterly impossible for me to wait all that time. Three months! Why, only the other day you yourself . . ." I stopped in time.

" Three months isn't at all a long time. Lots of girls think nothing of asking a man to wait a whole year for an answer. And they've not nearly as much to think over as me."

" What have you got to think over? Don't you care for me? Why, you . . ."

" Yes, I know. That's just the difficulty."

" There's no difficulty at all except of your making."

" There is. There is. Don't be so stupid and . . . and thick. Listen. Let me think. Don't you see? Why, years and years ago, Dorrie and I, we made a compact. And you reminded me so of Lewis Waller, and wore such nice suits, and of course it was all silly and schoolgirlish and that kind of thing, but when I heard you were wounded and — oh! it all came back like anything, and I could hardly bear the thought of meeting you, it was so thrilling and glorious, and when I did, it simply did for me, and . . . any one could understand that, I should think."

" But that only shows . . ."

" Don't chip in," she cried. " It's difficult enough to explain without your chipping in. Where had I got to? Oh yes. Any one could understand that. You did beautifully at the time — you know, when I burst into tears and all that. I'd really caught you awfully bad. You made me see. Cured me. I don't mean you're not a hero, and splendidly good and patient; but somehow it's different. And that's why I must have at least three months to think it over. Besides . . ."

" What? "

" To tell you the truth. . . . Of course I've enjoyed the fun we've had . . . but somehow it doesn't seem quite nice of you . . . I mean . . . to behave like that with a girl you really meant to marry. Fun's fun, but perhaps after all it was only clumsiness."

That made me wince, which she noticed; and impulsively she came to me and put her arms round my neck and said: " Oh, I didn't mean his poor maimed hand and foot."

I almost wished she had.

" It can't be helped," I said. " If you don't care, you don't care. It's my own fault, and there's an end of it."

" Don't be so hasty. I tell you I must wait. I feel it queerly all coming back."

" There's no use in waiting. I can't wait," I said rather crossly, because I had not expected the turns of the interview, and the idea of a three months' wait abashed me; suspense in a matter of this kind was intolerable.

"No," I said, "it's very sweet and kind of you but I couldn't allow it." I did my utmost to transform my crossness into grief. "No, no, I'm not as selfish as that. I couldn't allow you to put yourself to all that . . . all that nuisance on my account. I thought . . . but there, it doesn't matter."

"But it does matter. It's not selfish of you. I'm not worthy of you. I must wait. You must let me wait. How can you expect a girl to answer off-hand? And it wouldn't be a bit of a nuisance to wait. I should love it."

"No, no. You must take my word for it. You must trust me. Forget what I've said to you. Think of me only as your friend."

I held out my hand to her with a sad smile. She refused to take it, shaking her head angrily, and she looked entrancing when she was angry.

"I won't have it," she cried. "Oh, why must you be so stupid and inconsiderate? Can't you see how difficult it is for me? You seem to enjoy making things all horrid. I believe you enjoy being miserable. And you've never said you loved me or . . . or anything. Oh, I think it's mean of you! Why can't you be a little different?"

"I'm sorry. I know I'm a very ordinary sort of person."

"Oh no, you aren't a bit. I've had heaps of boy friends. You're not a bit like any of them. They're all alike. Some are naughty, and always

want to kiss you; some are serious, and pretend they
don't. It sounds silly, but it's true: just two kinds,
and you're completely different. First you're really
serious, and hardly know I'm there; and then I'm
serious, much more than I've ever been in my life,
and you're kind and wise, and then become just as
naughty as any one could be, though any one could
see you weren't used to it, and we have fun, and
then all of a sudden you become solemn as a judge
and ask me to marry you, and are cross when I tell
you that you must wait for an answer. Not cross
because you're . . . oh, I don't know . . . not for
any nice reason, that any one else would be, because
you're so much in love with me, but cross like . . .
like mother used to be when I was a little girl and
left the door open, and I wouldn't come back to
shut it. I almost expected you to slap me and say.
like her, it was for my good you were slapping me.
And you know you did say that if I were a small boy
you would smack my head. And now you declare
to me that you're a most ordinary sort of person.
You aren't. You're a most dreadfully strange and
peculiar person, and if it weren't that all through,
whatever you are, you're always somehow a great
baby, I don't think I should like you a bit. And
as it is, I must wait. I can't possibly decide off-
hand."

"Anyhow, perhaps we've said enough for now."
Strong were my own reasons for disliking her to call
me " strange and peculiar." I picked up the tumbler
which I began to sip.

"You make me desperate," she thumped the

table to exclaim. "Desperate. You've hardly said anything at all yet. That's just what is so upsetting."

"I've asked you to marry me. I should have thought that wasn't so bad for one morning's talk."

"Marry! That's just it. You see, I'd had ever such a long solemn mood of stepping softly round you as a holy sort of angel of mercy kind of thing. Settling down with a halo and a hush for ever and ever, Amen. Oh, well, and when you opened the window on that mood, I tell you, another came. More fun. I must have more fun. I'm twenty-two. I thought of marrying about twenty-five, say. That's three more years to be gay in. So it's not only you, but settling down at all yet, that I've got to think over. But you won't think I'm not most awfully proud and happy and flattered. It's really not so much you. You'd make any girl a simply ideal husband. It's just that I can't help my liking for what I call fun. And I'm rather strict and old-fashioned in some ways, and I do think it's hateful the way some young married women talk to other men exactly as though they weren't the wives of some one else. Perhaps a man can't realise how hateful that is. It's unfair, to begin with."

So she prattled on. I saw and admired the frankness in what she said. But as she prattled, a slow suffocating feeling came over me, and I remembered with intense vividness how when I was a little boy and made houses under the bedclothes, I used suddenly to experience the same kind of sensation, and used violently with legs and arms to fling off the bedclothes, shouting, " I can't breathe, I can't breathe."

Now there seemed nothing to be done to regain my breath. I could not even tell what was stifling me, for Amy in her animation looked more sweetly pretty than I had ever seen her look, and as I say I recognised and admired her frankness.

Misery came creeping over me. Common sense repeated that it was sentimental to mind what a pretty girl said, and deliberately opened the door to the most alluring visions of her. But so far were they from lifting this fog of misery that they increased its density.

And still she prattled on. Hardly above my breath I managed to say at the first pause, miserably:

"My own fault. The mistake. Rather insulting."

I had no strength left to withstand the flood of triumph, as she cried out with bright eyes:

"You see, we both must wait. Now don't you? You feel for yourself how difficult it is when you begin to think about it."

I could only venture without conviction on the answer:

"I don't think it ought to be."

"But it *is*. That's just what I've been saying. We must wait. I know I'm right. And you needn't be gloomy and depressed, because I'll be just as nice to you as ever I was, and I'm almost sure it will be Yes. Because we do somehow feel things in the same way.   Jimmie, what's the matter?   You're all white, Jimmie."

I made a supreme effort.

"It's all right," I succeeded in saying.   "Only I'm not . . . not quite strong enough yet for all . . . for all this emotion."

My head was swimming.   She stood watching me, staring in fright.   I was thankful that she did not rush out of the room for mother.

"It's nothing — nothing.   It's passing.   Sudden giddiness."

I motioned with my hand.   She could not move. At last the wretched giddiness left me.   I gave a sigh of relief.

"I'm sorry for being such an ass," was my apology.

Fright changed to rapture as she said:

"Oh!   To think you care like that!"

She turned away and began to walk slowly towards the door, her head thrown far back.   She was actually going, yet I was obliged to say:

"Amy, you won't mention any of this to the mater?"

In the same rapt pensiveness she said, still moving towards the door:

"Oh no, no.   How could I?"

At the door she turned to say:

"I'm almost positive now it will be Yes."

She went.

After my last attack of giddiness I had been sick. Relief at my exemption from that humiliation was indescribable.

I hopped to the sofa and lay flat on my back. Only then did I realise with boundless thankfulness that no mental or spiritual pranks had been at their subtle and secret work upon my personality, but that the simple homely truth was that the Sanatogen had disagreed with me.

"All the same," I thought, "I must be careful, I must be very careful, and keep a firm hold upon myself; or the most innocent facts will be pointing to some supernatural agency, and I shall be exposing myself to precisely what it is my main business now to overcome. That's the devil of the business: its ingenious trickery."

You can imagine my relief at knowing, as I did without trace of uncertainty, that the discomfort which became misery was solely due to a simple physical cause, to the oncoming of giddiness.

I closed my eyes to brood on Amy's prattle, on Amy's frankness, on Amy's common sense; and again I burned incense before the image of her girlish loveliness; in irreverent glee I allowed my imagination to touch in each exquisite detail of the lovely picture.

Not in love with Amy? I hooted aloud at the crude absurdity of the question, yet while I hooted, I heard his low voice ask, without reproach, yet with quite maddening distinctness:

"Wouldn't any young woman do as well as Amy?"

I started up; looked furiously about; saw nothing; shook my fist and cried:

"I know you now by that vile insinuation. Some

obscene spirit of evil. That's vile; that's base; that's filthy. Am I an animal?"

I waited. There was no reply.

"Answer me. Am I an animal?"

There was no reply. I summoned all my strength.

"You shall answer me. Be visible and answer me. Confront me and dare to answer. Am I an animal?"

My body trembled with excitement and anger. But I only heard the sparrows chirping outside, the wind fluttering the pages of a book, and on this book my eyes fell, as the fluttering stopped, and I saw the heron's feather which I had laid inside the book for safety.

My strength forsook me. I fell back and buried my face in the cushion.

"Oh, it's not fair," I moaned. "It's not fair. I shall go mad. I shall go mad."

V

THAT was the worst seizure that had so far caught
me. The company of others — the general company — helped me to draw down a barrier between
the thought of it and me. Accordingly I kept them
talking on after lunch with a vivacity that surprised
me, and blinded me to an undercurrent which I must
have otherwise perceived sooner than I did. But
even when Doris came up to me and pressed my arm
and said, " Oh, I am so glad! " I did not realise what
she meant. Her look of intense meaning did not
enlighten me. She ran out of the room to catch up
Amy, who was in the passage.

Alone with me, mother said: " My dear boy, you
could not have done a wiser thing."

I was startled.

" But I asked her to say nothing."

My mother smiled.

" I know. But with such news to tell! You
couldn't expect her to keep it quite to herself."

" But she said . . ."

" She *said*, you goose. Weren't you only a day or
two ago saying things to me? I was not to make
plans, and so forth."

" But this is different. Besides, nothing is settled."

" You mustn't expect a girl to be too brutally

definite. After all, she only gets engaged once . . .
for the first time," she added, in a way that under
other circumstances would have made me laugh.
She put her hand on my shoulder, and in all moth-
erly seriousness said: "Girls are girls, dear, remember. Don't bring your hard-and-fast boy's
rules of proper behaviour to bear on her."

"Can't they keep their words, then, for five con-
secutive minutes?"

"But why should she? Doesn't it after all show
that her doubts are slight? Oughtn't you to be
glad? Besides, she knows that you really wanted
me to know. Didn't you?"

"Yes, you perhaps, but Doris."

"Well, dear, that was really my fault, because
Doris came in just after Amy told me, and I looked
so happy that she practically guessed. She asked
me point-blank, and I couldn't tell an untruth,
could I?"

"I suppose it doesn't much matter," I grunted,
and was bidden in mother's most gentle manner not
to be a cross curmudgeon.

"What did she mean, then, by insisting she must
wait?" I asked.

My mother rubbed my cheek with her knuckle.
She has engaging ways that never fail to enchant me.

"I don't know how you asked her."

"What has that got to do with it?"

"Don't you yourself like a certain — shall we say
reluctance?"

"She did it to please me, then?"

"Not definitely. Not intentionally. Her anxiety to please you is instinctive; and you must own, crusty one, that she has been successful."

There was often something unmanning in my mother's manner. At that moment, weakened as I had been by my nerve seizure, I was completely unmanned. I felt as though I were a small boy, a little helpless kid, bewildered, lost and frightened. I should like to have climbed upon her lap and wept. As it was, I put my head on her shoulder and said:

"Why am I unhappy, mother?"

"Ah, darling," she said, "I know. I felt like that. It's really that you're so happy it's more than you can bear."

I stood up and smiled at her; and until that moment, as I looked at the tears in her eyes, I never knew what loneliness could mean.

"This is love," I said to myself. "They are right who say that love means grief. What else could it mean?"

I carried that trend of thought up to my room with me. It suited my mood.

I was learning the meaning of life as it is, freed from all illusion. How right I had been in seeing my salvation in Amy! Bare facts, stripped of all false pretty trappings, were as much my need as was bread for a starving man. To be bruised by them? What did a bruise or two matter for a man who was not a coward? I must harden myself against my subtle antagonist, who would trick me into his power. Only by facing the illusions of daily life could I wipe his influence from my mind, and heal

myself of hallucination.   He was only a visible form
thrown out by my sick mind and shattered nerves.
I must become whole and strong again.   I must even
make myself a little more ordinary than I need
otherwise have been.

And Amy — dear little Amy.   A little silly perhaps; a little foolish; but only in her talk, and that
was amusing, when you didn't listen too attentively,
or when she was sitting on your knee.   If you
wanted talk, clever or thoughtful, there were always
books; there were always men friends.   And Amy
was a girl, sweet and delicately, reluctantly willing.
Why talk to her?   Why worry about trifles?   Take
the good feeling while it lasted, and when it went.
. . . Hundreds   of   good   respectable   men   and
women passed before my eye, and I reverenced their
dignity and their forbearance the one to the other;
and I realised how fine it was that natural contempt
and human exasperation so rarely peeped through
their features.   Nature made each the plaything of
the other.   Playthings are very pleasant, but playthings are out-grown; then duty comes and the stern
affairs of life.

So I patted my unhappiness till the pain itself
pleased me.   This is love, this is life, I said; and
gathered enormous comfort from the view of myself as a brave man facing facts with an unflinching
eye.

Then Amy entered.   Was I cross with her?
Telling my mother?   She really and truly couldn't
help it.   My mother so understood things, and was
so pleased, which of course made such a difference to

all the thinking that was to be done. No thinking? Ah! that was all I knew. That just showed I was a bad impatient boy; and so on, and so on.

I hardly listened to her words, but played with her hair and her little ears, and enjoyed my delight in feeling that she was close to me, and that while she prattled on, she was, almost imperceptibly, of her own accord, edging closer and closer.

I did not listen to her prattling, because it roused in me the loneliness which I called the grief of love, and also a feeling of shame which I also called the grief of love; neither did I want to feel them, so I kept caressing her and enjoying the delight of her nearness. Common sense told me to take the good of the moment and not to make my own misery. But I heard her say:

" Now we're practically engaged you needn't be *too* good."

And to stifle the thoughts which her remark started in my mind, I began to kiss her lips. What better way was there of stopping the stupid words that would be coming out of them?

My kisses burned the remark into my mind; why should it have shocked me, as it did intolerably, when it expressed a thought which was fluttering somewhere in my own consciousness?

There is no rose without its thorn, was my answer. This is the grief of love, and I submitted to it all the more readily because I could never forget my familiar's question, " Would not any young woman be as good? " nor cease to be disgusted at its base inference. For that I had my reply ready. " I am a man, not an animal," and I looked forward to my next visit from him, that I might throw my answer, like a challenge, in his teeth.

I bore this grief of love all the better for my confidence that it was arming me against the insidious enemy. I did not hide from myself how much I hated him; but I resolved not to let Dr. Redman know how deeply my enemy affected me. For my own sake, too, I must preserve the cool impersonal manner which I had adopted.

I wrote to the doctor there and then, in order that I might help to create in myself the right coolness of attitude by instantly putting it into practice.

" DEAR DOCTOR REDMAN.

" I find my talk with you has been most helpful. I have, believe me, no fears of my wits becoming unsettled by this hallucination business. It interests me, and nothing more. It does not at all prey upon my mind. I look forward quite honestly to my next encounter. There is one I am keeping for you to see. I was quite truculent with him, you will be amused to notice, and also extorted some information which as far as it goes is worth having, but it does not go very far. The mystification business is still going strong; my answer to which is, ' Don't be mystified.' But though it is not ' on my chest,' I think it wise that I should lead as far as possible the sanest, most normal kind of life in my power. I have therefore proposed (I think, bashful lover, with success) to a dear girl whom I have known and liked from my boyhood. I am sure you will agree with me that it is a good step to have taken. It has already given me much confidence. A girl has such an extrarordinary fund of common sense. Hers is at my disposal to act as ballast. I have not thought it necessary or advisable to tell her of my nocturnal visitor. Of course, all this is in the strictest confidence.

"Yours very sincerely,
"JAMES WOOD."

His answer to that letter, which I thought an excellent letter, ended for some time my friendly relations with Dr. Redman. His answer I received next morning: a telegram which ran: "James would would he well I wouldn't but he is a white man and I remain Redman." Friendly relations you understand; I was not small-minded enough to take offence serious enough to affect my formal and family relations with him.

But of that later.

On my slow way downstairs I had plenty of time to realise that visitors had come to tea, and to wonder what it would feel like to be with Amy among strangers for the first time after my practical engagement to her. Would there be any difference? Of course, congratulations when our engagement was announced must be lived through. This gradual approach to the new state had many advantages. Amy doubtless had been helped by her woman's instinct to anticipate them.

I guessed that the visitors were the Combes, having forgotten that Doris had asked them to tea —

Emily and Corinna Combe, daughters of R. W. L. Combe, the journalist. I felt uneasy as I entered the room. I put my uneasiness down to this being my first appearance in a new though unknown rôle. Unknown. Unconfessed perhaps would be the truer word, for no sooner was the door open than Amy danced up and fussed round me as she had never done before, and as I could not understand her doing now. Her attentions were kind but most embarrassing. Is she showing me off? I wondered, and decided that if she were, it was a very harmless little pleasure, another little feminine instinct which would soon satisfy itself. And as for people knowing, sooner or later wouldn't every one be in the secret, until the secret passed, and not to be seen together would require explanation? But when it came to her putting a cushion behind my back I was obliged to say — but I said it gently and with a smile:

"No, really. I hate cushions, you know."

And I pitched the wretched thing across the room on to the sofa.

Natural antagonism of the sexes, I thought, his side of which a gentleman must learn to conceal. No doubt my dislike of cushions and my way of showing it was equally distasteful to her. I felt that every moment of the day was instructing me in the lesson of life as it is. This is the real thing, I decided; and remembering the pleasure of Amy's kiss, I added, it might be worse.

I liked Emily and Corinna Combe. They both danced beautifully — especially Emily. Corinna had given up dancing for a year or so. I had asked her why, and she had said that it meant too much to her; an answer which baffled me and which she would not at the time amplify. Emily studied singing in London. Corinna wrote (what I did not know) and managed her father's house, as Mrs. Combe had recently become an invalid. They had a host of friends, and we were on quite friendly terms with the family; but I rather fancied that mother did not wish to become friendlier: there had been some scandal about one of the daughters — I forget which — and she always told me that Doris was naturally old-fashioned like herself. I should probably have seen more of the Combes if I had had only myself to consider.

It was very strange how excitement spread; gave its note to the party, as though we were somehow celebrating an occasion. I noticed it particularly because Amy usually was quiet and subdued when the Combes were there. They teased her about it when we met, as we not infrequently did, for tennis, in the summer before the war. Emily gave the chief response, and she and Amy and Doris talked and laughed and made mother laugh so much that she could hardly pour out the tea. Corinna did not say much, but she entered into it. I listened and laughed, and was carried along by them. There are times when one feels how very pleasant it is just to talk and laugh with nice people. No doubt this pleasantness was emphasised for me by the agreeable interest of which I, being a man and wounded, was delicately made the centre. I was sunning myself in it when without warning anguish took me by the throat.

It was a chance remark. Nothing more. Corinna was standing by the fireplace, eating a sandwich. She said: "Oh, what's that? Why, it's jam," and took out her handkerchief to wipe the back of her hand. Now the connection was of the vaguest, and I had taken a firm hold of myself not to think of certain aspects of the war. As a sensible man I had reasoned it out with myself. The war had to be; war is not pretty, but to brood on horrors means lunacy. There is much heroism, much suffering; I have done my bit, and there's an end of it. I smoothed it all over, too, with patriotic sentiments and made the best of it. What else could a sensible man do? It was no good going about with a glum face as well as with a maimed arm and leg.

Now, Corinna's innocent remark brought to life another remark that I had heard. "God! What's that?" a man near me had cried out in the trenches, but he answered his question by violently retching, for the stuff that trickled down his face was warm and human, and my neighbour was new to the trenches.

There was no reason whatever why her words should have startled this memory, or why the memory should have overwhelmed me.

Luckily Roger was by me, and I stooped over him, stroking his head, while my head reeled. It was as though I were being beaten. Blow on blow fell on me; I felt I must cry out in my anguish; and yet after that first vision, no further vision came, no definite memory, no definite thought, only anguish battered at me, and left me weak and feeble.

Disgust took the place of anguish. Disgust at Amy, disgust at them all, but chiefly disgust at myself. I could not sit with them, could not look at them. I got up and went to the window. If Amy had fussed up to me, I think I should have struck her with my stick. There was a lull in their talk and laughter. Fearing my seizure might have caused it, I turned. Emily and Amy were talking again. I did not heed them. What I saw hit me with surprise, sheer surprise, like a blow in the face.

For Corinna was standing, not looking at me, poised, head erect, motionless, in precisely the attitude in which I had first seen my familiar standing poised. Her heels were not touching the ground. I stared. And then, to complete my discomfiture, she turned towards me as my familiar had turned, moving her neck only, that is to say, not her shoulders or any other part of her body. Then she smiled, and walked swiftly up to me.

I would not allow my feeling to outgrow very natural surprise at the similarity. Her movement helped in my effort to prevent it deepening to consternation.

I said: "Why do you stand like that?"

"Oh, it's the right way to stand. It's . . ."

I felt her realise my mutilation. "It's a fad of mine, you know. I won't bore you with it. How quick of you to observe it!"

"I've seen it somewhere else."

"Yes, of course. It's the poise of many figures in Greek temples."

There was nothing strange, of course, in my tracing a resemblance between the sound of her voice and his. They both had the same low but very distinct tone.

"Tell me more about it," I said.

"Some other time, perhaps, if you're interested."

"Now, you two," came Amy's cheerful voice, "what secrets are you having in the window together?"

I was angry at the interruption, and still more angry with Corinna for the look of amused contempt that flickered over her face. And as she moved away her back and shoulders seemed to taunt me with a "Now do as you are told."

"One of those superior women," I thought. "God help them! Slightly contemptuous of all men; and I'm no exception to her silly rule."

Still, she moved so lightly that she seemed without weight — wafted along. I was obliged to notice it, nor did it appease my wrath.

"Some silly trick," I fumed. "Why can't she walk like an ordinary human being?"

And such a few miles away, across a strip of sea, men in hundreds and hundreds were in the mud, smashing each other to pieces with explosives. The impulse nearly mastered me to cry out: "Do you know what is being done in the name of honour, in the name of God? Why don't you walk out in front of those trenches and tell those men to stop slaughtering each other?"

It was with an effort that I regained my composure, to feel weak again and feeble, lifeless and sick at heart. I wished the Combes good-bye and hobbled up to my study.

"I can't go on like this," I thought to myself, and I sat in mute dismay.

My father (have I said that he died when I was eight?) had known Henry Fawcett; the blind postmaster-general had been his chief hero; and stories of Fawcett jostled in my mind as a child with Jack the Giant-Killer and Puss-in-Boots. He still seemed to me a fabulous being, and his remark to his father at the moment of the accident, when after the shot struck him he was in darkness, was part of my earliest consciousness. For Fawcett's first words were, "It won't make any difference," and I realised, as I had not done before, how this story had bitten into my consciousness so that the feeling that my own disablement should "make no difference" was instinctive.

Now I sat again on my father's knee, a little boy in a velveteen suit, smelling the curious smell of velveteen, staring at my father's heavy moustache, that curled down and made him look like a walrus, hearing his emphatic voice hushed to say, "And it made no difference, Jimmie — none — either to his love for his father, or to his career, or to his cheerfulness. He rode. He skated. He laughed. He helped the people as much as any man has ever helped the people." And he lifted his head to announce, as he always did at the end of this story, "His, my son, was a hero's life."

I felt no pang at my father's being dead. I felt no inspiration to emulate Fawcett. I felt only a kind of dumb resentment that mine was not a hero's life.

A hero marched on with a permanent purpose unswerving to its attainment. I had no purpose, no permanent state of mind even before the most familiar facts of my life. I was like a leaf in an eddy, going round and round, aimlessly, foolishly. Every little effort I made to steady myself spun me more giddily round.

All my strength was needed for no great purpose, but simply to remain my ordinary reputable self, to keep sane, and escape the thing that wished to lure me along the path of extravagance to utter witlessness.

I don't know why the coincidence of Corinna's poise and my noticing it immediately after being battered by that vision of war should have affected me so deeply. It was a coincidence, of course, and nothing more. There could be no sort of understanding between them.

And again this time I found the greatest help in taking what action I could, and the only action that was possible was to enter in my notebook, coolly and impersonally, an account of what had taken place. One note which pleased me was, " Attack perhaps induced by nervous agitation at my first experience of being treated as my future fiancée's property." The last words of my entry were, " Must certainly make a point of seeing C. C. soon, and must pump all information I can from her."

What finally restored my peace of mind was the thought that these two — my familiar and the superior young lady — were obviously made for each other, and what fun it would be to palm them off on each other. Send him perhaps to her with a letter of introduction. They were destined by a beneficent Providence to assist each other's upward steps, hand in hand, heavenwards.

Yet I never took the idea seriously that I could join their hands and start them off together. Even then it was in my bones to feel that somehow the being was inextricably mingled with my own personality; somehow owed whatever earthly existence it possessed to me.

" It's quite harmless," I cheered myself to think, " and as for my disablement, what should I have done if I had been blind or deaf. The war would end; and I should find work, and life would resume its normal course." It was a little difficult to imagine — and then suddenly through my mind ran, à propos of nothing at all, as though some one had spoken it — but no one did: " They ought to send recruits to butchers' shops to inure them to the sight of blood; to develop their instinct for slaughter on beasts before they apply it to men."

I was glad of the thought, wherever it came from; it tested my newly-restored self-control, and I dismissed it instantly with contempt, as a foolish extravagance, unworthy of an officer and a gentleman. Nor had a pig's squeal when stuck the least resemblance to a man's shriek of agony when bayoneted. You might as well head the triumphal march past of soldiers with waggon-loads of bones and putrefying corpses, with troops of the maimed, the blind and the insane. The idea was absurd. War was a cruel necessity, and a sensible man must make the best of it. Shouts and flying flags and playing bands were the meed of the returning hero. Some public expression of gratitude for what he had done, for all he had seen and suffered, was only right.

The door was tapped: the maid handed me a visiting-card. "Miss Combe asked me to bring this up to you," she said.

I took the card off the tray. On it was written in Corinna's tiny neat hand: "Not a fad; liker a religion. Should hate to mislead you about it."

"What can the girl mean?" I thought. "She must be mad. Oh, these superior people! Why can't they behave like everybody else?"

I went downstairs and amused myself with Amy till dinner. I was walking along a secluded path in the garden with my arm round her, when she said, "You *are* beginning to make the best use of the one hand you have got, aren't you?"

It was one of the remarks which stung with sudden shame. Why, I could not tell. For there is nothing shameful in a boy holding his hand against the heart of the girl he loves. Of course from my past experience I knew that shame was a part of love; but why Amy's remark should so sting me with it I could not for the life of me understand. But it was so strong for a moment or two that I wished she were miles away and that I was never going to see her again, until I remembered that this was reality

—reality for which I searched — and reality was better than many a moony vapouring. I savoured reality's salt sting; my physic against ghosts and goblins and all extravagance. I gave my stalwart little champion of reality a gentle luxurious pinch on her soft arm: at which she uttered a tiny scream, and assured me that there would be a black mark there in the evening.

" I bruise so very easily," she said meditatively, and I cannot describe the amount of mysterious meaning she put into that innocent statement. And she added, " Such liberties to take, when you're not even engaged to me yet ! " I simply blushed crimson at the sting of that dose. " The primitive woman," I thought. " She'd like me to beat her when she's mine." But I never made any answer to her sallies. Even if an answer were ready to my tongue, which it never was, I should have kept it to myself. I knew where argument led by now. " Lovely Thais sits beside thee; take the goods the Gods provide thee," was my motto, and Amy was a very pretty piece of goods.

But above all, she stood for reality, and my antidote against all uncanny insanities. After an hour or two in her company I felt braced to face any figment of the fancy. Ah, that salt sting ! It was what I needed to season me. Shocked, was I? Precisely. And the shock was salutary as the shock from a plunge into cold water.

I looked forward that evening with supreme confidence to the visit of my familiar, certain that one more resolute exhibition of defiance would destroy his power over me, such as it was, for ever.

I counted on his coming. But he did not come; and his absence disturbed me more than any appearance of his had done.

True to my rule, I made a careful note of this; and added a rider as to my state of mind.

VI

BOTH the letters from my friends at Lloyd's and Oxford struck the same note of wait till the war is over and see then. There were sure to be a large number of openings, but at present. . . . Both letters were cheerful and depressed me.

The post, too, brought a request from a man, Saunderson, for me to appear at a recruiting meeting, and perhaps say just one or two words. They would have such a stirring effect, coming from one who, etc., etc. The writer apologised for leaving his invitation to the last minute, but he had only just heard of my convalescence, and that I was in the neighbourhood. The meeting was to be held in the Town Hall at Guilford. He would call for me in his motor, just on the chance. He was lunching with the Combes.

I was excited. Here was something I could do. I was not asked to speak, and even if I tried and broke down, my failure would be more effective than an oration.

Mother insisted that I should send a reply paid telegram to Dr. Redman, for permission. She seemed doubtful whether I could stand the strain. I telegraphed to please her, and the answer was favourable. Doris and Amy and mother all declared that they must be there. Such a to-do!

How was it to be managed?   They could not hope
to crowd all of them into Saunderson's car.   Was it
too far for the girls to walk?   Then mother could
cram in perhaps.   But mother would not risk being
left behind, and recklessly decided to dash the ex-
pense, war-time or no war-time, and send the gardener's boy on his bicycle to hire the car from the
Walford Arms.

Well, the meeting was packed.   There was a
Member of Parliament, a clergyman, and some one
from the War Office, who had been billed to appear.
A great many women were present.   They had been
specially invited, and the Member urged them to
send their reluctant husbands and brothers and sons
to serve their King and country on the field of battle
and to win for themselves an easy conscience and
eternal fame.   He fumbled with his words, and his
address was not received with much ardour.   The
clergyman followed him.   He was eloquent on the
war being a holy war; enlistment in his opinion was
a sacrament.   Christ died for mankind.   In the
present crisis our country stood for all that was
sacred in mankind; and to die for our country was
to emulate Christ's sacrifice.   I found myself being
profoundly touched by his words; he spoke them
with a passionate eagerness that was always restrained.   At the end of his most moving period, a
loud voice shouted, " And how about blowing the
b—— Germans to pieces, mister ! "

The clergyman was in no way embarrassed by the
interruption.   He rose to the occasion.   He raised
his hand, one finger pointed upwards.   " Remember

Belgium! " he said in a soft penetrating voice; " Remember Scarborough! " and then, to my dismay, he swept round and displayed me, and hardly above a whisper he said, "And look at our young friend here."

The effect was instantaneous and terrific. Men shouted. Women waved their handkerchiefs and cheered frantically; and during the uproar I discovered that he had helped me to my feet, and that I was only waiting for the noise to lessen to begin my speech.

Have you ever stood on a platform and looked at the staring, peering eyes? During the first few seconds familiar faces appear strange then. You seem isolated from every one, switched off suddenly into a world of your own. Your eyes play you queer tricks. There was Amy; there was mother; there was Doris; all clapping, all talking to each other. There were the Combes, Emily and Corinna, Corinna sitting very erect; and yes! there was an empty chair in front of her. Empty? No; yes, it was: a felt hat only, on a stick-handle propped against the chair. I kept staring at it, wondering whether it would appear again; for I had distinctly seen my familiar — seen him with absolute distinctness. I kept staring as I began to speak, for I was aware of an expectant stillness and silence. However, I saw nothing but the empty chair, which faded away and became only Corinna Combes' intent face; which was partly explained by the fact that she had leaned forward with her arms on the chair-back soon after I began.

I listened to my own voice, saying:

"I can't speak."

Another voice shouted: "Damn it, he can only fight."

The interruption sounded as remote as my own voice.

"But I want to say this. If there is any one here who thinks that force will ever destroy force, it is his duty to enlist. I wish I thought that war was glorious; I wish I thought that war was holy; I do not. And I don't know how war's to be avoided except by not fighting. So I'm in bewilderment, and not very encouraging. I really couldn't ask any one to go where I have gone, to see what I have seen. Still, there it is. I suppose it's got to be done. But what there'll be left of Belgium to restore, I don't know, after we've done driving the Germans out of it."

I sat miserably down. There was faint applause, through which a hiss seemed to creep like a snake. The chairman must have been too surprised to cover my failure. Seconds counted like hours to my dizzy head. And then with an enormous oath, which proclaimed the voice of the clergyman's interrupter, a burly fellow got up and shouted:

"That's the first bit of truth I've heard spoke yet about this here God-forgotten war: and blow me if I don't give in my name for a —— soldier, though I be an honest shoemaker."

"Go'n!" shouted some one, "they won't 'ave yer. Ole poison-bag!"

By that time the chairman had recovered from

his surprise. He got up and praised the heroic restraint of my speech; it showed the true spirit of a soldier's modesty. And he got properly launched when the catchword came into his head. "Shall we take it lying down?" upon which theme he improvised many vigorous variations.

During his speech I did not raise my head. I could not look again at all those faces. I was afraid Amy and Doris and mother must be feeling desperately ashamed of me. There might have been some truth in what I said, but to say it under these circumstances was not only unpatriotic but damned silly. Heroic restraint was the line of praise my platform friends took in the lobby after the meeting was over, and they complimented me upon my orginality, and the fine response we had obtained. I apologised profusely, of course. Couldn't think, I told them, what had possessed me to drivel like that, and I thanked the clergyman for his stirring tribute to the fellows at the front.

"I still feel one of them, if I may say so," it came quite naturally to me to say. · And they warmly pressed me to speak at other recruiting meetings. "That dry manner of yours, with a little cultivation, would· become uncommonly effective," the Member assured me.

I said that my nerves had gone all to pieces. And they said: "Oh, a little later, then; a little later." They spoke with cheerful energy, as though the need for recruiting rallies was likely to be perpetual.

As soon as I could I left my platform friends and went to find the ladies, who had agreed to wait for me in the car in the High Street, twenty yards or so from the Town Hall.

Just outside the entrance Corinna Combe darted up to me; she gripped my arm and said with more feeling than I have ever heard in a human voice: "Bravo! That was fine. Fine. That is what I call real pluck. I felt proud that I knew you."

Before I had time to point out, as I wanted, that nervousness had forced me to say the exact opposite of what I had intended to say, she was across the street again with her father and sister, who waved at me. They looked, after my platform experience, very friendly and familiar.

I rejoined my people. They did not seem to think that I had disgraced them, but were full of excitement about my reception. I sat between Amy and mother in the body of the car; Doris sat by the driver, leaning over to pour out her congratulations. Mother said: "Your speech was very short, dear, and a little damping. But after such an uproar. . . . I really wondered how you managed to speak at all."

Amy had been very quiet, till then. She said in a hushed voice, "Oh didn't he look wonderful! Standing there." And she whispered for my ear only, "My noble, wonderful hero!"

"Yes, even his mother felt a wee bit proud of him."

Somehow I could not share their emotion. The drive home was disagreeable. Amy I liked least in her present mood, and it made me cross to realise how much I disliked it. It was no good saying to myself that it was quite natural for a girl to feel like that, and any decent man ought to be pleased. Obviously he ought; and obviously I wasn't. I even disliked the expression of her face. The utter unreasonableness of my feeling annoyed me intensely. But do what I could — and I tried every device in my power — I could not rid myself of this annoyance. It steadily grew. And when on getting out of the motor she whispered, "This has been the happiest day of my life," my only response, which by God's grace I managed to keep to myself, was, "Hell! Hell!" And it boiled up all through me.

I quickly saw that Amy was not the cause of the mischief; she was merely the easiest object on which to turn my bad temper. The disturbance was deeper in me than anything dear little Amy could touch; it was not due to the momentary apparition in the empty chair; in my state of nervous excitement it was quite natural that I should have seen that vision, and a blink of the eyes was enough to scatter it; or rather to merge it in the face of Corinna Combe; probably Corinna had suggested the vision to my subconscious self, which connected the two after their queer similarity of poise, and certainly it was not due to her impulsive rush at me and clasp of my arm in the side street after the meeting. No, these things may have been contributory; they were not essential. The true cause lay deeper than any of them; it lay in myself. I had intended vaguely to say one thing; I had definitely said another. My wish was to say a few stirring words. The words I had said were flatly stilling.

I was not sure of myself. Nor could I become sure by taking thought.

I tried to dismiss it as a trivial matter. Don't we all, ran my pooh-pooh argument, like to see both sides of a question? Don't we all like to be broad-minded and tolerant? And more than that, isn't it an actual virtue? Quite sincerely a sensible man could hate war — all sensible men did; and quite sincerely a sensible man might think that this war was necessary and right, and even, if you were of a religious frame of mind, holy. It was clear as day to my reason, and yet I was as confused as a man might be who found himself walking in two different directions at the same time. As I say, I was not sure of myself. I had the sensation of being a shadow, of having been, in some mysterious manner, sapped.

I applied my usual corrective to moods of depression. I assured myself that nothing had occurred that could not be perfectly explained by the shattered condition of my nerves, but it was no good. For the first time this explanation failed to reassure me. The sapped feeling of nothingness remained. It was as though I tried to raise myself by something which yielded as I pulled; something, moreover, which previously had supported what weight I had put on it. I was baffled and hopeless.

Amy came to sit with me. I asked her what she had thought of my speech, really thought of it. She told me in her most adoring voice that my speech was lovely, and that I looked wonderful. I pressed her to talk sense, suggesting that it was not quite what I meant to say. She agreed with me warmly, and went on to declare that it was " Much nicer not to — well, in public, you know; all right for a clergyman, of course, but not quite the thing . . ."

"What do you mean? Show emotion in public, or what?"

"Yes, that's it."

"But didn't you hear the hissing?"

"Hissing?"

"Yes; after what I said."

"No, of course there wasn't any. Goodness, no!"

"Then why should I have heard it?"

"Oh, you were so excited! Enough to turn a sneeze into a hiss. Or a kiss?" she added, looking at me from under her lashes. I took no notice of the hint.

"What I said was something like this? What did I say?"

"Goodness, you don't expect me to remember. Besides, what does it matter what you said?" she pouted prettily, and sulked for a moment, like a too friendly cat you have put off your knee.

"It matters very much to me. And what I said was . . ."

"Oh, no, no. Really," she pulled herself up and laid her cheek on my mouth. "One speech is enough."

But word for word the speech was repeated within me, precisely in the same way as the interviews were when I was entering them in my notebook. I was so distracted that Amy became merely a weight and an encumbrance; and as she turned her face, her lips seeking mine, I turned away in disgust and tried to push her from me.

Suddenly to my horror she was on her knees in front of me, saying something about my being a great, strong, cruel man whom she worshipped and adored.   Roughly I put my hand on her shoulder and shook her, and told her to get up and not behave in that absurd way.   She obeyed like a little dog, and stood looking at me humbly with imploring eyes.

I spoke in a bullying voice.

" I won't have these stupid scenes," I said. " They're degrading.   This incessant harping on one's feelings is simply weakening and bad.   I won't have it."   And so I went on, not knowing and not caring what I said, but finding satisfaction in my bullying attitude.   The lower she cringed, the rougher I became, and the deeper grew my satisfaction, until at last when she crept close to me, begging me to forgive her, I was able to kiss her, and her clinging lips sent fire through my blood, and forgetfulness of everything.

Then it was I who cringed, begging her not to go, but she released herself and stood up, her head thrown back, mischief in her eyes, and said in a deliberate voice that sounded almost like a threat:

" I can always make you kiss me when I like."

I concealed my fear from her, laughing.

" A woman always can.   No need to be a witch for that.   Especially with me."

She stood in front of me, never taking her eyes off mine, slowly nodding her head.   What need was there for any dread of her? None at all that reason could find. Why should a man dread the airs and graces of a pretty girl?

"Do as you like with me," I said. "Nothing could be jollier."

"That's exactly what I do do, though you don't really believe it."

"Yes. I do believe as long as it makes you happy to believe it."

"Quibbler!"

I wondered why she should be readier in speech on these occasions; why antagonism should quicken her intelligence. It seemed as though her chief pleasure lay not in kissing me or being kissed, but in my subjugation to her will. I said in my most caressing voice, solely to reassure myself (as in a dream a man pinches himself to know if he is awake or asleep):

"Dear little. Amy!" and the ejaculation, expanded, meant, "However cold and unaccountable you may appear, you are really dear little Amy and no other"; and with pathetic trustfulness I repeated my mother's dictum that dear little Amy would make any man a sweet little wife. I leaned back against it for support, asking myself: If my mother didn't know, who did? And "any man" was precisely the plain average decent man I had been and was resolved, in spite of all experiences and fears, to remain.

"You don't know how I need you," I cried, stretching up my hand to her, to pull me out of the strangeness into which I was sinking.

"Ah, naughty!" she said with unction, and the two words thrust me deliberately under.

Slowly she shook her head from side to side, smiling. "I know what boys are," she continued, and her voice sounded far away in the distance.

Faintly, too, like a thin wail of despair, ran the usual argument through my mind: that it was foolish to take a girl too seriously, unfair to expect too much from her; that what she was was all sufficient for a sensible man, a delight for a sensible man; that the sting of actual fact her common sense gave me, pleasant or unpleasant, was the antidote by which I could keep my sanity; which would brace me to be a man. The argument had no power to restore me; it was a ghost's voice, whispering, and increased my chilling sense of nothingness.

Amy sat by me. I saw that she was at her sweetest and most attractive. I felt nothing. She said it was a shame to tease me, and wasn't it fun having a little tiff and making it up again; and no one must brood and be sulky, because that spoilt everything. I knew it was common sense she voiced; what I very well knew to be true; but as they came from her the words, for all their truth, sounded ghostly and remote, as though I had overheard them in an omnibus spoken to some one else.

Gone was the sensible self which was my pride; and what remained? Only his shadow that mocked whispering from the distance in Amy's voice. It was with the sensation of " coming to " that I answered a tap at the door, and noticed Amy spring to her feet.

The maid brought in a letter, saying that the gardener's boy had left it from Miss Combe.

I took the letter and looked at the envelope. The maid went out.

"Whatever can she have to say to me?"

"Open it, you silly boy, and see. I expect she wants to congratulate you on your success. Poor Corinna! It's awfully nice of her."

"Why poor Corinna?"

"Open the letter."

I did so. It was not in tiny writing, but in a large sprawling hand.

"What delighted me in your speech was not that I agree with what you said. I don't know that I do. But what thrilled me was that it was your utter self speaking out, through the layers and layers of the casual easy stuff that is everywhere now on tap. To do that at any time is difficult. Now, against the foaming, frothy stream, and then when it was at its foamiest and frothiest! it was thrilling, and I must thank you from my heart. When one man in these whirling, giddy, terrible times stands firm on his feet it helps others to keep their balance. You have helped me. I always thought you were an ordinary, nice, intelligent young man. Not that you aren't; but you're much more a definite person than I imagined. Not that it matters to you one way or the other what I think or thought, but it eases my mind to give you a hail — a salute almost — to say that I recognise you."

"I wonder what she can mean by that?" I said to Amy, who was reading the letter over my shoulder.

"Oh, she only wants to congratulate you. It *is* awfully nice of her. Poor Corinna!"

"But why poor Corinna?"

"I'm always sorry for these intense people, aren't you? However well they mean they can't help being awkward and peculiar. Most of them pride themselves on it; at any rate Corinna doesn't do that. She dresses quite nicely and doesn't talk much. But there it is. She is awkward. Why can't she just congratulate you like anybody else? But no, she can't. Out she must fly with this queer sort of stuff. No wonder she puts men off, is it?"

"Well, I hadn't thought about it."

"Exactly. You'd hardly know she was a girl at all. Fancy wanting to sit out a dance with her in a quiet corner. That's why I say poor Corinna. And there are so many girls like her. Hardly get any fun at all, poor dears. I've often felt so selfish, and tried, really tried, to give them a chance. But it's no good. They simply *aren't*. Boys shy. And of course the only thing left them is rather to despise us. I don't mind a bit; it's so natural they should. I know I should, if I were like them."

I listened to her in amazement.

"You have got a lot of common sense," I said.

She accepted the compliment in the same serious spirit in which it was offered.

"Oh yes," she said. "I know how many beans make five. Here's an instance. I met her once at Goodwood. I don't know how she strayed there. I hardly ever go to races, but of course I felt absolutely *in* it walking about and so on; but poor Cor-

inna! Oh, she wasn't badly dressed, but you could
see she was a fish out of water. Hopeless. She
pretended to enjoy it immensely. 'I love to see the
horses gallop,' she said. And you should have seen
the man she was with! Oh! I don't believe the
scandal about her; but it's just because of her awkwardness that it's there. A married man, you know
carried on with her, and his wife made a fuss.
Couldn't have been anything in it. Still, there it is.
And it's the sort of thing that's very unpleasant,
whether there's anything in it or not."

"I had no idea you kept your eyes open so wide."

"Yes, and I'm sorry for girls like Corinna.
You'd better answer her note at once; it's just the
sort of thing that gets forgotten if you put it off."

"It needs no answer."

"You must be nice when you can. It's only decent. And it was jolly of her to want to congratulate you."

"Whatever shall I say?"

"Oh, anything. It doesn't matter. Only not
quite so without a beginning and an end. Work in
'generous' and wind up 'yours cordially,' and sign
yourself in full, James Wood. Mrs. James Wood
—sounds rather commonplace." She led me to the
desk. "Pen, ink, note-paper, envelope," she said
as she put each ready in turn. "Just time before
you dress. I must go." She went. I began.

"My dear Corinna. Thank you very much for
your generous letter." There I stuck before I
added "I was very glad to get it," and stuck again.
I thought of all that Amy had said of her. I read

the letter through again. What did she mean by "your utter self"? And to call me a man who stood firm in these whirling giddy times, and helped others to keep their balance. Now of all times and on the strength of that giddiest of my giddy moments to recognise me as a definite person. What did it mean? What did it mean? What made the girl write like this?

I tried heavily to think it must be an elaborate joke. The effort failed. She was transparently honest.

"It's true enough up to a point what Amy says of her," I thought. "But there's more. She doesn't care a snap of the fingers what anybody may say or think of her. She's not an atom self-conscious about it. That's where she's different from other superior people. But they're all detestable."

I tore up what I had written. The letter needed no answer. Besides, why should I be dictated to by Amy?

Yet I wanted to answer the letter; I wanted to find out more clearly what Corinna meant; and what had given her this uncanny impression.

VII

I OUGHT to have been pleased, no doubt, and grateful that my familiar made no appearance. In one way certainly it was a relief. But in another it was not. Somehow I needed my enemy in visible shape; it roused my courage to resist. Then again I was in the position of a man who has made enormous preparations against an enemy which did not exist. Here was Amy practically a part of my life, and there seemed no reason for her being so, if I was my normal self.

All I wanted now was to be let alone; to sleep for six months. And there was at least a fortnight more in which Amy would be staying in the house. I could not understand why I had been so precipitate. Had I really been so badly frightened by the apparition?

In my present state I knew it was wiser not to think about the war lest I might be led to brood on horrors; wiser too, for that matter, not to think of my relations with Amy or with my familiar; and above all not to think of myself. In fact my field for thought was becoming limited, and more than all my energy would be needed simply to repel the advances of these three subjects. It was impossible not to read the paper in the morning. I confined myself to the casualty lists and the official reports: but such neutral phrases as " artillery duel," "the counter-attack was successful," never failed to present a vivid picture to my mind; and I could not read the casualty list without wondering where each man was wounded, and what was left of the dead. The process was involuntary and beyond my control to check. It went on even while I repeated all the good comforting thoughts about the war being a war of freedom, a war to end war, a war for the freedom of the world, all of which I fully believed, and all of which stimulated me, but stimulated in exact proportion at the same time the vividness of the picture which I would fain hide. It was the dead that haunted me and their burial or lack of burial. "The attack did not reach our lines." Common sense bade me take a wider view of the world struggle, but could not obliterate from my mind the sight of those tumbled bodies.

I turned to Amy for forgetfulness; but she was ceasing to have the power to give me forgetfulness, and with utter injustice this loss of her power exasperated me against her, as though it were her fault that she was unable to cure me of all the ills for which I took her, like medicine.

Everything seemed to turn against me, to become a weapon in some unseen hand to work mischief. What should have pleased me and encouraged me most deeply became most deeply mischievous. The recruiting meeting, Corinna's praise, Amy's growing devotion (the loftier and more supercilious my conduct to her, the more tenderly devoted was hers to me), the cessation of my familiar's visits seemed to accumulate distress on me.

Dr. Redman came, and was extremely friendly; but his face after the stupidly facetious telegram offended me. I lied about the familiar to him, saying it was all a trick of my imagination, as I found that I could take down conversations with it by reams, whenever I wished. He accepted my word without argument or protest of any kind, and after his usual examination suggested that change of scene would be a good idea — a day or two in London.

The idea appealed to me. I telegraphed to a friend, Keith Collins, in the Board of Trade, who had rooms in Westminster, to know if he could put me up for the week-end.

The mere action of writing on a form with a lead pencil made me feel less shadowy and unsubstantial. I mentioned the doctor's suggestion and gave grave reasons that made my presence in London necessary; but the truth was that the idea of a good dinner and a great deal of champagne sprang to life within me; and that was the only idea in my head, much as I tried to convince myself that to go was, as I said, " rather a nuisance," but perhaps on the whole best to fall in with the doctor's suggestion, and I had promised Collins to put in a Sunday with him.

He wired delight at the prospect of seeing me, but there were three days through which to exist before I went. The whole problem of life resolved itself into existing through those three days. I felt I could leave my skin and all my worries behind me, and take on a new mind. Crawl out of my old self with the natural ease of a snake and watch the shed thing from outside.

A little thing will show my apathy. I had often laughed at Brer Tarrypin's method of withstanding the fire in the field —" Sot and tuck it, Brer Wolf " — but now without the least flicker of a smile I gravely endeavoured to carry out the simple heroism of the Tarrypin strategy. Through two long days I " sot and tuck it." I made no effort of any kind; not one, to think, to speak, to do. I was witless and content as a dried leaf in the wind. I put up no resistance.

For example I read in the paper that a boy had hanged himself because people " chipped him " (that was the reporter's word) for not enlisting; that a soldier and his wife had put their heads into a gas oven, because they wanted to die not separately but together. Was the man afraid to die, or afraid to die alone? And was the woman afraid of life, or afraid of life alone? Which of the two had thought of the gas-stove? And which of the two had first suggested the escape of death together? And were either more insane than the man who could direct the wholesale slaughter of hundreds and hundreds of thousands of able-bodied men?

All these questions passed through my mind, meeting with no resistance and arousing no horror. I " sot and tuck it "; sat and smiled, and looked forward to Saturday as to the day of my release. To the thought of my familiar I was equally indifferent. If I went mad, I went mad, and one lunatic more or less was not a matter of much interest to the mad world or to me. The suggestion of " Patience," too, which Doris made came as an inspiration; for shuffling and arranging the cards for me was a quiet little attention that kept Amy occupied and pleased.

I woke on Saturday morning like a small boy on the last day of term. At last to be leaving this doleful place which I had entered a month or so earlier as an earthly paradise, blessed beyond all dreams of blessedness. What bad magic had changed the blessedness to dolour? As I made ready each little detail of my departure I had the sensation of unmistakably being the plain common-sense man I always wished to be. I saw him in motion, practical, suave, and alert. Nothing worried me; nothing slipped my memory; no unwelcome thought obtruded on my mind; and no apathy dulled it. I was myself. It was like sleeping in one's own bed again after much travelling. Everything, from the visits of my familiar to Amy and the war, assumed its proper proportions, and I felt ready for any emergency.

No emergency arose. My journey was uneventful, though I could not say what I expected to happen. Dear Collins met me at Waterloo and escorted me in triumph to his rooms, which I had no sooner entered than I was instantly switched away to ante-bellum days, for his rooms in Westminster looked and felt and smelled exactly like his diggings in the Broad. It was more than the two enormous armchairs and the huge Chesterfield sofa which suggested Oxford; more too, than the pipe-racks and photos. Some subtle hint came from Keith Collins himself which told you that whatever might be the circumstances of his life at whatever age, those

years at Oxford would remain his ideal of living for
ever.

He is a quiet able chap.   There are many like
him.   His mind had opened to receive the great
impression, and that impression would be indelible.
I envied him his assured habit of mind; I had often
done so before, but never so poignantly as now.   It
is, mind you, a habit of mind; he has no tricks of
speech, no affectations, which are known as the Oxford manner.

At tea-time when Keith brought in hot buttered
toast between two soup plates, and a jug of milk,
I could have sworn that he had just brought them
from the College kitchen, as we used to do two or
three years only ago.   The great black kettle which
boiled on the fire, the huge lumps of coal with which
the fire was made, the shape of the fireplace, the
sight of a chocolate cake and Bourbon biscuits, made
the intermediate years evaporate.   We were in the
Broad again; the only new things were an added intensity of appreciation at my good fortune in being
there, an intenser consciousness of the quiet peace of
the place.   I was back in the Broad again, with
this difference, that I took nothing of what it stood
for for granted.   The illusion cut deeper than any
reality could.   And there was Keith reddening as he
always reddens at the slightest or no provocation
(pleasure? shyness? embarrassment?   I never knew
and never know why), and saying as he poised a
packed spoonful of tea, " One spoonful; two spoonfuls; three spoonfuls."   And there was that queer
crooked smile of his that flickered wrinkles all over

his reddened face; and as though obeying some un-written rite he put in four spoonfuls, " to be on the safe side," as I was sure that he always would (and aim that he will) until the end of time, or at any rate his time.

I tell you, I hugged myself, to squeeze in the full flavour of it as I sprawled in that longest, lowest, deepest of armchairs at my utter ease.

Keith looked more boyish than any man of his age I have ever known or seen. Evidently some-thing was embarrassing him more than usual. His flush was more frequent and more scarlet. I lazily waited, confident that it would soon be revealed to me; and it soon was. He nodded — no one else could nod so quickly and so definitely without rick-ing some small muscle in the neck — towards my left hand, and jerked out:

" About the neatest tweak I've ever seen, that. Do you have to wash it? "

I gave a hoot of laughter; it was too daringly Keith-like to be able to put so much feeling and sym-pathy into that absurd jerked-out, nodded-out re-mark. It was our first meeting since my return from the front.

He blinked so hard that I swear his ears moved, and snatching up his cup (big as a basin) he shot out between furious sips:

" My small cousin. Woke up in a fright. Dreamed he'd washed his hands. Family legend. Hurt, I suppose, like blue hell.   What? "

" A bit painful," I agreed.

The reality of my wound had no strength against

the reality of the feeling induced by Keith's presence.

"I'm blissfully in the Broad again," I said, and there was a crescendo of significance in his multitude of little nods as he blinked and said:

"H'm! Oxford. Good days, those."

There was a long silence broken only by the trickling gurgle that Keith's tea invariably made on its way down his throat — subject of many a ribaldry. He moved his eyes at me in recognition of this little weakness, but neither of us laughed or spoke for a minute or two, and I said without laughing:

"Look here, K. C., I don't believe any feeling is real without a touch of absurdity in it."

He frowned, and gave a questioning grunt.

"Back again into all this . . . after . . . I can't tell you what it means to me. This is what life used to be. Life was so good."

Screwing up his eyes, he gave a little tempest of nods. All the time he looked at me with the directness of a child.

"I'd almost forgotten how good it was."

"Must shake things up a bit. Such an experience."

"It's knocked me out. I don't seem to be able to get into reality again somehow."

"Dull, you mean?"

"Oh, no, not that exactly."

"After such doings. Humdrum, eh?"

I looked at him attentively. He was grappling with something. At last it came out. "Proud of you, Jim," he managed to say.

"Not that, please," I cried, very like a small boy when a bigger boy begins to twist his arm. It started a frenzy of thought against which the cherished feeling of the room would have no chance of resistance; it brought back all those things from which I was trying to escape, from which up to that moment I had escaped. But why should it? What power of malice lay in K. C.'s innocent remark? Besides, I knew that he looked upon me as a wounded hero. I was able to calm myself, much in the same way as one can still the first shoot of an angry tooth by holding one's breath, by saying with all the indifference I could summon: "Oh, it had to be. It's on my nerves, rather. Let's forget about it."

"*It* being?"

I could not answer.

"The war? Your share in it? The wounds? Best to know. Less chance of . . ."

"Oh, everything, everything but those good Oxford days. Where shall we dine? Is there anywhere in town like the Grid? Do you remember when we drank those two bottles of Lafitte? Fifteen bob a bottle. But I must have fizz to-night. Oh, buckets of the bubbly. I want some quiet place where we can eat too much and drink too much, and oh, a regular buck dinner, and forget and be jolly for once. The country gets damnably depressing. I've been dreaming of a really buck dinner. There's something so gloriously real, so solidly real, about eating and drinking well. But it must be somewhere quiet. Pagani's upstairs.

Or the Carlton Grill. Or what's that place in Jermyn Street?"

Keith took my mood not without a glimmer of surprise in his face. I seemed to see him in a flash of light at that moment, what he was and what he stod for, and saw with envy. For his attitude of mind, that cheerful, intelligent acceptance of things, was in the main the attitude I longed to achieve, with personal variations here and there of course. His great sanity, his large common sense, were a man's supreme possessions; they were the bases of character. No feeling could ever penetrate to shake those foundations or disturb them, so sure they were and solid. It was impossible to imagine that he should ever be turned silly, as I had been turned silly, by the sight of a bowl of primroses; or (so unpleasantly, so almost indecorously) by the sight of his mother and sister. He would never creep to church in comic fear of conversion or be overwhelmed with relief to find his fear blotted out by a trivial error of his own; he would never see strange beings or need to make elaborate plans to keep his equilibrium. I had been like him; my friendship told me that I had been like him; and now, by an explosion, I had been blown out of my real self. I was like a man out of his depth, unable to sink or swim, who in his spluttering, arm-flapping, neck-straining struggle watches his friend with feet firmly on the ground enjoying the waves and the water and all the circumstances which cause his own distress. The wonder was Keith noticed nothing, as my mother and sister had noticed nothing. That was my chief consolation; had they done so my shame would have been intolerable.

I staggered in by Keith's side (or so it seemed to me, so vivid to my thought was the swimming vision) my toes touched the ground on which he stood; I managed to share his foothold. He accepted me as he accepted other circumstances of life, and his acceptance supported me.

I was able to regain the well-being and comfort of feeling back again in the Broad once more.

Meanwhile we had agreed to dine in Jermyn Street, and to excuse my manner, I was able to say, with enough hint of apology to make him flush deeply:

" I'm still a bit jumpy, I'm afraid."

" That's to be expected," he answered in such a dear knowing way, with a nod so confidential, that I gave a shout of laughter, and declared he would have made his fortune as a family physician; his bedside manner was perfect.

Keith is never at his best at a dinner-party; never will be unless it may be at the head of his own table, if he ever have one. But for a quiet dinner with a friend I know no one to touch him. From the moment you start out with him or meet him, he has the right frame of mind, so that you know the dinner will be a success. There is nothing blasé about his manner, none of that painful drawl, the " suppose we'd better dine somewhere " of the young man about town; the " suppose it had better be the Savoy," as though it were a sin not to be a little bored by anything so usual as a dinner in town. To Keith a little dinner such as we were going to have was a treat, and he was glad to show it. His eye twinkled; there was a general air of expectancy about him, not to say impatience. He was delightfully and honestly greedy. He would throw out curt interrogations.

"Lobster mayonnaise?" or, with a cloud over his twinkle that he could not have both, "hors d'œuvres?" Or he would whisper, "A la carte," and you would know he was trying to solve the old puzzle whether a set dinner with a limited choice was preferable to your own free hand.

This evening, like a naughty boy divulging a pent-up wish, he exclaimed, "Just a salmon mayonnaise and a duck. Why not?"

"I'm with you," I declared.

"Heaps of green peas," he murmured, as he put his arms into his coat.

"Heaps and heaps," I warmly agreed.

Oh, it was jolly, that dinner. It was not the best dinner from the point of view of food that I have ever had, but from the point of view of mood incomparably the best. Gad, I was in the mood for it. The pleasant glow of anticipation sank tranquilly into my bones; the right prelusive touch to the pleasanter glow of the wine — liquid sunshine — that darkly sparkled through my blood. Delicious food, delicious wine! A good friend at a quiet table! The intimacy, the deep ease, the supreme composure, were feelings that I needed badly, and wholly, wholly enjoyed. Every little nerve in my body, long mutinous or distressed, was more than at negative peace; every little nerve actually tingled with positive delight. Oh, our talk was not brilliant; no special confidence passed; but everything we said took on our mood of happiness, and gained a kind of significance. Each knew the evening would never be forgotten, was, by some subtle rightness of circumstance, an event silently recorded in the annals of our lives.

Nothing jarred. We lived in past days with no effort, cut off by a rosy mist from every topic of disturbance. There must have been some tacit understanding between us, happy and perfect in its secret working. Opinions vary as to the best moment in a dinner, but mine has never wavered. That moment for me is when, having chosen the best cigar and listened to its gentle whispering crackle, you take your first deep luxurious pull at your preliminary cigarette. Anticipation and fulfilment are then in a perfect manner blended. It is the supreme moment, let your winebibber say what he will.

At first, after my recent experiences, I dreaded lest some unhappy accident might obtrude like some malicious djinn and transmute the mayonnaise into a deadly crustacean, sauced merely and be-leafed, the duck to a slaughtered bird, the wine to a gassy fluid, and my dear friend Keith to a commonplace man, complacent, dull and unseeing. But no such accident happened, and the dinner was as it should be, something more than merely eating and drinking, was, as I have said, an event.

At one time, just after I had lighted my cigar, my confidence was such that I was on the brink of telling Keith all the queer pranks my nerves had been playing me since my return, of my visitant even, and my resolve to lift myself back into the good region of common sense from which I seemed to have been blown. Especially was I tempted to speak to him about Amy, and open his eyes to all the vagaries of woman that I had lately learned. I felt pregnant with knowledge of the subject and with advice. But though I was sorely tempted I was strong enough to let it alone. What should I have done, had my visitant seen fit to have made a shadowy third at our table? I·was content to relish my ability to see all my late experiences without horror or dread, in a warm and rosy glow.

And then, as Keith was finishing his crème de menthe (he has a boy's disregard for old brandy), he suddenly asked me if I had seen or heard anything of the Angelic Leaders. Something in me as sensitive as a prawn's feeler sensed trouble in the topic. I had heard rumours of St. Michael and St. George and Joan of Arc having been seen on the great retreat from Mons, exhorting the Allies and fighting for them; but had heard no account that could be called authentic. My amazement at Keith's quiet acceptance of the truth of these visions kept me at the moment from worrying thoughts and inferences. That Keith, who was simply my embodied ideal of how a common-sense man should think and feel about practically all matters but clothes, should accept these heavenly visitors to the battlefield as calmly as he accepted the Dons at Oxford, did literally amaze me.

"I hoped you'd seen him," he said —" St. George in silver armour on a great white horse. Rather splendid, don't you think?"

"Who told you about it?" I asked.

He told me his sister was a nurse on the line of retreat. At first the gloom among the incoming wounded had been terrible. It was no good fighting the Germans, they said. They were not men, but devils, and in such multitudes that they seemed to spring up from the very ground. Then there came a change in the men's disposition so marked that all the nurses noticed the strange exaltation in their look, and thought that they had been supplied with wine. But the change was not due to wine. All the men told the same story: that they had seen in a luminous mist bright persons on white chargers waving them on to rally, and that the enemy had fallen back before them.

"Do you believe they were actually there?" I asked him.

"Sure of it," he answered, with an emphatic nod.

"Will it make any difference to your manner of life?"

"How do you mean?"

"The fact that there are spirits who can fight on our side — great warrior spirits."

"Why should it?"

"I don't know. But somehow I feel it ought."

"Nothing in my life to be particularly ashamed

of. What should I do? Go to church twice a
week? — or what? Wish I'd seen him."

" Where do you think he came from?'"

" Don't know."

" I should like to know what he'd been doing
since . . ."

" Since when? "

" Death."

Keith blinked and shrugged his shoulders.

" How do you explain it? "

" Explain it? "

" Yes."

" Just can't. And don't want to. Can't *explain*
a blade of grass, if it comes to that. Or the whirling poise of this old world of ours twirling among
the other worlds in space." I was filling his glass.
" Fair shares now," he said, with anxiety that he
should not have a drop more than me, and having
reassured himself he resumed his normal tone to
ask:

" Don't you believe in them? "

" That they were seen, oh yes; but in their actual
existence — well — I don't know. Belief's queerly
beyond one's control, somehow. I should awfully
like to, at any rate."

It was an unspeakable relief to me to be able to
include the supernatural in the rosy glow that surrounded ourselves as we were including it. What
gave Keith his fine power of acceptance? If I could
surprise and capture his secret! This power of his
was what I most desired, and I felt that I was quietly
assimilating it, taking a sun bath, as it were, in his

calm and confidence. My cure would be complete
if I could discuss my own visitant with him in this
quiet unemotional way. But the very thought excited me, and as I knew by now where excitement
could lure me, I didn't dare.

"Not logical, that, is it?" smiled Keith with
pleasantly uplifted brows.

"Logical? No. Silly and indefensible, quite,"
I smiled back, fairly lolling in security, and as a
matter merely in which two men should take an
intelligent interest I threw out the question with no
bating of the breath: "Do you think that God
takes sides?"

"Yes, certainly. Why shouldn't he?" said Keith
in beautifully the same spirit. And he leaned across
the table to say with exquisite emotion in his voice:
"Another half bottle would be right?"

"It would," I agreed with instant enthusiasm (I
at any rate had not been drinking crème de menthe) ;
and the half bottle was ordered. "Keith," I said
when the bottle was brought, "I can't tell you how
much good it's done me seeing you. There's something magnificently steadying and solid about you,
my boy. I was all shaken up, oh, but dreadfully!
This evening I've felt more myself — more my real
self, you understand — than I have since I came
back."

He blinked and blushed and nodded.

"Do you know," I said with absolute sincerity,
"I wasn't sure that I ever again should be able to
enjoy an evening so much as I have enjoyed this one.
I was afraid . . . well, never mind; but a man can

lose his power to enjoy things, and when he does he's just about done for."

" You never will," he answered. " Nor shall I," he added, tipping down the last of his wine. I never envied any man so much as I envied Keith Collins at that moment. He had the means of bringing everything comfortably down within his scope, and so he shed round him an atmosphere of poise and contentment. I remembered times in the past when I had been, for all my sincere affection for Keith, tempted not so much to sneer at him or to belittle him as to tick him a little lightly off as the perfect Civil Servant. Well, he was. But now I knew the full worth of his type. You may call it cut and dried if you like, but it's sane, sane, sane, and Keith's sanity was firm as a rock, firm as the impregnable rock. I tell you, I literally clung to it.

Why, that evening we discussed the war, as two intelligent men should discuss it. We took the broad view, and thought as men should think not of individual horrors, but of national needs. It was bound to come, Keith said, and it could not have come at a better time for us. We were unprepared, of course, in munitions especially; but we should pull through. War was a very dreadful thing; he would be the last to deny that; but after all what cement was there like a big war for the integrity of an Empire? As he talked, the weight of the war's oppression lifted. It became remote as an ethical problem. I had no fear of any sudden onslaught of horror upon my mind; I had no fear of any ghastly visions such as had afflicted me. I felt re-

pose and composure such as I had not experienced
for many a day, and thereby realised how rattled
my nerves had been.   I felt as we talked that I was
the man I wished to become, and the possibility even
of any relapse was absent.

I saw how rightly my instinct of self-preservation
had led me to steer between the unnatural extremes
of rapture and despair, and to cultivate common
sense.   My treatment of the strange visitant, my
engagement to Amy, my visit to London, had all
been far righter than I had realised.   I looked forward to the future with serene confidence.

After talking about the war, we talked even more
pleasantly about the scheme of my detective stories.
Keith was enthusiastic, and was sure that the market
for such stories was constant.   " And you've only to
show yourself to sell them," he added.   "No patriotic editor would refuse you.   Besides, the idea's
jolly good."

What starts the mind from one subject to another?
Writing, I suppose, was in this case the link; for it
occurred to me then suddenly, sharply as the prick
of a pin, that I had not written to Corinna — so
sharply that I exclaimed, " Oh, damn!" and Keith
asked me anxiously what was the matter.

" A letter I meant to write, and haven't," I said.
"Nothing of any importance."   And I began to
wonder whether Corinna would recognise my true
self now when it was running in what I knew to be
perfect order.   But I turned my thought from that
line, and began to question Keith on the working in
war-time of the Board of Trade.   On his own sub-

ject his calm was less definite. He had had dealings
with the War Office, and was very funny about the
incompetent old gentlemen, retired majors and others, who had been picked up off the parades at
Bournemouth or Torquay, and were expected to
transact important business. He spoke naturally as
a civilian, and I was pleased to see how very human
he really was. It put his great possession almost
more firmly within my reach than did his boyish enjoyment of a dinner in town. I was obliged to interrupt him.

"I know why I like you so much and find you so
refreshing," I cried. "You are so magnificently, so
wonderfully human. I don't care, it may be insular,
but of all the men in the world give me an honest,
intelligent, level-headed English gentleman."

"I'm a Scotchman, you know," Keith shot out,
nodding and crimsoning with delight at the aptness
of his score.

"If I weren't a cripple I'd do you a Highland
fling, I feel so happy," I said; and I did feel happy.

Moreover my happiness continued all through my
stay with Keith. I had only one misgiving, and that
was negligible in its immediate effect. I tried to
summon my visitant, for I was confident that if he
came, I could convince him finally that all further
interference with me and my life would be futile. I
was confident that I could dispose of him once and
for all and for ever. My disappointment in the
morning was great; my first waking thought told me
of it, and it lasted through the slow process of my
toilet. But my depression was scattered by the

sight of Keith and the sound of his voice telling me that we were going to have an Oxford breakfast — three courses, that is to say, without porridge, and a preposterous quantity of toast in large slices. I was swept back on the instant to good ante-bellum days.

VIII

I GOT home during the morning of Monday. There were one or two other people I had intended to see and one or two things I had intended to do on Monday, but I decided to catch the first possible train, because I wanted to take with me the full flavour of Keith's quiet antidote. I had no doubt as to its efficacy, and never feared that it could wear off like the smell of his bath-salts (it is Keith-like to be careless in his clothes and extravagant in toilet sundries) ; but I somehow felt that the sooner it was, so to speak, rubbed in, the more beneficial it must be, and also I was as anxious to test my new frame of mind as one is to try a new toy; and it was certaintly as definite and real a possession to me as a putter, say, or a cleek.

I had a practice-shot in the train. Two Tommies (superior clerks they had been, I should think), nice chaps with brown faces and tough limbs, were in my carriage. One passed the other his paper, pointing with his finger to some verses; the other read them slowly and with an obvious effort of concentration.

" Well, what d'you think of it ? " said his friend.

The other grunted, thinking deeply; their manner suggested to me that they were leading members of their chapel's literary club.

"It's all right," the other pronounced, handing the paper back. "It has the universal note."

His friend produced a pair of folding scissors and proceeded to cut out the poem, running his scissors up the paper with a quickness that showed he had made many cuttings from papers, and put the cutting in his pocket-book.

"But there's this," the slow other brought out, "to be remembered. That chap utters one side of the job only. Of course it's poetry right enough to think of dying for your country and so on; but it's business to wipe up as many Germans as possible, in whatever way the C.O. sees fit."

"You're so modern," said his friend. "But you can't have realism in poetry."

"I grant that. What I say is — and I've always said it: poetry's got to illuminate facts."

"I know you've said it. And this war just proves you're wrong, if nothing else does. How can poetry illuminate the effect of a well-placed shell on a unit? Not Milton nor yet Byron could do that."

"Well, if it can't, it's not much use to me. That's all I know. As soldier I mean. There's a sight too much of all this dying for your country to please me. I'm going to take every snitch of cover I can find, and do in every German I can pot; and if I'm done in, so much the worse for me."

"You don't mean you're going to give up reading poetry?" He spoke with awe in his voice, as though the other were a minister who had thought of giving up preaching.

"On the war, yes," he sternly declared. "Takes

the heart out of a man who's got to kill, and got to want to kill."

They were sitting in opposite corners, speaking in low earnest voices, leaning forward arms on knees. The device they took to shield their talk from the carriage carried it to my ear. Never having heard soldiers speak of the war before, I was intensely interested, so much so that I was tempted to join in, if only to congratulate my stern neighbour on the soundness of his common sense. I knew that I was all right, just as surely as I knew that had I heard that low-voiced talk before being armed with Keith's good weapon, the voices would have started wrangling within me, leading to Heaven knows what disturbance. But I listened with amusement and with strong approval of the stern speaker's common sense. Poetry illuminating facts roused in me the picture of myself, a very small boy, painting texts in red and blue on Sunday afternoons. I should have quietly gone farther still and said that the function of poetry was to turn the mind away from facts, to emphasise, for example, the glory of patriotism and war and sacrifice, so that no one should think of the dirty facts, the mud, the blood, the fear, the hatred, the lust, the terrible boredom and filth of war and the effect of high explosive on a unit.

It was good to be at home, free of that wicked ingratitude which had turned a paradise to a hell. My dear women-folk! I thought, as I entered the hall and found them drinking milk after a walk. They were surprised to see me, expecting me to return by a much later train, in time for dinner in the evening.   Their pleasure touched me, and showed with beautiful clearness how very dear I was to all three.   But there was nothing ostentatious, nothing exaggerated either, about their manner of expressing it or my manner of receiving it.   No, everything was sensible and right, delightfully right.

"Dear boy, what a nice surprise!" said my mother.

"How jolly you've come!" said Doris.

And Amy stood nestling confidingly near me after I had kissed her, holding my jacket, and she said with meaning, but simply and nicely, in a way I immensely liked: "I *am* glad you're back."

Trivial enough, no doubt, and commonplace. But it was precisely the triviality and commonplaceness round which I rolled my tongue.   The *vin ordinaire* of life; the "good little wine" of the country, which would not travel without turning sour. Ah, my womenfolk! my home! to think I could ever have been bored by them; ever found them irksome; ever allowed their place of habitation to get upon my nerves!   The memory of my past folly made me blush as I stood there in the hall in their midst.

They did not understand me?   Mother, in wanting me to marry Amy, that dear little wife for any nice man?   Amy, in the way she treated me? Doris, at all, in any way?   Why should they understand me?   What in me had I wanted them to understand?   My bad temper?   My nerves?   Precisely that exaggerating and exaggerated side of me that it was my wish to cut out?   I saw how unfair and how preposterous my former state of mind had been. I glowed in the consciousness that it had ceased to be.

"Oh, my dear good K. C.," I thought, "never shall I be able to repay you for the great good gift you have, quite without knowing, bestowed on me!"

There was no ecstasy about my happiness, no extravagance. It came, I assured myself, from a quiet, upright acceptance of facts. All the while I was making mental notes of my state of mind, so that it might become familiar and for ever within my grasp. This cheerful acceptance ought, I said to myself, to be laid on to a sensible man's consciousness as water or gas is laid on to his house. Both were necessities of a decent existence.

And always through my mind ran the refrain: "I'm being the man I want to be."

Every moment, moreover, of this right mood's duration must surely add to its strength, and lessen the possibility of relapse. The last stage of achievement was apparent, when the mood would be wholly, supremely mine and therefore unconscious and natural. My pleasure in savouring it as I did now was very like the pleasure of a man's first hour of relief from toothache, very like but not identical, for my recovery must be slower, and my thankfulness, as the phantom of insanity faded, must be deeper and more durable.

Two tags of my schooldays came upon me, and for the first time in my life I realised their beauty and significance. They were helpfully apt to my condition. Μηδὲν ἄγαν, nothing too much. *Mens*

sana in corpore sano. A healthy mind in a healthy
body. As a Christian might be inspired by a text
from his Bible, so was I inspired by these words
from my boyhood's grammars. Both served to
strengthen me in my course, to stiffen my attitude.
I had unsmiling sympathy with the Christian host
who could hang on the walls of his spare bedroom,
for the solace of any guest, "My God shall sup-
ply thy need." It was a declaration of faith in
which I no longer saw anything funny or discourte-
ous. That it might not prove efficacious was an
argument outside the point. But in my own house,
I should certainly resent any lack of control or exaggeration to conduct or any behaviour contrary to
what I now knew to be the necessary mottoes of my
life.

All this passed swiftly through my mind during
our quiet, enjoyable lunch, and I decided, as soon as
possible, neatly to print my mottoes on two corre-
spondence cards and pin them up on the bookcase in
my study with drawing-pins.

I had ruled the last line of the square which surrounded each, when Amy peeped in on me, and was
anxious to know what I was doing. I explained.
I welcomed the test of explanation. No mockery
and no misunderstanding should daunt me in this my
declaration of common sense. What is more, I was
not only to preach about my mottoes, but also to put
their teaching into immediate practice. For Amy
(she had become to me once more dear little Amy)
not having seen me for two days, was anxious, dear
girl, for a display of emotion, which I knew, for me

at any rate, to be far from sensible.   What was the use of this barren fervour?   No sensible man should play with his emotions.   It would strengthen my will-power to withstand her delicate advances.   Besides, Amy had said that she could always do as she liked with me, and that was an error that could not too soon be eradicated.

So I was kind but imperturbable.

She was lying on the couch, and asked me to sit by her to look at a line in her hand.   I looked at the line, but though she made room for me on the couch, and it was not easy to leave her with a single kiss, I went back to my own chair.

"I want to talk to you," I said.

"What about?" she pouted.

"Oh, just a nice talk.   There are lots of things to talk about."

"You don't love me any more."

"It's silly to say that."

"It's not silly: it's true."

"I love you just as much as I've ever loved you."

"That's not saying much."

"Darling little Amy," I pleaded, "do be sensible!"

"Don't patronise me!" she cried.   "Odious of you.   Of course you're a hero, and noble, and all that, but you needn't be so horribly superior, or at any rate you needn't show it."

"Don't talk like that!" I answered, shaken. "I'm not a hero or anything like it.   I'm only sensible, and want you to be sensible."

"You are a hero.   You are.   You are.   Why do

you want to take that from me as well? You are my wounded hero."

There were tears in her eyes. I had not the strength to be kind. I snapped out:

"Shut up! That hero rubbish sickens me. It gets on my nerves. If you talk rot like that, you must get out. I can't stand it."

"Who's being sensible now?" she asked with that sudden change of front that always amazed me.

"It's because I'm so easily *not* that I've got to make myself."

"And me, it seems."

"Oh, Amy, do try and understand," I said.

"How can I when you're always changing? — not changing exactly. But why ever can't you be yourself?"

"That's exactly what I want to be," I cried.

She shut her eyes, pretending to be asleep. I was silent. The silence lasted long enough for me to regain my composure, which I managed with far less difficulty than on any previous occasion.

Amy half opened her eyes, and stretching out her arms sleepily to me, said in a low voice — oh, adorably winning:

"Come to me."

I said, "You darling!" but I did not move, though I longed to hold her to me and kiss her soft neck and her soft hair where it waved up from her neck.

"It's no good," I declared. "I should love to. We've got to be sensible."

Her arms relaxed and dropped. Her eyes shut.

A little smile curled her lips. She was silent for a few moments; then she began to speak slowly, her eyes still closed, in a gentle purring voice:

"All this about being sensible. Why can't you be yourself? The danger of the wounded hero is that he may just become a prig. I expect you feel this really. That's why you're so touchy about it. Touchiness doesn't alter facts. You don't really think I should have cared for you if you'd merely been smashed up in a bicycle accident, do you? And yet you won't be yourself. You're always taking a new line, as though you were converted or something."

She got up quietly and stretched herself, yawning.

"I shall go and have a nap, I think. I'm sleepy."

She came up to me and stroked my head.

"Dear little Jim!" she said solicitously. "It's awful for you, I know. But you will try, won't you, not to be more of a prig than you can help?"

This was a test of my Keith-acquired composure far higher than my Tommies had given me. I can't tell you how crucial a moment I knew it in my bones to be. Composure conquered. I looked her quietly in the face and said without the faintest trace of irony:

"That's where I most need you."

A flicker of bewilderment passed over her like a shadow. I answered it, my hand on her arm:

"*You* must help me not to be a prig."

"Oh, I'll try," she said, and with mock-seriousness; "but I'm only a weak little girl, and it's a mighty task."

I laughed, and soberly said:

" You can't exaggerate its mightiness, even in fun. You've far more insight than you realise. You were teasing me just now, I know, but you simply can't imagine how it got me when you said: ' Why can't you be yourself? ' That's just the whole difficulty. You put your sweet little finger plumb on the point."

" Oh dear, oh dear! " she cried.   " My poor little head! You are talking such rubbish. You *want* to bewilder me. But for all that you really are rather wonderful. When I think about myself, I seem to be nothing; I don't think, and then I just am.   And now you're making me talk rubbish too. With your texts on the walls and all that. It *can* only make you sillier and more self-conscious. Who's to say, anyhow, what's too much or what's too little or what's enough. And it's all nothing whatever to do with what the real truth is.   I know that you'll think me horrid to know; but I do know, and you may as well know that I know — about your going to town and not wanting to kiss me."

She seemed working herself up to something.

" Whatever have you got into your pretty head now? " I asked.

" Oh, don't put on that air of innocence, for good-ness' sake! I know what men are, and why you were so gloomy and patient before you went away. I guessed your little game then, and I know it now."

" What do you mean? "

" Oh! Please! "

It seemed to me that she could only mean one thing, and I was ashamed of myself for probably wronging her in thought. She drew herself up, however, with a kind of babyish dignity that touched me, and proceeded thus:

"There you sit gaping at me. Why should you be shocked at a girl *knowing* what a man *does?* And I do know. I've only kept my eyes open. Besides, isn't every musical comedy more or less about it? And girls have talked to me; yes, and married women. Oh, I know, even if I hadn't read in one of the greatest English writers that any woman is better than none to a young man. Isn't what I'm saying true?"

"Yes, there's truth in it," I said. "But none about me. . . ." And I was obliged to add, "In this particular instance, at any rate."

I waited, because thoughts of the kind to which she referred had without any doubt passed through my mind.

"Whatever put such ideas into your head?" I cried.

"Ideas! It's simply common sense."

She stamped her little foot.

"I only wanted to be with Keith," I said. "And have a good dinner," I added lamely.

"Oh, do talk common sense! You ought to be glad I'm not an innocent baby. Aren't you a man like other men? I'm much too modern to be shocked. I think it was very natural for poor Tom Jones, always getting into a state with his darling Sophia, when he did see the country girl; he simply couldn't help himself. And who's Keith Collins, anyhow? — and a good dinner! Fancy a man leav-

ing a girl like me for that! Let's talk common
sense."

I was flabbergasted. This from Amy, whom my
mother firmly believed would make any man a dear
little wife! And after all, perhaps she would.
Why not? Yet it seemed impossible that I could be
rightly hearing what she said. There was an incongruity about her words that left me speechless.
I saw a great deal of common sense in what she
said; I saw her babyish desire to flaunt her knowledge and discomfort me; I saw too a faint instinctive struggling towards honesty of intercourse with
me. Yet I sat before her horrified and speechless.

And how came she to use my own trick, as it were,
to beat me with? Why did she harp on common
sense? For a moment I had a dark suspicion that
she was somehow being used by the thing that had
appeared to me, that she was somehow possessed.

I had not, however, reached the top of my perplexity. For suddenly she was on her knees, nestling against me, pleading in a pitiful voice:

"Oh, you are my hero. You are. You wouldn't
have left me — so gladly — just for a good dinner?
Do say you wouldn't! A hero can be bold and
wicked and masterful. He can't just be greedy.
And I do so want to care for you. It's so lovely to
be in love."

I cried out, raising my voice almost to a shout:
"I'm not a hero. I'm not a hero. I'm merely a
greedy prig, a greedy pig; a pig and a prig!"

I had no idea what could happen next. I was at
an utter loss. If she had left the room turning

somersaults I should hardly have been surprised.
As it was, it really seemed more ludicrous that she
should get up, as she did, tidying her hair, as though
nothing had happened, and should say as she did, in a
matter-of-fact little voice:

"Well, I suppose I'd better go and have my nap,
if I'm going to have one at all."

Then, blowing me a kiss, she ran out of the room.

"Ha, ha!" I said to myself vacantly. "So that's
that," and for some time I sat like a mummy. Then
I got painfully up and stretched myself and hobbled
across the room to the window. I breathed the
fresh air with relief.

No girl could understand what friendship could
mean to a man, and could not in consequence appreciate the pleasure of such a little dinner as Keith and
I had had. She thought of it merely as food, and
of herself as a daintier dish. And after all that was
very much how I thought of her; so her idea tallied
with mine and with what common sense told me was
the bare truth, stripped of sentiment.

But why, after all, bother in the least about what
she did say? Talk! What sane man could honestly say that he wanted to *talk* with a pretty girl?
And Amy was a pretty girl, who fully agreed with
me as to the purposelessness of talk. That was
sheer luck, and nothing at all to deplore. I must
season myself to her common sense, however unexpected and even shocking it might appear in a pretty
girl. Wasn't mine to be a common-sense marriage?

Still, the fact remained that I could not always be

caressing her; and the practical question instantly
arose, upon which I fastened with relief: what must
I do to fill in the time? About this question there
was nothing misty and hazardous, and very soon I
found the satisfactory answer. Games was the key.
Games! But which? Draughts, poker-patience,
golf, tennis (my hand and foot would be a decent
handicap), backgammon, chess? No, chess was too
strenuous for her, with even the gift of a queen;
and billiards? No, not much fun when you had to
give ninety-five in a hundred and owe fifty. Chess
and billiards were too good to be spoiled. Of course
bridge when there was a four; she played quite a
good hand for a girl. Strange, I thought, that I had
never before realised the significance of games or
what an important place they took in the domestic
economy of life.

The air was so refreshing that I thought a stroll
in the garden would be pleasant, and, glad that my
mind had been so quickly put to rest, I took a stroll
along the most secluded path lest Amy might see me
from her window and join me. One thought especially served to support my mind as stoutly as my
stick served to support my body; that I had no illusions to be shattered by marriage.

The path took me in view of the road, and I heard
myself hailed by a woman's voice.

"Hullo, Mr. Wood," it cried. "May I come
trespassing in?"

Leaves were being rustled in the ditch by the
hedge which separated our bit of wood from the
road; but I saw no one. I guessed it was Corinna,

and in my politest voice I made the best of it and answered: " Oh, please do, by all means! "

And Corinna Combes' hatless head appeared in a gap in the hedge.

" What fun to find you! " she cried.   " Do you mind?   I so wanted to see you."

I wondered why neighbours should nearly always be a nuisance, and replied genially, " That's very nice of you."

The swift grace of her movement along the path to my side reminded me of my visitant, and how remote and unreal he had become to me.   Such a reminder was therefore very pleasant, and mollified my resentment at the girl's intrusion.   It was clear from the first moment that she was jollier and more at ease alone in a wood than with others in a drawing-room.

" I've been meaning to write to you," I said.

" My little outburst needed no answer," she laughed.

" It was only partly to thank you; I meant to confess that you were off the track about the . : . keeping my feet and being myself — do you remember? It was the queerest thing in the world.   I said the exact opposite practically of what I wanted to say."

" What did you want to say? "

" The usual recruiting stunt.   I've never spoken before, you see."

Corinna was looking intently at me, not at all unpleasantly.   She was so completely at her ease that I was completely at mine.   She was dressed in brown and green, very neatly, with a neat little brown hat; her face was red-brown with the sun and wind. A wood was certainly her setting: there was something gnomish and elfish about her appearance. It seemed a thousand pities that she should ever be superior, or give the impression of being superior.

"Of course I believe you; but I must also believe my own ears and feeling."

"And what did they tell you?"

"That the deepest honesty in you . . . only the last sincerity in a man . . . what does move? Not rhetoric in your case. Isn't it the trembling truth that sheer sincerity forces out of a man? Each word came charged tingling full of reality to me."

There was nothing assumed about her eagerness.

"I never felt more uncertain, never shakier than at that absurd moment."

"Oh, that has nothing to do with it. There's something deeper in one than reason or one's habit of thought."

Her interest was so active and yet so impersonal that I had the sensation of talking about some one other than myself. It was a new experience to me.

"Do you know," I said, " that I was so far from being myself that I listened to my own voice as though it were the voice of another man?"

"That's just it," she cried. "What is this self of ours? It takes a big thing to shake us up to find it. Otherwise we bunch along like sheep. The big thing comes, and this real self at last has its chance. It comes to life and is at first a stranger guest unwelcome, and the habit self does all it can quietly to smother it."

" I can feel what you say is real to you," I said.
" My feeling about it explains in a way what you
began by saying — about what moves one in what
any one says — but honestly all this about real selves
and habit selves has no meaning at all to my reason."

" Haven't you even felt a sort of pull in yourself? "

" Yes, but . . ."

" Well, that's what the pull's between, only my
names for the sides of the tug of war.   There comes
a bang, a shock, and one is aware of the bunching-
along part and the something else."

" If the bang came to me," I said, " I should
plump for the buncher."

She laughed.

" Oh no, you wouldn't," she said, smiling.
" Your saying that proves it hasn't."

" Why does it? "

She raised her shoulders and spread out her hands,
like a Frenchwoman.

" I know," she said.

" Are you a theosophist or something? "

" No; why do you ask? "

" They always seem in possession of some private
key, that sets them walking through the world with
a quiet superior smile of contentment on their faces."

" That's an unkind way of putting it, isn't it? "
she said, with laughing eyes.

" I hate them," I quietly announced.

" Have I struck you as superior, then? "

" Yes, but not now."

" When? "

" In a drawing-room."

" Oh yes. I know. I'm shy, and hate being shy, so I put on airs to show I'm not. It only happens when I feel there's no one at all who can see through me. When there's one person *with* me I can be simple and natural."

She got up.

" Why not come and have tea with us? " I suggested.

" I'm afraid I can't, thanks. But what's the time? "

" Ten to four," I told her.

She sat down again.

" It was love shook me up, gave me the rousing bang," she said with absolute simplicity. " Opened my eyes. Yes, that's really the truest way of putting it."

She seemed to be thinking aloud as she said:

" The parting of the ways. Drifting one way, living the other. Living with intention."

Something stirred within me; I did not want to be drawn too far into her confidence, jolly as she was in a wood.

" Look here," I said firmly, " I'm awfully interested in what you say, but to be quite frank, after all's said and done, I believe in common sense."

" Oh yes, of course. It is that."

What made me angry I don't know. But I was angry.

" I'm not with you. It's too crazy and fantastic."

She jumped up with laughing, combative eyes.

"Common sense is the rudder," she said. "I'm speaking about the direction, and mine's not crazy or fantastic."

She stood erect before me, poised, her body like an unsheathed sword. She said in a low voice, no strain or pant in it:

"My attitude of devotion."

The antagonism in me answered:

"Mine is a humbler attitude."

"As fine as possible for life to use."

Resentment hardened; the likeness to my visitant was too uncanny.

"Life's crippled me," I said with brutal candour.

She shrank up, she drooped.

"Oh, forgive me," she cried. "I forgot. But it's not life that's done it — not life."

I had got up by then, not lessening, I'm afraid, the difficulty of rising without the help of one foot. Before I knew what she was doing, she had seized my hand and kissed it. I was aghast, but before I could speak she had fled away down the path, and with a flying leap cleared the hedge like a hurdler.

"Good God!" I said aloud, partly at the madness of her jump, partly at the madness of her sudden pity.

"There's something in common sense after all," I thought, and the absurd exhibition of the lack of it reassured me profoundly as I made my slow way back to the house. I was glad to own that she was quite a nice girl at heart. I was able to accept her, you see, and acceptance is far less disturbing than anger.

"Whatever theosophists may be," I thought, "I'm jolly glad to have my own key." And my whole being glowed with a kind of universal affability, so perfectly established did my security appear.

All through the day my confidence lasted. My mother noticed it.

"I'm sure your little change has done you good, dear," she said after dinner. "You seem ever so much more your old self."

"Oh, streets better," said Doris.

I looked at Amy.

"Do you think I'm better?" I asked her mischievously.

"You feel better, don't you, darling?" she answered, without betraying the least embarrassment.

"Much better," I replied cheerfully.

"Ignore a thing," I thought, "and it ceases to exist," and the thought pleased me, as though I had stumbled on a great truth. Only supposing I had taken seriously all that she had said! Whereas now what might have been stumbling-blocks were simply steps up which I climbed to composure.

Another step was waiting me, however. For on going to my bedroom I found a fat envelope, with my name written on it in Amy's handwriting. I opened it at once and read:

"I don't know what possessed me to talk like that just now. You must try and forgive me. Really I don't know much, not even what I want. I expect it comes from reading horrid books. I do want to

have a good time, and I manage to all right, only
there are times, especially with you, when everything
I care for seems stupidly not worth while. What is
worth while? Settling goodly down to look after a
house and have babies? What is love, anyway? —
I mean real, actual love. Not the sort of dreamy
happiness I get when I think of my wounded hero
and all that; that's glorious, and I can't think why it
makes you cross for me to talk to you about it, except that you're a man, but it's thin and shadowy
somehow — I mean it's like breathing air when you
want a good substantial meal. Oh, I do wish I was
a man! It would all be easy enough then. You
don't know how difficult it is to be a girl, especially
if you want to be a nice girl as much as I want it.
And I could see I shocked you, and in a way I dreadfully shocked myself too. Yet when you remember what you want from me, it really does seem
funny that anything I could merely *say* could shock
you. Why do we all think *saying* things is horrid?
Men do and say much worse things, don't they?
Oh, things are difficult. Really I am such a hopeless half-and-halfer. I mean there's part of me
that's utterly Victorian and *pot-au-feu,* and would
like to have a goody, sedate life in a little home of
my own; and for that you would make a perfectly
ideal husband. Oh, my dear Jim, ideal! You'd
be a wounded hero and have to be a stay-at-home.
And then there's part of me that doesn't want
to marry at all ever until I'm — oh, very much
older, and simply obliged to settle down. It's the
old pull, I suppose, between Duty and Pleasure,

that's all the rage in good books. Wouldn't life be nice, if they were ever the same?—D. and P. I mean. Not, dearest old Jim, that you stand wholly for Duty. It would be quite nice, I'm sure, for a little time at any rate. But you do know that re-signed look husbands and wives get. A sort of reso-lute cheerfulness when any one else is there, which becomes Heaven knows what when any one else isn't. Nursey used to say to me: 'When he's court-ing, you don't know a man nearly well enough, and when you're married you know him ever so much too well.'

"What is a girl to do? If you could answer that, I'd marry you to-morrow. Truly I would. I think I only said those outrageous things to you to see if I could find out what you were like. I'm not really such a — what is it?— such an '*enfant terrible*' as that. Of course I don't want to bore you with the Woman's Question and all that. They're all frumps mostly, and besides, with the war and so on, it's frightfully *démodé*. But there is most decidedly a 'question' about girls like me. Girls, I mean, that aren't clever and independent and manly, and jolly well able to look after themselves, but nice womanly girls; not the stuffy sort of womanly girls, you know, but girls like me: modern as anything, but not selfish or strong enough to snatch what they want; only wretched if it's not given them. Do understand what I mean. I'm not thinking out what I'm writ-ing, I should only be silly and self-conscious if I did that. Besides, one only thinks when one's got to be careful what some one else may think about one, and

I'm past all that with you, after what I've said, and we've done, which is a comfort.

" You see, the point is I shouldn't at all mind being the nice innocent little Early Victorian miss who curtsied (or is it courteseyd?) acceptance to the husband her kind parents found for her.   It's not my fault that it can't now be done.   I'm a sort of betwixt and between.   I guess a lot, but all I know is that there's a lot to be known.   I'm dragged in two ways really, and it's so difficult that I simply don't know what's to be done.   That's why I try to think as little as possible, and just go on trying to have a good time while it lasts.   I could go on writing screeds and screeds, but it's not much good.   Only I don't want you to think worse of me than you can help.   You couldn't talk to me ever, I suppose, just as though I were a man?   I suppose it's hardly fair even to ask you.   If a girl really knew all about men and life beforehand, she'd never, never marry one.   Why should she?   Some one told me that. I forget whom.   But it didn't make me dislike men. Not a bit.   It made them quite tremendously fascinating!   Oh, it is difficult being a girl like me, when I think about it, and it's funny how things you say do make me think.   You are rather a wonderful person, though it's too lovely of you to pin up those little text things in your room.   Now they'd work quite differently on me.   They'd very soon make me go and do the most awful things — they would really, I'm sure, as soon as ever I'd got used to them, and that would be dreadfully soon.   But then I'm a girl, and not a bit like you.   You do feel friendly to

me, though, don't you, as well as the other thing?
I should so like some one to treat me seriously as
a human being, and not just as a pretty girl; and yet
those who do are *so* stuffy and boring. I do wish I
was like your mother. Things were much easier
when she was a girl. There was hardly a choice
then. But now! Oh, believe me, it is most awfully
difficult! Anyhow, please do take this letter seriously, and don't think worse of me than you can help.

"Toujours à toi,

"Amy."

I don't know why the letter should have pleased
me, but it did. She's just a naughty child, I thought
demurely, worrying her pretty little head about
things which it is no good worrying about. Talk to
her as though she were a man, indeed! I shouldn't
dream of insulting her like that. No, no; she was
annoyed at not being kissed and boiled over a little.
Nor was she, I smiled to myself in my composure,
any the worse for being slightly wanton. Times
certainly were changing. Would my mother faint if
she read the letter? I appreciated the child's difficulty. It was rather sweet of her to be so candid,
and after all no man of common sense wanted a
girl to be an alabaster saint. There was a lot of
sense, too, in what she wrote, though her joke about
my being an ideal husband was somewhat heavy.
Her girlish ignorance was as charming as her
naughty resentment. And what a time the letter
must have taken her sweet little hand to scrawl!
Her writing sprawled, but she was no fool; far from

it. Would mother term all this her airs and graces, of which she confessed ignorance, and would she persist in her opinion as to Amy being a dear little wife for any man? Why not? A thousand times, why not?

Thus I tiptoed, preening myself on the highest step, in boundless security. I read the letter through again from beginning to end, chuckling, and went to bed, and almost immediately to sleep.

I woke from sleep with a start, as though an ice-cold hand had stroked my neck.

There, to my horror, standing not erect, but bowed before me, with eyes full of sorrow, was, in his own white light and clearer than I had ever seen him, my visitant.

I could not speak. I could not move. Literally I felt that my body had become a great stone. Something held me in its power as I stared into his unflinching eyes.

I had the sensation of falling, falling, falling. I made a desperate effort to take advantage of his deep dejection. I was strengthless. He looked feeble and sad, but I could not resist. It seemed a long hour that I lay there motionless under his sad eyes. At last he spoke.

" I am so sorry," he said, " but it has to be. The other way was no use. Such a pity! Such a great pity! "

I made a convulsive struggle to ask what he meant; my lips would not move. He faded and was gone.

IX

THEY used to feed the snakes in the Zoological Gardens on little live animals. In the glass case the little animal scuffled away from the man's hand in its new freedom and hopped about for a few minutes, until it came under the snake's stare and its movement ceased. On waking in the morning I felt very much as one of those little animals must feel when first its eye catches the snake's eye and he knows that he has escaped from the man's hand only to meet a worse enemy. I was in the glass case with the snake. A mysterious horror had me in its hold.

When I got up and tried to dress myself, I was obliged to sit as much as I could owing to actual physical weakness. It seemed, too, that my heart was beating faster than it should.

To put a brave face on the matter, I said to myself: "This is really getting past a joke."

I told mother, who immediately noticed that I was not so well, that I had slept abominably. Amy's letter had entirely passed from my mind, but it flashed back when I saw her, and I was able to take her on one side and tell her how much I had appreciated its intention.

"And you don't think too badly of me?" she asked with very dear timidity.

166

"Not a bit.   Not a bit," I replied.   "You're human, human."   She looked at me askance on account
of the intensity of meaning which I put into the
word.   I answered her look of fear with a hearty
"To be human — that's what I like my friends to
be."

She must have known what I meant, but she was
obliged to assert herself and say, as she drew herself
timidly and prettily up (she always looked fresh and
lovely in the morning) :

"What else can human beings be?"

"Oh, millions of things!" I laughed back.

All through breakfast I was continually on the
verge of the horror that brooded deep within me.
In lulls of the talk it was clear to me that measures
must be taken, drastically and speedily, to tackle it.
I put off thinking what those measures should be,
and I spun out all the little details of breakfast to
their finest.

After breakfast, chiefly to gain time, I suppose, I
wandered into mother's sitting-room and announced,
à propos of nothing at all:

"I say, mater, I proposed to Amy, you know, and
she said she must have three months to think over
her answer."

My mother was making lists on half sheets of
paper, as she always did after breakfast; she has always been a great believer in lists.   She looked up
at me, pushing on her spectacles with gentle firmness,
and said:

"Well, dear?"

"Oh, I thought I'd tell you.   That's all."

She smiled her dearest smile to say slowly: " I don't think that you have any cause for worry in that."

I never could understand why I always felt such a very male man when mother spoke to me about Amy. " I don't worry, of course," I said.

Suddenly, on the spur of the moment an idea came to me as I was turning away:

" Oh, there's another thing. Aren't there some papers or something that belonged to Grandfather Albert? " That was how we used generally to refer to my father's father.

" Yes: there are some notes and writings: a pile of old exercise books and letters."

" Do you know where they are? "

" Yes, dear. I keep them locked up in the cabinet."

" Could you let me have a look at them some time? "

" Certainly."

" You couldn't now, I suppose? "

She took a key from a drawer at her desk and went to the cabinet, which from my earliest childhood had been a thing of awe to me, and mystery. It opened like a bookcase, but inside there were no shelves, only drawers, many and deep. One of these she pulled out, and extracted a bundle of paperbacked exercise-books, tied up with faded pink tape, and a bundle of letters in one fat envelope, also tied up with faded pink tape.

" These are some of his notes and jottings; these

are his letters to your father. He was a very fine old man before he. . . . Always strange in his ways."

" Dr. Redman spoke to me about him."

" Dr. Redman almost worshipped him."

" Somehow one doesn't expect devotion in a man like Redman."

" No? " said my mother. " But he's coming to lunch."

I laughed with pleasure; the inconsequence was so exactly like her; and something in me was pleased that I could still laugh with pleasure, in spite of the mysterious horror which was somehow set stirring by the sight and touch of those old papers. As I held these bundles in my hand I dared not think of the connection between my grandfather and my familiar, betwen the old man's tragic end in an asylum and my own secret terror of insanity. I dared not think of it, I say; yet I was deeply aware that in some way, by the mere recognition of their existence, I was taking a definite and important step, though in what direction I did not know. For a moment I hesitated. It was on the tip of my tongue to give the bundles back; but I waited and watched my mother push in the drawer, close the doors of the cabinet, turn the key and replace it in the drawer of her desk.

I waited, while my mother resumed her lists. She said:

" Father intended to write a life of Grandfather Albert."

" I know."

" It would please him if you were able to do so. There are lots of diaries and things."

" I say, mater, was he really mad? " I asked.

It was the tone of my voice, I expect, that caused mother to turn to me with a look of scrutiny; and she surprised me by saying:

" Many thinkers have, I believe, gone too far. Have crossed the line and been unable to regain their footing.   In such cases there's no tendency . . ."

" I never dreamed there could be," I stoutly interposed.

" Your father was very frank about it before he married me."

At that moment I touched something more definitely real in my mother than I had ever known before.   Had she some subtle instinctive means of guessing what was in my mind?

" It made a terrible impression on your father, seeing his father when his reason first lapsed. When you were a tiny baby, there was a time. . . . You were terribly excitable . . . we had the shadow of a fear, but, thank God, it passed when I found the right food and you've always been your dear, sensible, intelligent self."

That drew me far back into mother's life; I seemed to see the two not as my mother and father, but just a young couple fighting a bad fear together. A wave of intense thankfulness passed over me that I had never mentioned to her the visits of my familiar.

" The fear was never quite real to me," mother

went on, " except through his feelings. I never could understand about heredity." She stood up in all her quiet diginity. " I am a woman," she said, " and I prayed."

She came to me and kissed my forehead, and as she kissed me I felt a very little boy again.

" I had no idea," I said with apology in my voice, if it is possible to apologise for the behaviour of a life-time, " that people thought of those things then."

" Your father was in advance of his time," she answered proudly, and added, like the darling she was, in case I might have a wrong impression, " though he was a good man and a Christian."

"How that dates!" I thought as I kissed her. Yet there was absolute sincerity in my cry: " You're the dearest mother a man could have."

For I realised that if ever I were in abject distress (other than that in which I was) I should be able to put my head in her lap, as I loved to do when I was a small boy, and cry my eyes out. A dim fore-boding caused the thought to be an inestimable com-fort.

My hand on her shoulder, I said: " I'm glad of the impulse that made me ask for grandfather's things this morning."

Stroking my hand, she answered, smiling: " Run along now; you've wasted quite enough of my pre-cious time." And the impossibility of my ever run-ning again must have cut into her heart, for with infinite tenderness she exclaimed: " Oh, my dear boy ! "

I went away very slowly, because of the bundles under my arm, up to my study. I took with me the good knowledge of having come closer in touch with mother than ever before; but the pleasure in that good knowledge, although it was keen, could not stand up against the blunt fact which had been revealed to me that father had had misgivings on my account. Who does not know that tendencies are apt to skip a generation? Why should this mysterious horror be brooding within me? But why connect my vision, my dream, my hallucination, whatever you like to call it, with such an awful catastrophe as insanity?

What was madness? Blake saw visions: was he mad? Or was he saner, for instance, than the man who in the prime of life could devote all his energy to cricket or golf? What was madness? And my grandfather, what form did his madness take?

I wanted to know what was the meaning of my familiar's depression. What did he mean by saying, " The other way was no use." What other way? And why did the icy grip in which I had been held in my dream seem to persist now that I was awake? Why should my dreams be so painfully vivid?

Faster and faster ran these questions within me, carrying me away with them, faster and faster, and I felt exactly as I felt when as a boy my bicycle ran away with me down a hill, and I couldn't stop it. And a voice shouted a warning as I sped on; " Madness," it shouted, " is loss of control." I held my hand tightly before my eyes, pressing tight fingers against my temples. Then I knew that Amy came into the room and stood by me and stroked my head with a shy hand. She said:

" What *am* I to do? '

It sounded like a joke. I answered without stirring:

" What are *you* to do? What are *you* to do? Why the deuce don't you train for a nurse? "

" If you think that why didn't you suggest it before? " she gasped.

" Why should I? You never asked me. Besides, I never thought of it."

Nor had I. And what induced me to fling it out on her I did not know nor have I up to this very day discovered.

" Oh, you have; you have; and you've thought me slack and a shirker, and never said so, and all the time you've been playing with me. It's not fair. It's brutal. Suddenly to blurt out the truth."

My mind stopped; I still felt giddy with what I can only describe as my mind's rush through space. I looked up at her.

" Amy, I've never thought of it before, I swear; and I don't know why I said it then."

" You couldn't, offhand, want to change my whole life."

" No, no, I didn't mean it. I don't know why I said it."

She was silent, thinking; then she said:

" It's the obvious thing to do, of course. Only do you think I could? "

" Of course you could. You'd make a jolly nurse. The men would adore you."

She was still pondering, as she said very seriously:
" They're not all at death's door, are they? And
the costume's pretty. Well, thank you very much
for telling me." Then she held my face between her
hands and looking me straight in the eyes, said:
" For all that I think it would have been friendlier
of you not to have sprung it on me like this."

There was nothing babyish in her dignity at that
moment, or as she turned on her heel and walked out
of the room. In spite of my uneasiness I genuinely
liked and respected Amy at that moment, and incredible as it may seem, knew that I had never liked
or respected her before. I laughed at the idea as
fantastic and absurd, but no mockery of mine could
diminish its basis of firm fact. The possibility of
indifference to everything but her prettiness had been
her attraction for me.

" And what if it be so?" I said to myself with
defiance. " There's nothing to be ashamed of in
that. Besides, like and dislike! A girl was a girl,
and either attractive or not, and no one knew what
made a girl attractive." I did not worry for long
about that, but I did worry about the sudden impulse
which caused me to blurt out things of importance
without, previous to their utterance, their having
touched my consciousness. This had happened
three times in succession now in one morning —
twice with my mother, once with Amy.

By itself there was small significance in my bald
announcement to mother of Amy's wish for delay;
but why should I have suddenly asked for Grandfather Albert's papers? Why should I have sud-

denly flung out my suggestion that Amy should become a nurse? There the two bundles lay before me; the paper was turning yellowish; the faint musty smell that old papers get from long storage in an airless drawer was as noticeable as the faded pink tape with which they had been neatly tied. There was something ominous about their presence on my desk which kept me from untying the faded tape. Moreover I felt it ominous too, the certainty I had, that Amy would become a nurse because of what I had said. Could it be that there was an insidious connection betwen these spurts of speech and the threat in my dream? The question found no direct answer. But aloud I said to myself in a clear voice:

"It is a dream. A dream and nothing else. Queer of course in its recurrence, but entirely without consequence."

That reassured me. I was able to feel confident that it had no direct power over me in itself, if I did not allow it to prey upon my mind and to become an obsession. I decided to speak frankly to Dr. Redman; to ask his advice and to follow it implicitly. Even as I took the decision I leaned forward, resolutely pulled the end of the faded tape which tied the bundle of note-books, untied the knot, and picked up the top book.

The pages were ruled with lines which had not been utilised. Thin, minute writing, packed together and leaning this way and that, covered each page. Something occult, cabalistic almost, about its aspect increased my disquietude. So Cagliostro

should have written. I didn't like it. I didn't like
it at all.

Were there evil arts, black magic? Had this
strange old man, my father's father, some secret key
by which he gained access to the other world? And
was there another world? And if there was truth
in these sinister, uncanny happenings, how would
the honest man of plain common sense face them?
What ought I to do? If only they had not been
thrust upon me I could have continued quietly to ignore them. What weapon was so good as the
power to ignore? Had it been finally snatched from
me? After all, it was only a dream; anything might
happen in a dream. No man has any control over
his dreams, and nothing was known about dreams.

Because my father's father had had queer notions
over which he became so excited that at last his
senses wavered and went, was that any sufficient reason that I, his son's son, should be haunted? Was
such malignant injustice possible?

Oh, for Keith's calm power of acceptance!
There was nothing for it; that power of his must
be acquired — acquired — acquired. If only this
dark sword of fear were not dangling above my
head, how much easier it would have been! But
if it were not, I should after all be like Keith and
most other people that I knew, and have the possession homely and within, with no struggle, and in consequence, it was some consolation to remember, without realising its priceless value.

I wasted no more time. I began forthwith its
acquisiton. I resisted the *malaise* the queer little

old copybook gave me, as it sprawled on my knee with its yellowish corners and faint mustiness, by saying to myself: " He must have been an interesting old gentleman, this grandfather of mine.   Pathetic, too, that he should have been at such pains to write all this and should never have seen a line of it in print, not even a letter to *The Times*.   Why did the old boy write and write and write ? "

There were few signs then of my having inherited that scribbling symptom at any rate.   A rough reckoning showed that he was able to squeeze four hundred and fifty words into a page, which meant fifty-thousand words to a note-book, and there were six note-books here and heaven only knows how many more his frantic industry had not filled.

Not till then did it occur to me to try and decipher the tiny scratchings of the script.   Only the headings in printing were legible to the casual eye. " Milton "; " Folly and Freedom "; " Blake and Milton"; " The Blind and the Mad "; and so on. An effort to decipher the text showed me that I could only read a word here and a word there without making a study of his script, and in spite of my accumulating dread the romance of writing so much with so little care of its ever being read appealed to me.

My eye caught a quotation that seemed less carefully illegible than the rest: two lines apparently of blank verse.   I made them out.

> *" Six days they shrank up from existence*
> *And the seventh day they rested."*

And with the utmost difficulty I continued: " *Any*

*lines more final or more scathing in literature I
should be glad to know."*   *Final* I was sure of, but
whether it was *scalding* or *scathing* I could not decide.   It went on, *" And they still rest,"* or exist or
something.   What, wasn't clear, but the exclamation marks, three in number, were quite clear.   One
indeed had pierced the page.   I looked about for
more exclamation marks, and found them, plenty of
them.   Before one regular little bunch of them, I
made out: *" Lack of (something illegible) leads to
common sense, the bane, the chill-bane, of speed."*
That made me turn to the beginning to find a date
and discover how near his end the poor old boy was
when he wrote that; but there was no date.

A printed heading thickly underlined was " Mind
and Mutton."   It began as far as I could make out:
*" Not for nothing do muttons abound in Xt's par-
ables of man.   Munching muttons!   We behave
like sheep, we look like sheep, we smell like sheep.
Man is clothed and nourished on mutton.   Who
knows whether most of his misery may not be traced
to mutton?   In the process of digesting countless
legs and ribs and sides and backs of millions of muttons may no man have soaked his spiritual system
with the poison of muttonish qualities?   And the tail
is a titbit!"*

He did go it, the old boy; but I could find no reason for his crossness.   He wrote, it struck me, as the
best means of talking to himself, who would be far
the most sympathetic listener to such extravagance.
Was it madness that had made him angry, or anger
that had made him mad?   (Oh, my comments were

cheerful and jaunty enough, but underneath them
fear was creeping and gathering, fear vague and uncanny.) Yet I had heard nothing about him that
could give the impression that he was an angry man
at all. On the contrary my legends had him eccen-
tric, it is true, but alive, amusing and lovable, and
Dr. Redman had told me that I ought to be proud
to have his blood in my veins.

Dr. Redman! The man's name made me shud-
der, but I resolved to overcome my distrust of him.
Why should the patent frankness of his manner rouse
my distrust? Somehow I still found it difficult to
dismiss the feeling that he was playing a part with
me; for my good, of course, to ease my mind, but yet
playing a part. Why should he have made that remark about my self-satisfaction, and why should he
have sent me that silly telegram? Nevertheless talk
to him I must.

My eyesight was good, yet it must have been
peering at the tiny handwriting that had made my
head ache. I put away the note-book and lay down.
The pain was heavy at the back of my head just
above the neck, and got worse. It seemed as though
that were the seat of this bad sense of impending
calamity. I had been amused by the story of Sinbad
and the terrible old man of the sea who clung to his
back. I was not amused by the certainty that the
story symbolised the approach of madness. There
was no doubt of it, I must be entirely open with the
doctor.

Yet mark this well, the stronger grew my resolve
to speak to the doctor, the more acute grew my dis-

trust of him, the more intense my fear of taking him into my confidence. What if he said, in his blunt cheerful way: "Yes, my boy, this is probably the first stage. You must be careful not to excite yourself!" And I was positive that he would say something of the kind. What should I do then? What power had I not to excite myself? That latest dream had taken me by the neck and shaken me. Did I not still feel the effect of that cold touch on my neck?

Till lunch-time the pain persisted. At sight of Dr. Redman the struggle grew fierce between my rising resolve to speak to him and my rising fear of doing so. There were moments when, without exaggeration, it was all I could do to keep myself from screaming. These moments were when I caught Dr. Redman looking at me with what seemed anxious scrutiny. "He notices something!" I thought. "He notices something already!" and I held my breath in an agony of suspense.

How I should have got through lunch, I don't know, if it hadn't been that Amy told Dr. Redman that she wanted to become a hospital nurse and I was interested in their talk. That interest saved me; how or from what, I cannot rightly say, but it diverted my mind (and as I write the phrase I realise afresh the intensity of meaning it had gained for me since that experience), and the crisis passed.

Dr. Redman told Amy that the number of applications was large, but that he would do his best to slip her in somewhere, if he got the chance.

" She'd make a capital nurse, don't you think? "
I asked, really anxious to know his opinion, because
I was surprised at the readiness with which he wel-
comed her offer.

" Yes, I do," he answered promptly.

" Do tell me why? " I said, and Amy pouted:

" Every one hasn't got such a poor opinion of me
as you."

" Certainly I'll tell you why," said Dr. Redman.
" Miss Amy can stick to what she starts. She has
tenacity written all over her."

Again I was surprised. Instinctively I looked
from him to mother, who thought that Amy would
make a sweet little wife for any man, and I remembered that ever since I had ceased to accept Amy's
presence in the house as a matter of course like a
piece of furniture, and had begun to treat her more
or less as a human being, I had never ceased to meet
in her the unexpected and the unforeseen. Mother,
too, with whom I had lived on and off for some
twenty or more comparatively conscious years, had
shown me something in herself that very morning of
whose existence I had never dreamed; and that in a
perfectly normal way, and not as on that unpleasant
occasion when I had seen in her, with indelicate distinctness of vision, a type of all woman and motherhood.

Did the calm I envied in a man like Keith run all
through him? Or was it only a layer, and was
there in every man, however gifted with common
sense, the boiling cauldron I had become all too painfully aware of in myself?

I regarded Dr. Redman's neatly-shaped head and compact body with interest, and tried to think my symbol of the boiling cauldron wild and exaggerated. But it was not. One glance into my mind proved it startlingly exact.

My reading of Grandpa Albert's book gave a queer twist to my mind. Who has not dreamed of slipping slowly down, down, down an endless hill, with the view beneath ever broadening dizzily out on the ceaseless descent until the horror and loneliness of space become so awful that you force yourself to wake? With the cold feel of such a dream on me, I surveyed the party, all nicely dressed, nicely brought up people, discreetly clattering knives and forks, discreetly chewing meat and bread and vegetables in nice proportions, with a little mustard and salt and pepper, perhaps (no, no mustard; we were eating roast mutton), and the maid too, who was handing Doris potatoes, and we were all munching and swallowing and filling our stomachs, soon discreetly to be relieved; and there seemed something inextinguishably funny to me in the incongruity of it all: munching, munching, munching, men in trousers, women in skirts, three times a day, carefully chosen, carefully cooked, carefully served food. . . . And to what end? Altruistic were we, careful were we, to make ourselves into seemlier food for worms? Was all this care to make richer earth, richer dust? No wonder, with these facts of life to hide, we decked ourselves out with all the prettiest conventions we could find. No wonder, when exasperation at our mortal state grew too intense, we should hasten in our millions to blow ourselves to pieces with high explosives.

But why should any one get so angry as my grandfather, with his muttonish fancies, had become? No man could help the indignity of his entry into the world, or the indignity of his departure, or the indignity of his continual need for sustenance, and if his little life were foolish and undignified, who should blame him, who should be angry with him? No fellow-man, surely.

All this while I was of course carefully eating (more carefully than any one, as the fork was fixed by such a neat contrivance, into the palm of my dummy left hand) eating and talking, and I wondered whether any of the others were, like myself, except for smiles and words, far away in regions private to themselves. Here we sat, a friendly intimate party; yet we knew precious little about each other, uncommonly little, except Dr. Redman, who knew, I was convinced, more about me than I cared that he or any one else should know.

Oh yes, I would be frank with him. Why not? What need was there to rage as I had done? And was my mind easier because my stomach was full of food and wine? Very likely. The doctor was there to postpone as long as possible the inevitable end; one might as well make use of his services, such as they were.

No effort at unconcern was needed. I was completely unconcerned, exactly as though the rage of anxiety that had been accumulating during the morning had never been. Nor did I feel any surprise

or pleasure at my unconcern, so natural and simple
did it seem.   I waited for Dr. Redman to finish his
coffee without the least tremor; nor when we were
at last alone did I trouble to interrupt a long spy
story with which he saw fit to regale me.   The story
finished, I began:

"Last time we mentioned it, I tried to put you off
the scent, I'm afraid, about that hallucination business."

Instantly he became attentive.

"I was touchy about your telegram, I expect."

He said nothing; his eyes searched into me.

"Partly that, and partly . . ." I hesitated.

"Well!"

"You must forgive me, but partly I distrust you.
I want you to be entirely open with me."

"Explain!"

"Not to take a line with me.   For instance, I
know you noticed at once my nerves weren't so well;
I felt you looking at me during lunch.   And didn't
you, too, give me the long story just now to turn my
thoughts from myself?"

"Certainly.   What of it?"

"Only I do wish you wouldn't," I said, and without any warning I burst into tears.

Dr. Redman threw his handkerchief across to me
and said:

"Quite a good thing to relieve the lachrymal
glands."

"I can't think why I'm so damned silly," I said,
sniffing.   "I've got one of my own, thanks."   And
I pitched his handkerchief back to him.

" Pooh! I'm not a fool! " he said. " You need not mind me. It's just a physical affection. Nothing in it."

" I've been most horribly upset," I said, " and it all seems so childish and stupid. Dreams and fearings and . . . I don't know. Anyhow, I'll tell you. It came again last night, or I dreamed that it did. It is most damnably uncanny. Its reality, I mean. It was drooping and sad, and seemed to hold me in some ghastly force which I still feel somewhere about. I couldn't resist or speak. It said — it does sound senselessly idiotic to be telling you this solemnly in the daylight — it said, ' I am sorry. The other way was no use. Such a pity! ' I woke up with a boding sense, a kind of mysterious horror, which has been at the back of my mind ever since — something I might fall back into, lose myself in, somehow. I shouldn't mind if it weren't so silly, so incredible, so paltry. What am I to do? I have a definite fear that I am actually on the way to go out of my mind. Tell me plainly, please, is anything known about the approach of insanity? "

" Of course it's much too complicated a question for a plain answer." He dismissed my question sharply and sat brooding. " My God! How interesting! " he said softly, and after sitting rapt for a moment or two, he leaped to his feet and began pacing up and down the room, murmuring every now and then: " Great God! How interesting! "

His excitement gratified me: it was as sincere as a boy's at a school football match.

At last he stopped opposite to me, and, knees bent

to bring his face on a level with mine, neck stretched
out towards me, fists clenched and moving up and
down, he brought out in a suppressed stutter of anger
and excitement:

"Man! Man! Can't you see how hellish interesting it is?"

I resented the question and the emotion with which
he put it.

"A little too hellish interesting for me. Perhaps
if it were the other fellow's shirt that had fallen into
the water, I might see the joke."

He had swept round on his heel and was pacing
the room again.

"Oh, you dolt! You dolt! What's the good of
fear? God, what wouldn't I give to have this happen to me!"

The worst of a doctor who's a friend of the family, I thought, is that he thinks he can be rude to you,
and I shouted: "You don't understand. It's not
knowing makes me afraid."

"That's precisely why you're such a dolt!" he
cried. "If you only knew a little more, and weren't
so self-satisfied, you'd realise how damn little you or
any man can know about anything. What is the
thing we call life? What is the thing we call death?
Why is a tree green? Why does a rose smell?
Why has a worm no legs, and a dog four, and a man
two? What's memory or mind or matter? What's
anything? We only guess, we only guess and believe, and don't do much more than name our ignorance."

I drew myself in, drew myself together.

" That's all very fine," I said coldly, " but will you answer definite questions? "

" Yes, if I can," he answered, and stopped his pacing.

" Is this hallucination business a usual preliminary of insanity? "

Dr. Redman held up one finger of his left hand, pressing it, bending it, forcing it back.

" Firstly — firstly — how do you know it is hallucination? Has no existence of its own, that's to say, outside your fancy? Secondly "— up went the next finger, with which he dealt in the same fierce emphatic way —" secondly, what is insanity? Now listen to me. You have as yet no organic defect of the brain. None. Of that I am as certain as it is possible to be of anything. But your whole system is in a state of acute sensitiveness, and fear and worry may induce actual mental derangement. To use simple language, the chief cause — not cause, concomitant — of insanity is egoism, selfishness raised to the nth power. I could give you all sorts of scientific reasons for this, but they would only obscure my meaning. The danger is that you may feel set apart; that the unknown powers — God, nature, the world, I don't know what names you use — have a down upon you. Such an idea induces megalomania, or melancholy mania, according to your temperament. The remedy is to try and see beyond your own personal case. To be able to take an interest in it as a part of human experience; then you get into line with humanity. Service means not only happiness, but health, but sanity. Here we are on the borders where the spiritual and physical meet in their manifestations. I can and will give you medicine to quiet your brain and strengthen your nerves; I can help; but the true cure lies within yourself. Do you in the least tumble to what I mean?"

I resented his manner of speaking to me.

"No, I don't," I answered, quite unresponsive to his earnestness. "May I continue my questions?"

"Oh, if you like," he said, shrugging his shoulders.

"Do you imagine this . . . this visitant, this thing, has life and power of its own, and can derange my mind, as I could stop the works of my watch with a hairpin?"

"It hasn't yet, at any rate. If that was its game, I don't see why it shouldn't have done so before."

"Have you any idea what it is?"

"I can't say. It's something intimately connected with your own personality, I suspect; some part of it perhaps. No one knows what personality is. We all feel, more or less vaguely and indistinctly, different people at different times. Why shouldn't it be that some part of your personality has got loosened, as parts of your body were loosened?"

"Oh, don't talk like that," I cried, coldness and formality dropping from me. "It's not that I'm conceited or self-satisfied, but when you talk like that, I hear your words, but your words mean nothing to me — nothing, nothing, nothing. It's as though you opened a door and pushed me out into the darkness and mystery where any one might go mad."

"I know, I know," he exclaimed, and he was trembling with eagerness. "That's just my point.

If only you could realise the unutterable mystery of
all things in life this particular manifestation of mystery would not be so shocking.   Don't you see you've
been bumped against the main problem of life?   Our
ignorance and — how shall I put it? — our attitude
towards the Unknown.   You are outside, through
that door, in the darkness and mystery.   It's not me
or anything I've said that's pushed you out.   But
being out, you can't get back.   It's bad for comfort
and convenience.   On the other side of that door is
the danger certainly of madness, but also it is there
that the beginning of life is, of life in great company.   Away for ever from the herd who love their
ignorance and are satisfied with themselves.   You've
got to live up to the pitch of your experience."

"It's no good," I said plaintively.   "I'm very
sorry I was rude to you.   It was only nerves, I expect.   But I can't follow you.   I can't catch any
clue to your meaning.   How does all this help me
to face the possibility of another happening like last
night; another seizure, or visitation, or whatever it
is?   How does it help me not to dread the shadow
of insanity that darkens my future?   All I want is
to be let alone; to be an ordinary decent human being."

Dr. Redman came over to me.

"It's rotten bad luck, I know," he said, with
extreme gentleness in his voice.   "Let me help you,
young James, let me help you.   Think of me as
your friend, which I am far more than you realise.
Try and forge your own weapons against your two
worst enemies, Fear and Worry.   Man's third

and greatest enemy — indifference — is not yours. That's something. But they're shadowy, sly, horrible enemies. Another way of putting it is, you've got to find your own faith, your own worship, your own religion, your own guiding star. Your self, really. Good luck to you, my dear fellow, in your quest. It is the quest of all men who are men."

Dr. Redman went comfortably off in his motor, soon afterwards. Things were easy enough for him, simple and straightforward. But I was left with the help of some medicine and much counsel to face as best I could the mysterious horror within me; to go on with the queer mixture of the humdrum and the uncanny, the unfortunate ingredients of my life.

"A mental case. That's what I am," I thought bitterly. "Me, of all people, a mental case! Me, a feeble neurotic!"

It would have been so much nicer and more interesting if it had happened to somebody else.

X

> "Alone, alone, all, all alone,
> Alone on a wide wide sea."

I SAY that those who can read the "Ancient Mariner" merely as a romantic fantasy are very fortunate. As for myself, it describes with dreadful reality the adventures of my soul at this period; and my uncontrollable impulse to write this account tallies with the old mariner's determination to tell his tale, to stop even a wedding-guest to tell him. My tale must be told, once and for all told; without its telling my purgation will not be complete.

> "Alone, alone, all, all alone,
> Alone on a wide wide sea."

The couplet beat and beat through my mind.

Don't think that I did not see the ludicrous lack of proportion in my distress. When millions were suffering horrors compared with which my troubles were paltry — women raped, women waiting for their sons, their brothers, their lovers, in a long agony of suspense, children starving, families wandering homeless; when slaughter, destruction and desolation were everywhere — I knew all this well. I had seen things which it would not be nice to describe, in the legitimate business of war — not what are called atrocities (the distinction is between hor-

191

rors done carefully in cold blood, backed by the
blessing of each country's branch of Christianity,
and horrors done in hot blood by men inflamed by
drink and blood and lust and fear.   I knew all this
well, and I saw the absurdity of bothering in the least
about my wretched little self; I saw the absurdity, I
tell you, but I could not laugh myself out of it.   The
sight of it only added venom to my bitterness.   It
seems funny, no doubt, that any man could suffer
from such a lack of proportion; it was funny, like
being tied up and tickled on the soles of the feet —
fun, hellish fun, that begins with laughter and ends
with madness and death.

My state was not acute.   There was a queer
trembling quiet over me for the most part, ominous
in its stillness, which was torn from time to time in
quite unforeseen ways.

For instance two incidents — not in themselves
terrible or of any personal significance, as incidents
in Flanders have been (not that I saw anything at
all extraordinary in my experience of war; only men
filthy, men verminous, men wounded and killed and
blown to pieces on the field of glory) — two incidents
played havoc with me, and there was nothing in them
to affect me as they did, if my nerves had been in
decent condition.   Both happened on the same
morning.

I was reading the paper, properly and without un-
due sensibility; and a seemly wave of patriotic pleasure passed over me when I read the official announcement, told with quiet pride, that " our heavier guns
found the range, and the enemy battalion was, as we

learned afterwards from a prisoner, practically wiped out "; and I noticed a pleasing touch of realism in the quoted letter of a soldier, about a cat who visited his trench and was made a pet of, but preferred to sleep on the body of a dead German officer in front of the trench. But then I read a paragraph, with one small heading, at the bottom of the page, stating that a girl had killed her baby and had been sentenced to death; that she had been recommended to mercy by the jury, on account of her youth and the trying times which might have affected her reason.

The reading of that small paragraph seized and shook me. It burst upon my mind like a shell. All the symptoms of a nervous attack came upon me, a feeling of sickness and extreme exhaustion, followed by sharp pains at the back of my head. In my frail and shaken state it really seemed as though the fabric of our august state was a tissue of frantic absurdity, and I began to laugh hysterically. Twelve good men and true, worthy citizens to be sure (and how many others with the counsel and the judge and the clerk of the court, the constables and other officials?), all engaged with proper solemnity in condemning a girl of nineteen to death for having taken the life of a ten days' old child, her own, which she did not want, and for which she would have lived in disgrace, when all the brains and energy of the whole country's manhood was employed in the work of destroying human life; when indeed any man between the ages of eighteen and forty not actively engaged in destroying human life was a shirker and a slacker, an undesirable. As soon as the hysterical laughter passed and my nerves ceased trembling, common sense reasserted itself. I, of course, saw that war was war, and peace was peace, and that the laws of peace must be upheld all the more stringently during the unfortunate period of war, and that there was nothing sinister or ironical in the small paragraph which had so fiercely smitten me.

After my recovery, the effect of the shock persisted, as one feels weak after a fainting fit, and my weakness was the cause of the worse collapse that followed.

By the second post I had a letter from a friend, a nice chap who was going to be quartered in the neighbourhood and wanted to look me up. Towards the end of the letter, with a " by the way " introduction, he told me that he had met the father of two English girls who were caught by Prussians in a Belgian town. " The worst happened, or nearly the worst, and the little strangers are expected daily. Strangers they will indeed be, if you come to think of it."

Under ordinary circumstances, I should have dismissed the matter with " a very sad " or " very horrible," or some mental sigh on the horrors of war, and made arrangements to see my friend, for he was such a nice chap. But in my present condition the news laid me out. " Is it possible," I thought, " that these results of hatred and violence are to be allowed to survive? Is such life sacred, too? Will girls and women who have suffered outrage be obliged to perpetuate their misery and hatred on the world? What sort of life would it be that sprang from such a beginning and was nourished during its young days in such an atmosphere? Was all human existence a farce, a grinning, incredible farce?"

Why it should have stunned me as it did I do not know. I was not inclined to be sentimental as a rule. I knew, as we all know, that the proportion of children born of their parents' love, desired and cared for, is under any circumstances small in proportion to the number of children who are born haphazard, and that nature was as lavish and careless as mankind. I knew all this, and yet the few facts of my friend's letter stunned me, and I could find no comfort.

"Life is futile and disgusting," I cried, "bestial and evil. Filth we are, filth. War is the great cleanser. A few millions less of us will be crawling over the earth's surface, dirtying the face of the earth with our nastiness."

There was no pleasure in the bitterness of my thoughts, only horror, horror that turned to pain I could not bear, and for which I had no remedy.

"It's not my fault," I whined. "I don't know why all this should have happened just in my lifetime. All I want is to be a decent, respectable man."

Next day Amy was summoned by a telegram from Dr. Redman. Her pleasure annoyed me; her fondness horrified me. How could she expect me to answer her caresses with anything but disgust? How dared she fondle me? Oh, men and women were nasty little animals! Gladly I watched her go, and immediately after her departure I began to miss her, to want her back, and my missing her, my wanting her, filled me with disgust at myself.

Of all men's indecencies love seemed to be the
vilest.   What man or woman of the least intelligence
could honestly want a child!   Yet men bred, men
bred, lured on by this sham, tricked out with all the
false finery of love, until at last, sickened with the
mess and the sentiment, their honesty broke loose
in destruction, and all their energy was given to the
work of destroying each other, of killing, killing,
killing.   That instinct was fundamental, underneath
patriotism.   An excuse was needed.   It was in the
good hands of parsons and professors to fabricate a
fine excuse; and the others went stiffly at it, to vent
their rage at the trumpery business of life in killing
and being killed.   What else could set the nations
of Europe at each other's throats?   Not for nothing was all man's ingenuity in invention used for this
end of destruction.   What became old-fashioned so
quickly as a battleship?   Destruction inspired discovery.   Flight through the air, speed of movement
over the earth, high explosives, torpedoes!   What
could match the wonder of man's power of invention
when he was impelled by his one deepest, truest instinct — the wish to destroy, the wish, somehow, to
gain release from the base bondage of this life?
What were poets and artists and musicians?   Poor
folk, duped by their senses and their hope of gain
into trying to perpetuate the lure of life, and life's
chief lure was this indecency, this love.   What would
music and poetry, what would any of the arts be
without love?   God is love, they dared to proclaim.
But men were not deceived; men knew better.   They
let the songsters chirrup and sing; the display was

pretty, and did not keep them for an instant from what they knew to be a proper man's work. Hatred of the enemy might be deep; but hatred of life itself was deeper.

The mockery of it was that I saw it all too late, when I had been thrown up by the war, useless for everything but existence. If only I had seen the meaning of the war, when I was training, when I was fighting, I should have put more heart into the business. I might conceivably have suffered less from that insuperable boredom; but then I was deluded by the glamour of life, and I wanted to enjoy its prettinesses. I wanted even — how the words made me grin! — to be a decent respectable man. And yet there was something in man that kept him from suicide; something, even, that induced him to make the best of his condition; to cover the stark facts of life as decorously as possible, his own brutality, for instance, and all the pitiable indignities to which he was subjected from hideous birth to painful, uncertain death, to hide them under a robe of decorum, as he hid his own nakedness, that fools and children might not be alarmed.

This view of life which I describe in a few sentences descended upon me slowly, in intervals of a coma of insensibility.

I spent my time in the usual sort of way; only a little more vacantly than usual. Mother said: " I am afraid you must be rather depressed, dear." And I smiled and answered: " Yes, I am a little." I believe that mother was so glad that I had come back at all, that, so far as she was concerned, the war was really over. I wondered why she was so fond of me, and whether, if I hadn't come back, she would have missed me much. I doubted it. My heroic memory would have been a far stabler resource than my unromantic presence.

I spent most of my mornings in trying to decipher Grandfather Albert's note-books. It filled in the time, and his angers and enthusiasms, when I made them out or took them in, gave me a queer satisfaction. The pathos of his end, too, ceased to frighten me as it had done; madness, like death, seemed a release from this abominable life, might possibly be amusing. I felt that he realised the abomination, and though I could not share his angers or enthusiasms (my disgust was too radical for either), yet I felt there was a community between us.

I read him idly, and to pass the time I transcribed passages which were legible. One passage indeed indirectly influenced me. It ran:

" *The Church.— This curious institution exists to support the customs of the majority. It exists to flatter and sanctify convention and convenience. It has become the hose-pipe with which authority sprays its stupid actions with holy water. Think of Christ's attitude to the Sabbath; of Christ's attitude to custom; of Christ's attitude to the Scribes and Pharisees; and contrast it with the Church's attitude to Marriage. The Church is (O immortal irony!) the stronghold of the Scribes and Pharisees. Let us sing Hymn No. 565, ' The Church's one foundation is Jesus Christ her Lord.' "*

The aimless vacancy of my state of mind is seen

in the fact that though the words struck me as being
a monstrous distortion of the truth, my gloom was
only pierced by a faint smile; and my first act was to
turn up the hymn to see if its right number had been
given.   It had not.   And I was as annoyed, no more .
and no less, with this numerical inaccuracy as I was
with his extragance of statement.

The Church was, of course, perfectly justified in
joining the conspiracy of acceptance, and it existed,
as every one knows, to point towards a future life in
another and better sphere of existence, the prospect
of which was a consolation to many.

And why not for me?   Why should I not find
consolation in religion?   In spite of Dr. Redman's
exhortation, the tone of which, coming from a friend
of the family and a doctor, I resented, there might be
consolation here for me also.   Perhaps there was
more in my past fear of conversion than I had realised.   Yet there seemed something ludicrous, something almost impious, in the idea of going to our
vicar (the cherubic curate was out of the question)
and asking him for guidance in such a matter.   Was
it done?   Wouldn't it be an aspersion upon his min-
istry?   Under ordinary circumstances it would certainly have been unsuitable; there were the Bible and
the Prayer Book and works like " Holy Living and
Holy Dying," and the services on Sunday, and to
have wanted more would have been a liberty.   After
all, he was a man like other men, and his time was
limited.   Still, if your body was sick you went to a
doctor, and if your soul was sick, you ought surely
to go to a priest.   Yet the vicar and the Church of

England . . . somehow I could not rid my mind of a feeling of incongruity in a man's wish to make such use of either institution. But what possible reason could there be for a man of average intelligence finding incongruous or absurd his wish for an hour or two's quiet talk with his vicar?

Moreover Mr. Beach was a thoroughly nice man; with whom we were on friendly terms. He had bushy eyebrows, and wasn't fat, and didn't talk too much; and though this was of secondary importance, no doubt, in his calling, it was all in his favour, so far as I was concerned, that he came of a good family and was a gentleman. An apostle, no doubt, could afford to be a fisherman; a clergyman was all the better for a little breeding.

I was in such a desperate condition that I seriously thought of asking him for an appointment, as a man might his dentist. But I somehow felt that was too abrupt a way of getting into touch with him; so I suggested that mother should ask him to dinner. She did; and he came, with the unmarried sister who lived with him.

After dinner I approached the subject by asking him, when we were alone, if he saw the likelihood of a religious awakening in England owing to the war.

"An awakening?" he countered. "Of the Church do you mean, or of the people?"

"Oh, of the people," I said hastily, noticing that my question might be taken in two ways.

"I think perhaps there will," he answered.

An atmosphere of shyness on my part and reserve on his thickened coldly about us. I fingered my spoon and said as thoughtfully as I could: " Yes, yes."

With an effort at spontaneity, he remarked: " We're there, you know, when we're needed."

Questions that I longed to ask came thronging: Is life sacred? Is it right to kill? Do you believe in a future life? What does it all mean? and so on; and I knew that to ask any one of them would be an act of discourtesy and worse. So, merely to cover the silence, I pondered, " Yes, always there."

It was not the thing, of course, to talk religion over a coffee-cup and a cigarette at the tail-end of dinner; and I felt guilty of a plot against him.   Mr. Beach came to the rescue of my indiscretion by saying how disappointed one of his nephews was that his regiment had been ordered to India; and I thought what a large family they must be.

Uneasiness, however, lasted on between us, and very soon I took him off into the drawing-room.

There, to my surprise, he opened out and talked very sensibly about the immense good the war was doing to a large number of idle rich people who used to hunt and play bridge and amuse or bore themselves in the pursuit of pleasure, and who were now thinking of others, moved by a great ideal, and doing hard work, hard manual work, even.   These people, he said, had been brought face to face, for the first time, with the realities of life and death and suffering, and he did not think they would ever return to their old manner of life.

" One thing the war has shown us is how much better people are than some of us thought; far more unselfish, far kinder, and even anxious to do quite menial work for their country. Look, too, at the glorious rally of the lower classes to the colours. Who before the war would have believed that bank-clerks and shop-walkers had in them the true heroic stuff? These are great days to be living in, when the whole nation is united to crush tyranny and to end war."

He spoke quietly and reasonably, without any un-pleasant excitement, and his words kept me from sinking into my slough. Yet they roused in me the wish to put certain other points before him, in no argumentative spirit, but because I was sure that his patriotism and faith would be proof against unset-tling facts that would be cropping up while he talked in my own unbalanced mind. Of course the Allies were fighting against the spirit of militarism and, tyranny, and the Boer War, the Tripoli business, the Russo-Japanese affair, were unfortunate incidents that in no way lessened the justice of their cause; but I wished somehow that he would have mentioned them in passing. I didn't like, however, to remind him of them; to do so at the moment might have appeared rude and unpatriotic. Everything, I quite saw, that did not help the great cause must be forgot-ten. It was the time for action and eloquence, not thought. Eloquence halted when explanations be-came necessary, and halting eloquence meant lack of resolution, when all the nation's resolution was needed at its best and sternest to win through the noble struggle before her. What could be nobler than to sacrifice ideals in such a cause, to take up arms against militarism, to offer up freedom of speech, of trade, of the press, to destroy tyranny?

He looked at me in a way I liked very much, and said nicely and shyly: "You asked me after dinner if I thought that there would be a spiritual awakening. I wasn't quite honest with you, I'm afraid. Your question struck home. I was settling down like many men of my age into rather fixed habits, and the war has brought an awakening into my own life, made me in fact quite ten years younger. I am certain that my experience has been shared by many other middle-aged men besides myself. Why, I've heard of a man just my age, the working editor of a big daily newspaper, with a wife and eight children, who dyed his hair, shaved his beard, and went off to join the Sportsmen's Battalion."

I liked his manner, and I liked what he said, and I was disgusted with myself for thinking: "How that fellow must have been bored by his wife and his work!" It was an unjustifiable thought to have when a man was speaking whose words were a hand to support me from sinking into the swamp. Punishment followed swiftly; into the swamp my weight took me.

The vision came to me of whole nations bitten with madness, in raging war fever, rushing, like the Gadarene swine in the Gospel, down the hill to destruction, while all the middle-aged men, roused from their rather fixed habits, goaded them on, blessed them, extolled them, wept over them, and every woman who had lost a man — son, lover, husband or father — cursed in her heart every whole man

and added to the impetus of the madness-onrush.
" Shall the gift of all that we have in life be for
nothing? " they cried, stirring the pandemonium, and
the politicians shouted, " To the last man!   To the
last penny! "   And then —— Oh, I was in the
swamp! and from its depths I cried in a dead
voice:

" The last instinct in human nature is the desire
to destroy."

" I do not agree at all! " Mr. Beach quietly said,
but I went on speaking in a dead voice:

" Our only reaction against the bad farce of life
that is forced upon us."

Mother hastened to explain: " His nerves, you
know, have had a terribly severe shock."

" We call it nerves! " I said bitterly.

" What I say is true, dear."

" I'm in a bad way, anyhow."

Without any unction in his voice, but honestly
and kindly, Mr. Beach said: " I am so very sorry."

I managed to smile and say a little less boorishly:

" You must forgive me.   I'm apt to get despond-
ent."

" But very naturally! "

On this occasion there was not sufficient time for
any recovery from my damper, and soon afterwards
the Beaches rose to go.   I apologised to Beach in
the hall for being in such bad form, and no doubt
the immediate prospect of departure gave him a new
little access of friendliness, for after begging me not
to mention it, he, with many blushes, said:

" Of course, my dear Wood, you have the best

medical advice, and it's perhaps a liberty on my
part, but I happen to know of a most wonderful
nerve tonic, made up in tabloid form, to be dis-
solved with your food. Mercury is in it, and iron.
I've recommended it to several friends, and its effect has been really quite wonderful. Not good for
our nerves these anxious times. You must, please,
allow me to send you a small box."

I thanked him warmly, and ventured:

" I thought of coming round to have a chat with
you. I might fetch them."

" Do," he said. " That would be capital. Let's
see," he added hastily, " are you a chess player? "

" I do play a little. But, as a matter of fact, I
was meaning . . ." I dried up with a stupid little
laugh.

" We must fix it up. Does lunch suit you best?
Or tea or dinner? "

I stammered on:

" I was meaning — more informally. That's to
say . . ."

" I understand. Most friendly suggestion, my
dear Wood." He reassured me with a nice frank
smile.

I was vexed at the muddle. But it was too late to
clear it up. His sister appeared. Anyhow, there's
no need to be definite about it, I said to myself. Yet
I felt that if I paid him a professional visit, he ought
to be prepared for it a little beforehand. Or would
preparation increase the awkwardness of the interview, as well as double the awkwardness of its approach and of its beginning? My perplexity, per-

haps, showed the smallness of my need for his professional help.

By this time their cab was to be heard in the drive. The sound of the wheels made me take a plunge:

" I suppose a great many people now come and have private talks with you."

It must have been the wrong moment for my hint; at any rate it was not taken, if it were noticed; but instantly the veil of frigidity fell:

" Not more than usual, I think," and he began to shake hands in his courtly fashion with my sister, and to thank my mother for an exceptionally pleasant evening.

He gave me on leaving what I took to be a meaning look, that he understood and would write to me; which I thought was tactful of him and sensitive. I fully expected a letter; but no letter came.   And his sermon on Sunday — once a month he preached at the little adjacent church — was devoted to the needs of the Church Missionary Society.   He spoke as always without rhetoric or gush; simply, quietly and reasonably he made his appeal.   He knew, of course, how many calls there were at the present time on our purses, but we must not forget how necessary it was for the good of mankind that Christ's gospel of love should be spread among the heathen. And he introduced very neatly a letter which he had received from a friend, an ardent missionary, describing how he was drilling his native converts, and how the natives were pleased as children with the old-fashioned rifles which had been discarded from a neighbour's fortress, and which his energy had obtained for their use. Many of them had never handled a rifle before.

I was disappointed, even annoyed at his choice of subject, but I put a shilling in the plate, largely to still the mocking voice of my misery, which would insist the drilling converts was not the best way to spread Christ's gospel of love; and that when Europe was in such a mess of blood and hatred, as it was, we had better keep our precious religion to ourselves. It was a warm spring afternoon. After the service I sat down in the wood, among the pine-trees, in the sunshine which came dazzling through gaps and branches.

It had been a favourite place of mine. I used to call it, laughing, my temple among the pines, for thick aisles of pine-trees lead up the slope of a hill in regular lines, to converge in this more open space where only big pines grew, large-trunked and stately. The wind whispered through the tracery of their twigs; the screech of a jay or the chatter of a pigeon intensified the hush of silence. But the still weighed upon me. Loneliness crushed my heart. I felt a man and an outcast from this beauty; and worse than an outcast, that my presence was a desecration.

Black thoughts stirred within me — that I had enlisted only because it was " the right thing " to do, and that " the right thing " was nothing nobler than what everybody was doing. To think was an individual process, and made a man in little matters peculiar, and in graver matters wicked or unpatriotic. My thoughts ran on:

" ' So don't let's think. Let's do as others do.'

That is the common cry. Let us believe. But in whom, or what? In steps the Church and says, ' In me ': in step the politicians and shout, ' In us '; and each are backed by positions in their gift, with money attached to them and influence, to help to make belief in them easy. For human nature being what it is, it is easier for a man to believe in that to which he owes his income and his position. So in place of faith comes credulity, and in place of men sheep."

Why should such detestable thoughts afflict me? Was there in them a sign that my familiar was at his sinister work? Was this the intention of his last message—to cut me off from all human intercourse?

I knew what I wished to become: a man like Keith; a man capable and intelligent, kindly and of sound common sense; who took things as they came; and yet I felt myself somehow drifting farther and farther away from that safe shore, sucked out to sea by some power as mysterious and elusive as a current, taken away to loneliness.

I dragged myself home in ever deepening distress, Thoughts made my body so tired that I almost fainted. In my room I decided that I must get into line with humanity; and the only way of doing so was through the Church. I would not waver and hint. I wrote forthwith to Mr. Beach, asking whether I might call upon him on Tuesday at twelve, as my mind was troubled, and I wanted his help.

He answered that it would be convenient — a cordial letter — and twelve o'clock found me at the Vicarage gate, far too sick at heart for shyness or embarrassment. In very truth I felt that within that gate lay my last hope of sanity.

I was shown into what seemed a nice room, but I took no stock of it, nor of Beach's manner of receiving me. I sat myself down in a chair and pitched my trouble at him.

"I am going pretty well mad with misery," I declared —"literally mad. First there was the shock of my wound. I was getting better from that; then I was plagued with dreams, horribly vivid, recurrent dreams, and now I'm plagued with thoughts that cut me off, that drive me into loneliness. You know my grandfather went off his head. All this life seems unutterably disgusting to me; and the war an outbreak of honesty . . . life that culminates in this! Oh, please give me more of your point of view, that enables you to talk as you do, to look as you do, to feel as you do. Can you visualise the effect of a shell on a party of men? Do you know what 'missing' generally means? Or the little hole of a bullet through a man's head? Or how he falls when he's hit in the stomach? I want your peace of mind. It's really the war that's on my brain. All the rest is foolishness and hallucination; merely the outcome of this appalling awfulness."

Words came in a rush from me. He remained silent after they stopped. He sat far forward on the edge of his chair, clasping his knee and swaying a little to and fro. There was something restful and confident about him that filled me with hope, and his voice was soothing and low-toned, as he said:

"I am glad you've come to me, Wood. If I could

be of any use to you, I should be an awfully proud man. Don't you think, perhaps you are inclined to dwell too much on details, and not enough on the great cause."

"That's just it. I am. Things I've seen, things I've touched, things I've smelled; and the whole putrefying boredom of it." I spoke doggedly. "I want the broad view. That's why I've come to you."

Beach did not answer at once. Then he, still slightly swaying, said: "At first I was staggered by the horror of it, as we all were. By myself I should never have come through. I looked for guidance to those who are my superiors in spiritual insight and intelligence. I found it. A word here, a word there, that strikes a spark. How else does help come? and prayer, prayer — that is, the attitude of being able to receive guidance — humility."

He seemed to get nervous; but gave no foolish sign of it, no giggle or blink, and I liked the way he drew himself up to say: "I'll say a collect, if you don't mind. Beautiful words, so rest-giving to the mind and spirit."

He stood up and bowed his head; on my making an effort to rise, he said quite naturally:

"No; close your eyes. That's all that's necessary." And he went on:

"*Lord of all power and might, who art the author and giver of all good things, graft in our hearts the love of Thy Name; increase in us true religion, nourish us with all goodness, and of Thy great mercy keep us in the same; through Jesus Christ our Lord. Amen.*"

There was a short silence.

"That is rest-giving," I said, and kept my eyes closed. "Thank you."

There was a longer silence; then Beach took a deep breath and continued:

"Almighty and everlasting God, who art always more ready to hear than we to pray, and art wont to give more than either we desire or deserve; pour down upon us the abundance of Thy mercy, forgiving us those things whereof our conscience is afraid, and giving us those good things which we are not worthy to ask, but through the merits and mediation of Jesus Christ, Thy Son, our Lord. Amen.

The simple reverence with which he spoke refreshed me like a cool hand on a hot forehead. I had not sufficiently realised before the beauty of the collects; I suppose they were too familiar. I should have liked him to have gone on saying collects in that low clear voice of his. More than by the good words or by the good thoughts I was impressed by something which came from Beach to me, while he said them; a vague feeling that I was somehow better. I felt that if I were in my own room I should be able to have a delicious sleep. I had the same "comfy" feeling as when, a very little boy after a bout of naughtiness, while mother bathed me and gave me my supper, I became good and sleepy, and listened, forgiven and curled up in her arms, to the story she would tell me. Perhaps the Church was really the mother in need of whom the grown man went. Did a man ever outgrow his wish to forget, his wish to be comforted and forgiven?

Beach opened a drawer in his table and took out an envelope in which were cuttings from papers.

" This is from an article in *The Times;* so finely written, by Mr. Ernest Barker of New College.   It is called ' England and Easter Day.'   There is much about the memory of bells on Sunday ringing through the length and breadth of the land.   I will not read you the whole article, but just the words that came to me like sparks of hope: *'We all need to pray, and to pray earnestly, that our hearts may be established in quietness, and our eyes opened to see the thing that is right, and our hands strengthened to do what in us lies for the sake of Christ's Church militant here on earth. For to that Church this England of ours belongs; by her membership of that Church this England of ours is strong. The times of England are in His hands, and so far as England serves his plan so far is she justified of her labours. . . .*

" ' " *Oh, let England bless the Lord; praise Him and magnify Him forever." That is the last, the truest, the most authentic voice of our English bells. Let us therefore highly resolve that whatever we have done and whatever we may do shall be done in His name and unto His praise. If we think meainly of our cause, we shall make it a mean cause by our thinking. If we think that our cause is only the gaining of trade, or the destruction of a rival navy, or the security of our vast possessions, we shall make our cause and ourselves no higher than our thoughts.' "*

He stopped, and while with damped finger he

sorted cuttings and papers, he said: "That is very fine, I think, and very beautifully written. Ah! here we are. This is my second corner-stone. From the pen of a young writer who has come to the fore lately with his books on Russia — one S. Graham. Listen: '*Religion is never shaken down by war, but logicians are shaken in their logic, agnosticism is shaken, materialism is shaken, atheism is shaken, positivism is shaken. The intellectual dominance is shaken, and falls, the spiritual powers are allowed to take possession of men's being.*'"

Beach looked at me; his enthusiasm was growing, but there was no change in his voice or manner.

"He makes no bones about it, does he? But it's true, I think. No brittle structure can stand the shock of war. Now listen to this. This established my peace of mind. It is written by a man I know slightly, I am proud to say; a man of great attainments; head of a college at Oxford, editor of an important journal; you may have heard of his book, 'Mad Shepherds'; it had quite a success. The article is called: 'The Peacefulness of Being at War,' and has the pregnant sub-title, 'Chaos Succeeded by Calm.' I am proud to have shaken the man's hand. I will read you only the passages whose truth has sunk into my mind."

"I suppose you couldn't let me take these few papers away with me," I said. "I should like to copy them out."

Beach's manner was quiet and convincing. He had, without doubt, passed through a very real experience.   He was glad to share it with me.   I was glad to share it with him.

"To be sure I could.   Nothing would give me greater pleasure," he said, and began to read:

" ' *Our inner state in consequence was marked by profound unrest.*' — That was before the war," he interposed, looking up at me. — " ' *I doubt if there ever was a time when in general the minds of Englishmen were so agitated as they were in the few years preceding the war.   Rest for our souls was hardly to be found anywhere.   In religion, in philosophy, in politics, we were all at sixes and sevens, fighting one another in the name of our ideals, or striving to rouse the lethargic masses who cared not a button for any of our idealism; and often, it must be confessed, we were in a state of chronic irritation; and to make matters worse, a school of writers had arisen who made it their business to irritate, and, incidentally, to confuse, us still further.*

" ' *I believe that these months of war have brought to England a peace of mind such as she has not possessed for generations.   This statement, I should like to say, is not an experiment in paradox, but a sober statement of psychological fact.   It is to some extent a personal confession, but one which I should not dare to make were there not abundant evidence of its being a common state of mind.*

" ' *It is a literal fact that millions of men and women who some months ago were at " a loose end " and living aimless lives have now discovered that they have a mission.   The effect of this discovery is greatest, of course, upon the individuals who have made it; cases are known to the present writer which might be described as veritable conversions. But the whole temper of society is affected by the presence in its midst of so many people to whom a vocation has come at last, and the change is in the direction of mental steadiness and equilibrium. To that extent it may be claimed that we are happier than we were.*

" ' The individual is not more gloomy. He is brighter, more cheerful. He worries less about himself. . . . There is more repose in social intercourse than there was. Indeed, I venture to think that our manners are somewhat improved. The tone and substance of conversation are better. People are glad to see one another, and eager to hear each other's thoughts. . . . The spirit of fellowship with its attendant cheerfulness is in the air. It is comparatively easy to love one's neighbour when we realise that he and we are common servants and common sufferers in the same cause. A deep breath of that spirit has passed into the life of England, and no doubt the same thing has happened elsewhere.' "

He kept gently nodding his head in warm appreciation for some moments after he had finished reading. I waited for him to speak. He said:

" I cannot describe to you, my dear Wood, the effect of this upon me. It smoothed out the creases in my soul. It restored me. Did you feel the wonderful spirit breathing in these words? Do you see how the various passages I have read you fit together, and how they made a defence for me against trouble and doubt? I do hope and pray that they may do something of the same kind for you. Do you think they may?"

"I believe they will," I answered, for I had caught the quiet glow of his enthusiasm. There was something that appealed to me in his unassuming sincerity, in his honest humility.

"I can only help you in the way I have been myself helped," he said shyly, and I thoroughly liked him. It may seem a little thing, but it struck me as significant (and I am bound in consequence to record it) that, though I had placed him in the difficult position of spiritual guide, he never took advantage of it, and remained throughout the interview an absolute gentleman. It immensely impressed me.

"You have helped me," I answered; "and by lending me those extracts you will help me still more."

I made a movement of rising, but he got up, saying, "If you don't mind," and bowed his head. He spoke and acted so simply, so naturally, that I was wholly with him in spirit, and the short silence that ensued seemed right and not strange. I sat with closed eyes, and then in a low clear voice he repeated another collect, that took me back into times of remembered peace; to my school chapel, to my mother's knee:

"*God, who as at this time didst teach the hearts of Thy faithful people by the sending of them the light of Thy Holy Spirit; grant us by the same Spirit to have a right judgment in all things and evermore to rejoice in his holy comfort; through the merits*

of Christ Jesus, our Saviour, who liveth and reign-
eth with Thee in the unity of the same Spirit, one
God, world without end.   Amen."

On that I withdrew as quietly as possible in order
that I might retain the peace that glowed within me.
I simply said, " You have helped me," and I nearly
added " sir " from respect for him as much as from
association.   I was deeply moved, and confident that
I had been drawn back into line with humanity.   I
felt that I had been, in a very real way, cured — yes,
cured, though no one who has not suffered from it
can know what a malady loneliness may be.

I had found a fountain to which I could come for
refreshment.   The churches I saw dotted here and
there in the valley took on a new meaning to me,
almost a new shape; and I trusted my hope that my
cure would be permanent.   My spirit had been
soothed as with a caress.

I was waiting at the cross-roads for the brake that
passed about that time, when Beach ran up without a
hat, and, pressing a small parcel into my hand,
blamed himself for being so foolish as to let me go
without my nerve tonic.   I shook his hand cordially,
for he did not stay with me, and I was glad that he
did not.   I did not want him (with ordinary chit-
chat) to trouble the feeling with which he had filled
me.

In the brake I felt a pleasant brotherliness to the
men amongst whom I was seated.   Two men were
speaking of the war.

" When's it comin' to a finish? " said one.

" Humph! " grunted the other.   " When? "

" And what'll we do with Germany when it is? "

" There ain't goin' to be no Germany."

" Not much loss, eh? Nice fellers, them!
D'you know what I've heard of them? "

" No."

" Well, I'll tell yer, though it's 'ardly believable.
They talks of Mr. God and Mr. Jesus Christ. Fa-
miliar like. Same as they was Mr. Smitt or Mr.
Hans."

" Do they now? "

" They do so. 'Hair,' the word is too. It takes
all sorts to make a world, they say, but the less of
that sort, say I, the better."

Their patriotism might not be very intelligent,
but they were sound fellows, and my sense of brotherliness with them was not shaken. When a great
cause had so many followers as a nation involved,
there must naturally exist many various shades of
sentiment; besides, these worthy yokels only put into
plain English the politician's vaguer, less downright
cries of " No inconclusive peace! " or " Germany
must be beaten to her knees! " and so forth.

At home I spent some restful hours reading collects; and I resolved to learn collects that appealed
to me and to say one every morning and every evening. The last collect Beach read to me was the
collect I began to learn. " A right judgment in
all things and evermore to rejoice in holy comfort. . . ." The words spoke directly to my heart.
They explained the peace that radiated from the
vicar; he had found a right judgment and so rejoiced

in holy comfort, even though his eyes were not shut
to the savagery that devastated Europe.

Then I began to copy out into my note-book the
beautiful passages which had brought calm to Beach
and were bringing calm to me.   So sure was I that
calm was on its way to me that I read without the
slightest anger the last outburst of an entry from my
poor grandfather.   It ran: *"Emerson would have
been a great man if he had written nothing else than
the one sentence: 'God offers to every mind its
choice between truth and repose.   Take which you
please — you can never have both.'"*   I smiled
merely at his habitual exaggeration, and with my collect in my mind wondered what Emerson knew about
God.

I took a new nib, sucked it and began to write
without the least qualm.   But I had only reached
"and our hands strengthened to do what in us lies
for the sake of Christ's Church militant here on
earth," when a voice in me which I knew to be the
voice of my misery said, "Slaughter men, for instance."   I merely muttered, "Ass!" as I might to
an impertinent schoolboy, and continued to write until I came to "justified of her labours," when the
whisper prompted, "*I.e.,* the blowing as many Germans to pieces as possible."

I put the pen down.   "Oh, this is crude," I cried
—"silly childishness."   And I decided to pay no
attention to these interruptions.   That was in my
power, at any rate, though it might not be in my
power to control the voice, which pierced my rea-

soning with the blasphemous sneer, taken from the collect itself: " Holy comfort, forsooth, holy comfort ! "

I wrote stubbornly on to the end of Mr. Barker's beautifully written thoughts, and at the end the voice ran away with me: " Only think highly enough of your cause and the rest shall be added unto you, O fighters for Christ's Church of England — the rival fleet destroyed, your vast possessions secured and enlarged and huge trade gained. Then indeed shall England bless the Lord, praise Him and magnify Him for ever; and once more shall the church bells toll happily throughout the length and breadth of the land."

I listened to the voice exactly as I might have listened to an agitator in Hyde Park or to some low fellow whom I disliked and despised. My mind stiffened against its sneers; and I proceeded carefully to transcribe the next piece, which Beach had read to me. The voice was silent until with ever-stiffening mind I approached the last sentence, sure that I had silenced its impertiences.

As I laid down my pen, however, it spoke again, quite gently, almost sweetly, and without the least hint of malice: " Here is a man, a wise man, a man of influence and standing, to whom the war has brought calm after chaos. For him the war must be a great blessing, and the Hun the great benefactor. No thinker worries him any more. Thought is silent. Every form of thought is shaken by the horror of war; but religion is never shaken. The intellectual dominance totters and falls; truth bows to the censor's idea of expediency, but religion is never shaken. Religion smiles. Religion finds holy comfort. Established religion strikes new roots and is more deeply established in the earth. These months of war have brought to England such peace as she has not possessed for generations. Oh, let England bless the Lord and bless the Hun, the Lord's minister, for the individual is less gloomy; a spirit of fellowship with its attendant cheerfulness has been spread abroad. Religion is never shaken by war. Religion finds holy comfort. Religion can convert any sore to the stigma of martyrdom."

So this voice persisted, softly, sweetly persisted; and I knew it for the voice of the intellect, the voice of the devil, the wicked voice of my madness. At that moment I knew what my familiar had meant by his affection of sorrow. I stood up, hot-eyed in fury. I knew him what he was.

I cried out: " Mocker, tormentor! Get thee behind me! "

But my Byronic mood would not stand the sound of my own voice in an empty room. I collapsed, shuddering.

" It's not fair. It's not fair," I moaned. " Why can't you let me alone? Why need you infect my heart and mind with these rank thoughts and feelings? I should be ashamed if any man knew I harboured them."

I became, without resistance, limp and weak; and all comfort was beaten out of my heart and mind by thoughts, as the strength may be beaten out of a man's body by rods.

Men like Beach don't know. They dare not suffer. They take good care to find immediate consolation. The Church resembles Nero, fiddling over burning Rome.

" Let me go mad," I whimpered. " Let me go mad sooner than take such holy comfort."

And there, on the instant, before me, in a brighter light than I had ever seen him, stood my familiar with a look of triumph in his eyes.

I knew towards what he was luring me, and I lost consciousness in terror. My last thought was the conviction, the hope almost, that I should come to myself in an asylum; be done for ever with this intolerable fear of madness which must be worse than madness itself, and even as I tottered my surrender was complete.

But I was not released from the responsibility of supposed sanity. I awoke on the floor to the one dull fact that I must get into my bedroom somehow before I was sick.

XI

I SAW no meaning in any of these happenings. The
only thing for which I was grateful was that Amy
was busy, and that I was left alone. I wrote to her
once a week, and trusted that she would find some
wounded hero more to her taste than myself. She
was working hard, and her letters shortened. They
lacked, I was thankful to find, any such appeal for
intimacy as had disconcerted me in the letter she
wrote me while staying in the house. The fact is
I abandoned the effort to become the man I wanted
to be. I felt that it was no use, though I still felt
that my intention with Amy had been as right as my
intention in turning to the Church for support. But
the failure of the effort in both cases left me in a
worse plight than that in which I had been.

I forced myself to go to church so that Beach
might not suspect that his comfort had been unavail-
ing. At first I felt that I must go and denounce
him, so furious was I at the fall which had come to
me through trusting to his support; but luckily I had
the grace to do no such selfish thing, and I carefully
hid my misery from his view.

I shook his hand, when next I saw him, and with
a lingering pressure I said, " Thank you so much for
all you've done for me "; and I grinned inside, with-

out a thought of my grin's injustice, at the ease with which it was possible to make him believe what he wished to believe.

"And the tablets?" he inquired, returning my tone of voice and my hand's pressure.

"I take them regularly," I assured him.

The allurement of my grandfather's note-books increased for me, and I continued idly to read them, idly to transcribe passages here and there. There was a satanic pleasure in sandwiching the extracts which Beach had kindly lent me between the poor old fellow's savage outbursts. I came upon a quiet passage, however, which touched me more closely than many a tirade. It ran:

"*Man has even forgotten how to stand. He stands now on his heels, which throws the belly and neck forward. His base should not be the heel, but the ball of the foot, and she should use the diaphragm to support the top weight; then, stretched, he can move as one piece, using his weight to help him instead of dragging it after him. The Greeks knew this; a blind puppy could see, if he looked that they possessed a secret of movement which has been lost.*"

A proof of my apathy was that I read this passage with only mild interest, though it recalled the odd connection between my grandfather, Corinna and my familiar.

Day followed day of dead endurance. Summer came, and still men blew each other to pieces with explosives, and seemed likely to continue to do so as long as any explosives lasted in the world, while

the neutral nations busily fed the combatants, and
the clergy of each nation blessed the great fight for
freedom.   It all seemed natural enough and inevitable.   I didn't much mind.   I was quite certain that
I was slowly going mad, whatever that might mean,
but what did it matter, when the full energy of
every sane man among millions of men was given to
the making of explosives, poisonous gas, bullets,
bombs, rifles and the other contrivances of destruction?   I only wished that the process of going mad
was less tedious.

I laughed — I could not help it — when I read of
an army lecturer on hand-grenades, who was explaining, full of ardour, how they were to be lobbed most
effectively, and, to illustrate his point, lobbed one.
The illustration was too good, for the bomb burst,
killed three of his audience and wounded six others.
Unfortunate, but *trop de zèle* marked that act of the
farce.   I laughed, and heard the echo of madness in
my laugh.

The days dragged by.   The different outrages
that were committed, the sinking of the *Falaba*, the
sinking of the *Lusitania*, left me hideously cold.
They were only a device, like the taunts of Jack
Johnson, to lure England deeper and deeper into
the war, and to increase her anger and self-righteousness.   When you were killing thousands and
thousands a day, it didn't seem to matter much (as
much, I mean, as it ought to have mattered to a
right-thinking, right-feeling man) whom you killed
or how you killed them.   Was it worse to kill a
man who was fighting or a man who was urging

others to fight, a man who had lived three months or six years or twenty-six? Would a woman rather die than live without her sons or without her lover?

I felt myself steadily nearing madness, and my one wish was that it might not tarry.

I suffered most during the loveliness of the summer evenings when I sat in the garden. Looking at the flowers and the trees, feeling the wind and the warmth on my face, watching the slow pomp of the sunset, hearing the birds sing, I felt in the presence of holiness from which, being a man, I was driven out, as our first parents were driven, according to the old story, from the Garden of Eden. It wrenched my heart, this exclusion, as a man's heart might be wrenched if he were passed by a woman he loved with no look of recognition.

One night I could not sleep. When dawn came, I got out of bed and watched the night pass and the sweet approach of day. The first breeze of the morning, like the happy sigh of the awakening earth, brought the earth's full sweetness upon my every sense, and its sweetness stung me to frenzy, to an anguish of shame at being a man, who could use all his powers for mutilation and destruction, hatred, filth and desolation.

I hobbled up and down the room, cursing the cruel loveliness of nature, cursing the irony which made me realise it only when I had been for ever shut out from its sanction.

Anguish did not leave me, and as a man with raging toothache starts off on an impulse, appointment or no appointment, to the dentist, so did I after what seemed an eternity start off that morning defiantly to Beach. He must help me.

He was in his study. I was in too great a state of excitement for any preliminaries of courtesy or apology. Before I spoke he looked frightened, so the mask must have fallen from my face. I found it difficult to speak.

"It's here," I said, "and here — my trouble." And I laughed unpleasantly as I touched my heart and my head. "I'm going mad with misery." I said in a whisper, which sounded uncanny after my laugh, "Nobody must know. But I'm going mad with misery. It's the war, that's all it is, just the war. Nothing more. I see things: the same thing, a cold, mocking spirit creature. But that's nothing, that's nothing. Not the cause, I mean. It's just the war. All this slaughter, slaughter, slaughter. Do you see? And I'm ashamed to be a man. You must help me. You're a man, and you've got hold of something I must have. I felt it, and I must have it, or I shall go mad. And madness isn't always happy, smiling lunacy, the village idiot on the green, you know; it can be anguish so intolerable that a man loses control in sheer agony, hot wires in the brain, that can burn him slowly up."

I babbled on in wild excitement, explaining that I had not made the war, that I had always disapproved of war, that I believed our cause was just, that I had done my bit, and that I could find no reason anywhere for the torture of my mind.

Beach, after his surprise, stood his ground without

flinching. He came up and put a cool strong hand upon my forehead.

"It's a war to end war," he said in a soothing voice. "The nation has risen like one man to end war and the spirit of hatred which is devastating the world; has risen in support of the weaker nations, to put down the dominance of militarism."

"Is Christ the God of war or the Prince of Peace?" I asked.

"There is good and evil in the world," he said. "It is terrible that we should have to fight at all, but we're fighting for the right."

"But don't the Germans think so too? That they're fighting against the evil which made the Boer War, the Russo-Japanese War, the Tripoli business; the evil that has joined forces to crush their nation?"

"They may think so; but they are mistaken. Their pride must be humbled."

"But how can you humble by military means a military pride which has put up such a fight against the world? We hand over the conduct of the whole people to men who think war is the only means of keeping a nation from decadence. They've had no work to speak of for years: and now they are in supreme authority; they rarely get killed, and is it likely they'll go out of authority before they're forced? We're being sucked in, sucked in, deeper and deeper. These military potentates on each side want to go down to posterity with glorious records, and meanwhile men are slaughtering each other, blowing each other to pieces."

" I'm not in a position to discuss the conduct of
the war," he said; and feeling the coldness in his
voice, I stretched out my hand in supplication and
cried out:

" Don't leave me. It's just these thoughts that
are driving me mad. Don't you see? I know that
they are wicked and wrong. How is it that they
come to me? I don't want them. I want to be a
plain sensible Englishman, I do really; and I love
England. It's not like me to be excited like this and
shaking; bursting in upon you. It's no good saying
these thoughts of mine are wicked. I know they
are, as surely as I know that they tear my mind like
brambles. Oh, give me your faith. Show me the
light you see. Show me the star you follow. Silence this mocking spirit that torments me. Oh,
don't let me be ashamed to be a man; you are not
ashamed to be a man."

Even at that moment my admiration for Beach
was great, and it has increased since. It must have
been most distressing for him to have a man raging
in the way that I raged. His presence of mind
never forsook him; his sympathy hardly faltered.

" Wood, my dear fellow, I am so sorry," he said.
" Believe me, I don't think argument will lead us
anywhere — talk, I mean, about the rights and
wrongs of this awful business. We can only pray, if
you will let me."

But I could not let him. My eye fell on a poster
that lay on his table, on which he was billed to speak
at a recruiting meeting. Why the sight of it should
have flicked me like a whip lash on a raw wound I

did not know; but I struggled up to my feet and exclaimed:

"It's no good. That would be blasphemy. I don't believe in your God, and I don't want to believe in Him."

I was far beyond minding whether my words were civil or rude.

His wince, however, touched me, and I cried out:

"Oh, forgive me! Do forgive me! Something has happened to me. I don't know what it is. I'm driven here and driven there, as though by some avenging fury. I can't help myself, and no one can help me. I ought to have known. Any effort at comfort makes me worse."

"My dear Wood, there's nothing to forgive — nothing. I'm only so very sorry that I'm no use to you."

"Don't you let me upset you," I implored him. "I know that all I've said is folly and wickedness. But it comes, it comes, and I can't stop it from coming. I want to be myself again and I can't be myself."

And I knocked my fist against my head.

I went home in too deep despair to think for an instant of what a dolt I had made of myself, and when I reached home, my mother met me with news, that Corinna Combe was coming that night to stop with us for a few days.

If my gentle mother had slapped me on either cheek, she could not have startled me more profoundly. What this girl's connection with my cold evil one was I could not say; but that she was con-

nected with him I did not for an instant doubt. She
was in some sinister way a part of his machinations,
a medium, shall we say, to his power; and she was
coming to stay in the house, just when my last support had failed me.

At the news I was the wild beast in the net, cower-
ing and strengthless, watching the careful approach
of the hunter with his knife. Mother met me in
the hall, which is dark even in daytime. I stood in
the shadow. She neither saw my face nor noticed
my start.

I contrived to say, " Really! " with the right note
of surprise; and " Of course," to her question as to
my willingness that Corinna Combe should come.
War-time, she explained, and neighbourliness, and
her father was unexpectedly called away as a corre-
spondent, and her mother was in a nursing home,
and we couldn't let the girl be alone in the house —
could we? — and it appeared that no friend could
be found free to keep her company for four or five
days at the soonest, if then, and her sister was nursing, and she must be within reach of home and so
on. The explanations seemed endless, and I believed them all implicitly; yet I knew infallibly, as
one does know some things, that it had all been arranged and that Corinna was somehow an agent,
even though she might be a wholly unconscious agent.
I say that part of me saw in this coming of Corinna
Combe exactly what my mother said, a neighbourly,
natural action, while part of me knew as surely as
that a thrown stone will fall that her coming had another significance.

I nearly cried out: "Don't let her come! For God's sake don't let her come!" but I restrained myself in time, and the cry only sounded on through my consciousness, all the long time my gentle mother was speaking.

"When will she be coming?" I asked.

Mother answered, "This afternoon, in time for tea."

My apprehension grew acute, and was sharpened by an utter ignorance of what I apprehended. I had the sense of impending calamity. This coming of Corinna topped a series of events by which I had been lured to the brink of a precipice, and down that precipice I might at any moment be pitched. My mind groped for some clue, and as it groped the sense of doom grew ever stronger and ever blacker. There was a tightening of my brain, a tightening of my muscles. The skin across my forehead felt as though it would tear.

I heard Corinna come; I heard mother take her into the spare bedroom; I heard them chatting through the open window, and I heard them go downstairs. The gong rang for tea. I could not move. I was fully aware of the absurdity of my position; and the absurdity rubbed poison on my distress.

"I've got to go," I thought. "They'll soon be coming to fetch me." I went. The first time I went into action I was afraid; the fear I knew then was nothing to the fear I knew as I descended the stairs.

I opened the drawing-room door and went in.

There by the window Corinna stood, poised as was her wont, head erect.   I knew that she would be standing like that.   Custom came to my help, as I went forward to greet her.

She laughed gaily and said: " I always come trespassing in upon you, don't I? "

" Oh, I'm always charmed to see you," I answered.

Nothing happened.   The ordinariness of it all appalled me.   If only I could have found any grounds for my fear, half its weight would have been lifted.   But there were none, and fear oppressed me.

I left the drawing-room as soon as I could.   In my own room I lay flat on the sofa, in a stupor, until it was time to dress for dinner.

All through the evening fear gripped me with gathering intensity.

" Have you a headache, dear? " mother asked me.

" Oh yes," I said, " nothing to speak of."

And I dared not look at Corinna, who was looking at me.

" I should go to bed early if I were you," she went on in her gentle purring way.

" Yes, I think I will," I said, and almost screamed aloud: " Oh, can't any one of you see that I am going mad? "

I sat on.   Habit kept part of me talking satisfactorily.   I wanted to go to bed, but I was certain that I had not strength to leave my chair, let alone go upstairs and undress.   But habit set me moving when mother rose to go; and habit took me upstairs, where I stood, holding the banisters, and watched mother and Doris (they slept together) walk down the long passage at the end of which was their bedroom. I often did stand there, to wave them a last good-night as they closed their door.

Doris waved and came racing back along the passage to me. " You are quite all right, old darling, aren't you? " she said, and kissed me. She rapped on the door of the spare room, which was next to mine, shouted a cheery good-night, and raced back again.

The proximity of Corinna's room, then first realised, gave the last touch of ominousness. Something hidden and unknown within me must, during all that evening, have been resisting the encroaching fear for the simple reason that something within me broke at that moment, and fear came rushing in upon me. Fear, do I call it? Rather was it horror.

I stood there holding the big knob of the banisters. Below me the hall was in silent darkness; above me glared the hard eye of the electric light. Only familiar objects could carry such a chill of horror as began to freeze me, just as only a sensitive person can find his way well into your heart to sting it.

If I had only known for certain that I should be crossing that strip of passage for the last time, be turning for the last time the handle of my door and for the last time be entering my room; if I had only known for certain that death or madness awaited me behind that closed familiar door, and in what guise they were likely to come, I honestly believe that I should have gone straight in with my head up; for I have faced death, and am no coward. It was uncertainty that held me in terror's grip.

What would it feel like to die? What would it feel like to go mad? Why hadn't I been killed outright, instead of being left mutilated and shattered? I had shot a man and seen his face as he fell. Was his spirit clutching at my life and enjoying somewhere my anguish of terror? Should I know that I was dead and watch my body, stiff and still, be carried silently out, the men careful not to rub the white paint off the door? Should I know that I was mad and hear myself screaming and feel myself struggling and fighting and see the grief on my mother's face and still be obliged to scream and struggle and fight?

I knew the humiliation a man must feel who is bidden dig his own grave before he is shot, and obeys.

The silence spoke: " You must come in; we are waiting for you." And I obeyed.

As I crossed the strip of passage, the air was thick with horror ranked against me. A dead body changes the appearance of a room. My familiar room looked unfamiliar; it was my room of death. But even there habit kept me going, and I set about undressing, though what strength I had was draining out of me.

At last an end came to my strength; slowly I subsided like one of those little air-blown figures. First strength left my legs; then the arm which clutched the wardrobe, and I lay stretched on the floor.

But within me remained a thin thread of consciousness which told me that I had not fainted in the ordinary manner; that there was no power in my body, no feeling; that I lay on the floor and was not floating in the air as I seemed to be; and which wondered dimly what would happen next.

I wished I could turn off the staring light, and idiotically I remembered that I had not brushed my teeth or my hair, and thought that I should probably do neither again.   Some time, after all, every one must brush his teeth for the last time.

What would they do with my body?   Who would lift it on the bed?   A nasty job, that, for some one. Life was like a candle which some one blew out.   I was guttering.   And all the care and money spent in getting me a mechanical hand and a mechanical foot had been wasted.   That seemed a great pity. Would my hand and foot be buried or burned with me?   I ought to have made a will.   But who ever does think that he is going to die?   I had not learned much during my life — muddled along more or less as I was told.   Funny I should have been so afraid to die.   There was really nothing in it.   Nothing much in life either, if it came to that.   Yet what was it that one was always groping after?   Why did one care for the sky and the sun and the sea and the earth?   Winter, spring, summer; the coming of night, the coming of day; rain, sunshine, the wind; fruits and flowers; birds and the stars and the moon; the smell of a cloverfield and its colour; women and children and friends. . . .   There were good things in the world. . . .   Not a bad old place, the world, really, when you came to think of it and leave it. It almost seemed as though there might be some link of meaning running through all this life, in spite of the fact that millions on millions of men were taking such pains and enduring such hardships in their eagerness to blow each other to pieces. Why were they? Men were ingenious little animals. And whoever was God whom all these explosive-mongers were so careful to have on their side? God made the sun and the moon. If He approved of a war it became a holy war, and in a holy war men fought with fiercer hatred, so the rulers must keep in close touch with the priests and professors and other experts in the will of God, or there might follow some misunderstanding about the true nature of a war. Pity I was dying; it would be interesting to see how it would all end. . . .

And then my little thread of consciousness became a white hot wire of pain. How long that lasted I did not know, but my next sensation was of being lifted; and of my being unable to tell them that I was dead and that it was of no use putting me to bed, of no use smoothing my forehead.

I was so comfortable and warm and still, being dead, that it was unkind to wish me alive again.

But consciousness came back to me, and came as slowly as it had left me. I knew that my head was as sore as though it had been scalped and scraped, and that I must on no account move it. I knew, too, that my head was being soothed, and that the pain and the soothing were there together, and that the pain only made me more sensitive to the soothing;

as once before when, a little boy, I had badly burned my hand and they had put it in a soft bandage of cool oil. And then I knew that an arm supported my neck and my head was held against a breast; and a little afterwards I came to know, and to know without amazement, that it was Corinna's arm and Corinna's breast, and that she was stroking my forehead and crooning to me as though I were her hurt baby; saying that I must shut my eyes and go to sleep, and not be talking nonsense about going mad or being dead, or being frightened of her.

A new-born baby, pulling at its mother's breast, is not more in its right place than I felt in Corinna's arms; and unlike the new-born baby, I knew this well, and knew it without surprise. I was too weak and too tired to feel surprise, or anything but the warmth and peace without which I should not have been living.

Corinna was not just a girl, to my blurred sense: she was woman, woman and life and love.

So I put out all my strength and managed to move my lips and tongue in a whisper: " Shan't go to sleep."

And I thought: " I shall live, and I shall not forget; but I won't go to sleep yet."

And even while I struggled against the gentle oncoming of sleep I fell into the sweetest sleep that I have ever known.

.   .   .   .

My first thought on waking was that I must have recovered from a very long illness; but with the obscure memory of what had happened during the

night returned the queer sweetness into which I had
fallen asleep, and I lay in it quietly as one lies in
spring sunshine by the sea. I remembered my fear,
too. I had been taken into the heart of it, and
found there — what? Freedom from it? Was
that all that this enveloping sense of peacefulness
meant? But farther I did not question. I was too
content to enjoy, and too sleepy.

Mother looked anxious. I tried to reassure her.
" I'm much better, really," I said.   " As though an
ulcer had been forming and had burst."

I had no apprehension about seeing Corinna. I
merely looked forward to her coming without a
tremour of anxiety or of impatience, so deep was my
present enjoyment of what she had somehow been
the means of giving me. What this was I could not
say; it was new in my experience.

" Perhaps she'll know and tell me," I thought.
" And she'll tell me what happened."

Meanwhile I lay and waited, and wished I could
lie for ever in that state of peacefulness, which deepened when Corinna came. As she closed the door
behind her, she looked embarrassed, and there was
a touch of resolution in her walk across the room
to my bedside, as though she were telling herself
not to be silly. But she sat down and took my hand,
which was lying outside the sheet, and asked me how
I felt.

I wanted to say, " Delicious "; but I said, " Much
better, thank you," and after a little pause I said:
" Tell me what happened."

She said that she must not excite me: I assured her

that she wouldn't, and promised not to interrupt
her.

"Well, there's not much to tell," she began.
"You see I heard a great bang, and could not bear
the silence that followed it. I don't know why. I
felt obliged to open my door and listen; then to come
out into the passage and listen at your door; then
to tap at your door; then, getting no answer, to open
your door; and there you were lying on the floor,
staring with such fright at me and moving your
mouth, as a bunny might look at a stoat or something. I had an immense great impulse not to call
the others, but to lull your fear away myself. So I
put you to bed and held you in my arms and sent you
to sleep. I've seen some one else have a complete
nervous collapse. All the evening I'd watched
something wrong with you. I always obey an impulse. You were half wandering, half sensible. I
think that's all. You must have been going through
an awful time lately."

"Yes, I have. I thought I was going mad."

"Don't you think so any more?"

"No, I don't. Why don't I?"

"I don't know."

"I hoped you would. There's been a change in
me. As though I'd been falling, falling, falling
down a hill, had reached the bottom, and was beginning to climb up again."

"I've felt like that once."

"I feel I've found something, and don't quite
know what it is. I hoped you'd be able to tell me,
because it's somehow through you I've found it.

Everything in some queer way does not *seem* different; everything is different; as though something had died or something had been born. It's not my fault, this change, or whatever it is. I've been taken by the neck and chucked into it. Do you know — please don't mind my saying this — but I feel a sort of worship of you; the room feels the holier for having you in it. I woke up into that sense of holiness, and was almost afraid to breathe lest I might scatter it, but it lasted quietly on and deepened perceptibly when you came in. Queerest of all I can tell you of it quite unshyly, quite naturally, quite quietly, like thanking a rose for smelling sweetly. I mean it's accidental that I should have noticed it. It's there for every one who likes to notice it. So is the smell of a rose. O Lord! I wonder, can it be that it is everywhere? This . . . this . . . this . . ."

" Don't worry now. There's lots of time," she said. " I'm quite sure it is everywhere. I mean, don't worry about its name. Whatever it is you've found won't be more yours by naming it. And you're weak and your brain's weak and you mustn't perplex it. Once one has felt a thing so deeply as you have this, one never loses it. Of that I'm quite sure. One definite thing you've found is a friend. Now please try and go to sleep."

She leaned over me and with simple naturalness she kissed my forehead and both my eyes, saying softly as she kissed them, " Keep them shut." I did as she told me; but I held her arm and said:

" Corinna, I need you, you know."

"Yes, dear, I know you do," she answered.

"Just one more thing," I begged. "Why is it that I can speak to you without the least trace of the least fear of being misunderstood." I added reverently, "Almost as though I were talking to God." And she answered reverently, "Where else is God but in ourselves? To speak with, I mean. To be seen, of course, everywhere; in primroses for instance."

"Primroses?" I said. "What made you say primroses?"

"I particularly love them," she said. "That's all. No, keep them shut, dear, and sleep. I'm going now."

"It's true. You are much more than a girl to me. We'll find out, won't we?"

"Yes, we will."

"Oh, just one more thing," I said sleepily, for I was very tired. "I'm as much *in love* with you as an infant in arms is with its mother, and my need of you is as great. Can you understand *that*, too?"

"I think I can."

"Imagine an infant who's been able to talk some twenty-six years, and that's really what I am. Heavens! how I want to go for my first walk!" I snuggled down. Corinna stroked my forehead.

"Worship. That's it. Worship," I said drowsily. "How funny!" I heard the door close, and almost instantly fell asleep, feeling as though I should sleep for at least a week.

XII

I SMILED so often, and I dare say so idiotically, during those first days that I am quite sure mother had fears for my reason. Her own cheerfulness was forced, and once or twice, when she thought I was not looking at her, I surprised on her face a look of anxiety.

I spoke to Corinna about it without hesitation.

" Mother thinks the collapse has left me a little dotty," I said —" a little soft in the brain. Do you? "

She laughed, and said she didn't.

" I'm not so sure about it myself," I went on, " though I don't fret about it. I simply feel that I'd rather be what I am now, crazy or not, than what I was. I can't remain as I am though, can I? I mean, I must either become more what I am now or get back into what I was. Which do you think I shall do? "

" I don't know. It rather depends, doesn't it? "

" Depends on what? "

" On which you wish to do."

" Does it? That's just the point. Does it? My wishing's not had much to do with it so far. It's just been pitch and toss, and here I am. And what does getting more and more so mean? Does it mean getting dottier and dottier? What'll hap-

243

pen when I get up and leave off lying here and being petted and waited on?"

"There's a difference between ' wish ' and ' will,' Miss Rinnie, my nurse, used to say."

"I like the Miss Rinnie awfully."

"She was such an old dear. Any child can pull a chicken bone and wish for a pony; but willing means . . ."

"Means what?"

"Definitely making up your mind to a definite thing. And with me," she added, "now, it means prayer."

"I feel in the jolly old place where proverbs come from, and all the nice things we used to write out in our copybooks. Do go on talking like that. You're a mother and a nurse all rolled into one, and so young and fresh, and such a friend. Do you know, I feel almost on the brink of tears. It's so decent to feel a kid, and for you not to be any particular age or anything but just dearness and kindness and sweetness and trust; just some one to whom I don't open my heart but to whom my heart lies open. I've no memory for these things, but this is how I must have felt, when I was a little boy, to my mother."

"I always felt there was a friend for me hidden away within you; now we are friends," Corinna said.

"Yes, that's one way of putting it, but I've made friends before. With Amy, for instance. But Amy . . ." I stopped, and Corinna waited for me to go on, which I presently did:

"Why can't I talk to you about Amy in the same way? It's not that it's not done. To speak, I mean,

about one girl to another. It's not that." Again
I was silent. " I have treated her abominably."

A grief I had never known took possession of me,
but did not break through the mood of holiness that
was always present in Corinna.

" There's grief that doesn't drag you to gloom,"
I mused. " I was half joking about my being a kid
again; but joke or no joke, it's true. Am I a child
again? Is this the kingdom of heaven into which
I have been pitched? Is it you that have wrought
the change; or what is it? Has it been a slow
process of growth, quite against my judgment, or
has it been a sudden smack, like St. Paul's conversion? Do you imagine I shall feel the same quality in any other woman that I feel in you? There
is a thread of meaning somewhere. If only I could
put my thumb and finger on it, it would lead me
. . . where would it lead me? To you? And I
don't know if it's sense I'm talking or craziness. If
you are merely humouring a gentle wanderer, I must
say you do it awfully well. But I don't believe you
are, are you? "

" No, I'm not," she said; " the same sort of thing
has happened to me."

" You couldn't tell me about it, I suppose? "

" Yes, I could. Only what you've been saying is
true; one can't trace the steps of the happenings;
one finds oneself somehow there. I fell in love with
a man. I had a wonder of happiness; I believed
stupidly and was desperately wretched, and then
. . . one way of putting it is . . . I saw Love behind the man and behind my own longings. Any-

how, I had the same feeling as you have of beginning, of seeing the world for the first time."

"How long ago is that?"

"About eighteen months."

She paused, and then seemed to grow before my
eyes, as she slowly stretched herself to her full height
head erect, poised, as if all weight were taken out of
her, yet effortless, and swaying like a lily in a pond,
so that she seemed pouring herself up like a flame,
and might float away like a feather in the wind, so
that the lithe loveliness of her sang rapture and devotion in the same breath, like the work of a Greek
sculptor — and she said:

"Love will always be for me now a glad deliberate thing; a quickening of a state of being, not a
change of state. Only a more direct communion
with God."

I didn't understand exactly what she meant, but
her words and tone thrilled me with a kind of religious ecstasy; she went on:

"All shame died then, and all sense of sin except
lack of feeling and indifference. I shouldered the
full responsibility. I can't explain. I can't reason
it out. Only the deepest, realest thing in a man can
respond to love, is sensitive to love. All the rubbish
in you had somehow been battered out, and it was
your true self I held in my arms, your true self I was
able to lull back to strength. *In-Loveness* is the
usual beginning, and lovers love each other so that
each may free this deepest self in the other — the
ritual of delight, where duty and the passion for service and all good, active, energy-releasing things flame

through heart and body and mind, where the lovers are one with each other, and one with all the life of nature and the world, one with God. For God is love, and energy is eternal delight, and delight is loneliness, for there life lives at its highest pitch, and the God in man is free. And all the beautiful means of this communion lie within ourselves, ourselves; and are touched with the power and colour of joy and delight, for us to use. *In-Loveness* is the usual path; but the ways are infinite; anything in nature can do it, from a flower to the great sky. By a miracle, without *In-Loveness,* you have been able to see God through me. A note only, a note; a glimpse compared with the chorus when every fibre of your being sings through love the full praise of God."

She seemed to soar into the air as she spoke, and when she finished, to drop like a rose-leaf, as she stooped over me and laid her hand on my forehead and began to blame herself for exciting me, when she had been specially instructed to keep me very quiet.

"You don't excite me," I assured her. "But I can't pretend to understand; a thread of meaning glimmers here and there, but I can't yet grasp it as I want to. Oh, I wish I could lie here for ever and just see you and listen to you and be with you. I don't want to get up or grow up. I can understand now one reason why that nice old fellow sat on a pillar all his life, as much like a tree as he could manage. And it's worse for me than for Simon to climb down into the bustle; it means shaving, and wearing trousers and a collar, and all the queer stiffness and usualness, and I know you'll be merely Corinna Combe again, and life a passing from meal to meal and bed-time, over and over and over again, dressing and undressing, washing and getting dirty, on and on and on, till I brush my hair and teeth for the last time. All the freshness and wonder will go; no freshness and wonder can withstand such an encroaching heap of trivialities as a man's life seems to have become."

" I should wait till you do get up, and not decide offhand and beforehand what it will be like. Work and love keep a man bright."

" You will always stand by me and look after me? " I besought her.

" Yes, I'll always be your friend."

" I'm not depressed, but I do feel a sort of responsibility, as though I'd been shown something that must never be forgotten. It's like the algebra lesson at the prep. I followed beautifully when the math. master was explaining about factors or whatever it was; but it was very different when I was alone with home-work and the cold silent book. And in this case I couldn't say for certain what it is that I have been shown, what it is that I must remember and live."

" Aren't you putting it wrong? Isn't it that you're somehow conscious of a new standard of value which will be there to use in the everyday affairs of life; which will really as much use you as be used by you. You may get in its way by the wrong kind of forethought. And anyhow, now you mustn't worry and think and excite yourself."

"A long life won't be long enough to learn the
lesson I've been set.   Home-work with a vengeance.
One thing is settled, though: I must get up to-morrow.   I mustn't go on lying here, ineffably jolly as
it is."

"I shouldn't hurry," said Corinna.

"That's what I've been saying to myself for two
days now," I laughed.

"You must be careful."

"Being too careful is my danger, I'm afraid."

"Yes; but don't, don't, don't worry in advance.
Trust yourself and the thing you've found, or whatever it is.   Then it will control you, and you won't
muddle it from expressing itself in your life."   She
took my hand and held it and said, in the tone of
hers which sent an actual thrill down my spine: "I
believe in it absolutely, and it is the bond between
us."

And I began the attempt to keep my promise by
not worrying about what I should say to Amy, or
how this change in me would affect my relations with
her.

The average sensible man of my previous ideal
had been smashed like a tea-cup, and that was the
man who had wanted to marry Amy in order to preserve his common sense; but whatever it was that
was me had not the remotest wish to marry Amy
or any one else; had indeed still to learn to live alone
before contemplating sharing his life with somebody
else.   Explaining this to the matter-of-fact young
woman who was considering the question of accept-
ing me would not be without its difficulty.   Perhaps

the effort of explanation would make what had happened clearer to myself; if so, it would not be without its little benefit.

The news that Amy would be able to come down on Saturday finally decided me to get up on the next day, which was Friday. I could not let her surprise me, as it were, in the midst of my smiling daydream.

Rain poured down in torrents on Friday morning, driving rain which I kept stopping dressing to watch, shaken in waves over the tops of the swaying trees.

I was still weakish, as one is, say, after a bout of influenza, but I wasn't miserable, and looked forward to a quiet morning in my study with a relish that was new to me. Corinna said that she would come and talk with me at twelve, and though I was up and about (in the dreaded collar and dittoes), she brought with her the same mood of what I can only call holiness. But the word which I have often used pulls me up. If it suggests merely hush and solemnity, or anything essentially unlaughing or uneasy, it is the wrong word. There was hush, it is true, and solemnity; but it was also the incarnation of ease, and my whole being was a silent chuckle, as though all my power to enjoy were being gently, cumulatively quickened.

" It is ridiculous," I said to her, " but I simply feel happy, and upon my soul, I don't know why. Before, I mean, it was always connected with doing something or the prospect of doing something. Like wanting to kiss somebody, or kissing them, or looking forward to a good dinner and nice wine, or enjoying them. But in this there's a difference, though

I can't explain it. For one thing, this is complete in itself, and yet infinite. All the while, too, there's the funny sensation of talking a new language naturally. And there's this that I'm quite certain of, that if this happiness goes as inexplicably as it has come, no other happiness in all the world will ever satisfy me; just as, if it stays, every happiness in the world will deepen and gain meaning; and if it were a question of choosing between this and every other happiness in the world, I shouldn't hesitate to choose this. There would be no choice. This is the substance."

Corinna smiled, and when she smiled her lips hardly moved, but her eyes brightened, and little lines twinkled by the corners of her eyes, and nearly always a slight flush shadowed her pale face — an oval face with a round high forehead, and a wide mouth and a chin too big for beauty; a heavy face it might have been but for its gallant poise on the neck and its dearness — no, no, never heavy with such a sensitve nose as hers.

She could sit stiller than any one I had ever known; and at her stillest she glowed with energy. Behind everything she did or said there was tremendous intention and no self-consciousness.

"What makes me see you now?" I asked. " Before, you used to make me feel uncomfortable. I used to think you'd be all right if you weren't so intense."

"How horrid of you! I always liked something in you under your Oxford manner."

"Oxford manner!" I cried out.

"Well, under the little gentleman."

"I like that!" I protested.

"You always seemed so afraid of being yourself," she went on. "That was why I was so bowled over by what you said at the recruiting meeting."

"Stop, please," I said very seriously. "That opens the door too wide. To the war and to all sorts of things that I've not yet . . . not yet . . . oh, how shall I put it? — reawakened to? I'll tell you all about my familiar some day and lots of things."

Instantly she took me up:

"And I'll tell you all about my passion for dancing, and why it's a kind of religion with me, and lots of things."

Her quickness of response startled me. Again I was floating in the sunshine of her presence, after scraping on a sunken rock.

"That was a narrow shave," I said, thinking aloud; and, as though she read my mind, she answered immediately:

"Believe me, it's realler than you think."

"Won't the horror of war smash it?"

"No."

"Nor spirits nor the terrors of the night?"

"No."

"How do you know?"

At that she sprang up, and let out, not with a shout, though the walls rang with it; not with emphasis, though my mind and body thrilled with it; but rather as if the force of the words were let loose

from her, unimpeded, in their own right of life:
" Nor all world's wheels that roll crush one born
soul." She spoke in a soft voice.

" So that's it, is it? A born soul . . . I wonder
. . . I've heard of such a thing of course. Such a
very old, very familiar thing to take on such a crash
of meaning! I do wish I had had more of a say in
the matter; stepped into it, if only a little of my own
accord, and not been chucked into it."

She demurred; I insisted.

" Yes, chucked into it. I rushed about all over
the place, in every direction but the right one; and
then, bang! . . . in the heart of what I most feared
I find it. And all this that I've been saying to you
would have sounded mere vapouring if I'd overheard
myself a few weeks ago. Is there any end to the
mystery of personality? "

" None whatever. And no end to its power of
growth."

" I'm planted. My roots have struck. Is that
another way of putting it? "

" Yes."

" Oughtn't it to be the sole end of education to
do for a man what has been done for me? Yet I
feel that all my life I have been bent in another direction. Turned out to a pattern. Oh, every one
is. That's why it's the fashion at one time to wear
fancy waistcoats and the fashion at another to kill
Germans — for much the same reason, too — because 'everybody's doing it, doing it, doing it.'
Only there's this difference — that the parsons and

professors and high-souled journalists hasten to
prove that it is right and good and manly to kill
Germans."

Corinna was by my side, her hand on my forehead; she pressed my head to her breast, as a mother
her sick child.

" You mustn't talk like that, dear.   Wait to think
about the war till you're stronger.   Black hatred
weakens."

But I went on, shaken with passion:

" You've not seen an advance.   How all the lines
yell in the darkness, ' Give it 'em!   Let 'em have
it!'   And the blood and mud and devilry.   The
monstrous obscenity.   The dead men, the dead
horses.   Dead men piled four deep outside a church;
it took a week to bury them.   Scotchmen.   And the
prisoners we take, or don't!   We tried to wrap our
dead in a blanket.   All higgledy-piggledy in the
earth, as quickly as possible — dead Germans, dead
English.   And sometimes shells root out the corpses.
More men wanted; more men wanted.   Men and
guns and munitions.   What for?   What for?
What good end can slaughter and filth and destruction serve?   ' And how's poor Jack Smith or Bill
Thompson?' I've heard them say.   ' Oh, he's gone
west,' comes the answer.   And two little subs were
having dinner, right at the beginning, with some
friends of mine — mere children — and one said,
talking of another boy, that he was reported missing, and found dead two days afterwards.   ' Oh no,
it was a week.   I found him myself'; and to the
lady next to him, and in the same breath and in the

same tone, a little modified for apology, ' Would you mind passing the salt?' I heard it, I heard it. Oh! It makes a man of you, does war! It makes men of us! Or beasts, unthinking, unfeeling beasts!"

I pulled my head away like a naughty child.

"I don't want consolation. I don't want to be soothed or lulled from the black horror of it. All my life long I shall remember and be cursed by the memory of what I have seen and what I have done."

But Corinna was neither grieved nor crestfallen. She seemed gay and hard as steel as she said:

"You must get back all your strength to fight this creeping evil. It does no good to lose your temper about it like a spoiled child. You must face the full shame of grief and misery of it, and not hide your face. Face it at your man's stature, alive to the full pain of it, strong-hearted and erect against all the lies and the false sentiment, and the self-righteousness, and the ingenious tampering with truth that skulks under the name of patriotism."

The words braced my spirit like a gust of wind, stinging, full of good sea-spray.

I stood up.

"I will face it," I said. "You wonderful great inspiriting creature! I will face it. I won't be any longer a mere maudlin, sickly driveller. You scatter doubt. You point the way. You inspire. I know the direction. I have strength to start."

She became a gentle mother again to say:

"Ah, but you're not strong yet, my dear. There's

plenty of time yet, and you will need every atom of strength to start a life's work. Quietly, steadfastly, implacably. A false start is the worst waste of time. There is no hurry, and I have no doubts of you. Have none of yourself. Let your resolve soak well into your very bones, and get properly well again, meanwhile. Rest, now, rest."

"I don't understand how it is you have such power over that and every other horror."

"It's not me."

"It is you."

"It's not me. It's Love's power working through me. God's power if you like. It will work through you too. You'll see. It's Love's power you're sensitive to in me, Love the Creator whom I worship."

"I wonder," was all that I could find to say.

Amy returned in time for tea on Saturday. As the moment of her arrival drew nearer the sense of the badness of my behaviour grew perceptibly heavier. I tried not to think out ahead what I should say to her, but the resolve began to form in me to do whatever she wished; it seemed the only fair course to take.

I could not expect her to understand what I did not properly understand myself. How could a man say to a girl: "I've been treating you as a convenience, not as a human being at all; and now I respect you far too much to marry you"? Yet that would have been true, especially if I had added that she had been right in her mockery of me, and that I understood much better now the spirit of the letter in which she had besought me to talk to her as man to man. Throughout my relations with her I spied efforts at honesty on her part, which I had done my best to thwart. And now, to be honest with her, I should be obliged to tell her that I didn't want to marry her or any one. Or was I in love with Corinna? Ought I to tell Amy about Corinna? And what could I tell her, or how could I tell it?

After all, perhaps, I wasn't so very much to blame; and if she were a human being, she could look after herself without my help; all is fair in love and war. And besides, she had begun by rather flinging herself at my head. Plenty of excuses for my conduct cropped up in my mind, and their number and apparent excellence convinced me not so much of my innocence (which they would have done before) as of the layer on layer of meanness that had been allowed to accumulate within me.

The sight of Amy quickened the vision of my meanness. I saw her only as a human being, if I may use the expression: a creature fresh and lovely, with the colour of health on her cheeks, with light in her eyes, with life in her hair, with untold magic powers of growth within her, waiting to unfold and blossom and bear fruit under the sunshine of love. And this creature I had decided to use for my own convenience, for all sorts of negative things, so that I might not be frightened, so that I might not be uncomfortable, and so on — buy it as a plaything that might afterwards be a useful piece of furniture; not troubling to know her; not caring what became of her, using, indeed, what power I had to mar her un-

conscious wish for growth in fear lest it might bother
my future comfort.

No doubt I idealised Amy and blackened myself
(and was at the time indistinctly aware of doing so),
but there was an amount of truth in the vision which
kept me from virtuous delight in being a splendid
sinner, and showed me to myself as merely rather a
mean and dirty dog.

When we were left alone together, as we duly
were, this view closed down on me to the exclusion
of all else.   She came and sat down by me, and with
a jolly challenge in her voice she said:

"A nice way you've been going on without me.
Dancing regular little breakdowns all to yourself.
Now then, what do you mean by it?"

I felt a damned old puritan to be able to make no
response to this provocative fun.   Something in me
asked if I had bidden farewell to fun of every kind:
and received a quite definite answer of "Yes," to
fun of this kind, because it cloaked dishonesty.

I blurted out, "I've behaved like a cad to you,
Amy."

"Now, please," she cried, stretching out her hand
adorably.   "I don't want gloom, and I won't have a
scene.   I've been working harder than a housemaid,
and I want to laugh and have a good time — be
petted, and made a fuss of, and spoiled.   Oh, I've
been serious long enough.   Hardly any of the poor
boys were well enough to be amusing.   And somehow — well — all of them lying there, and one of
them was delirious, and — oh, well, I know more
now, and am much older; and anyhow, I didn't feel

as though I wanted to be amused. I've learned a
lot. Oh, a lot. But I do want to be amused now
and petted — petted by you — because I've come to
see how awfully wise you were about your old common sense and all that — really and truly sensible.
I've had a whiff of war, and I see there's no room at
all in the world for nonsense, and a young girl's
dream of love, and all that bosh. I'll marry you
right enough like a sensible girl, and make you a
sensible wife; only whatever happens I won't have
more than four children; and if it weren't that I'm
public-spirited and know that the country wants children, I wouldn't have more than two. But that's
all settled. As soon as you find a decent job, I'm
yours."

I sat, mute with shame. She leaned forward, at
my lack of response, and said in a voice of concern:
"I heard you were much better, quite yourself
again. Isn't it true?"

"I've been simply a blackguard to you," I said
miserably. "What you've just been saying shows
. . . I mean . . . Oh, I can't explain. But don't
think it. A girl's dream of love is not bosh; it's the
holiest thing in the world, and with a man's help she
can bring the dream to life in the world. It's just
this dream of love that's wanted most of all in this
world of slaughter and misery, the dream and the
effort to give it its full life. All I said and thought
was silly rubbish, silly, blasphemous rubbish. I
didn't know what holiness meant. I put lewd fingers
on what is sacred."

Amy stared at me in amazement.

"Good Heavens!" she gasped. "What's the matter with the man? You're not crazy, are you?"

"I thought I was going crazy, literally. I may be, for all I know. Anyhow, the whole world seems crazy now. There is no love without worship. Without holiness there's no happiness in life except what money can buy, and that's nothing but unrest and disquiet and that awful boredom that leads to war; because money means more money, more and more; and you grasp and envy and snarl, and then at last the great festering sore of all the sloth and envy and discontent bursts in a war. Oh, it's awful, awful, awful! It begins with every one of us, in such little things! And the little wrongs and mean-nesses accumulate and accumulate, until at last they find a national outlet in a rage of destruction. Then war stalks through the land and all war's monstrous satellites — hatred, fear, malice, falsehood raise their dreadful voices. Every foul thing flourishes in all its blatancy. Lust and greed are noisy. And the last and most awful blasphemy is that the priests and professors bless this obscene hubbub of evil, and egg on the fighters, on either side, with the horrible old lies of glory and the false glitter of patriotism. I've helped to push you into it, with all that cold crafty stuff I talked about common sense. Come out of it. Come out of it. Stick to your girl's dream of love. It's a stock joke, I know, but it has more usefulness in it, more life, more reality than all this waste of war. It's in that direction that God lies and truth and beauty."

She came towards me with troubled eyes.

"I know, dear," she said, "how awful it all is. You go on talking. It gets many like that. Such a nice woman, who has been in the hospital ever since the war began, told me, because I was upset by a poor young fellow who went on in almost the same kind of way. And your head aches, I expect. I know you don't really mean it. It's not *you* talking at all. *You* couldn't say such horrible unpatriotic things. Just you kiss me a little and you'll feel jollier."

Her kindness affected me deeply. It was all I could do to keep back my tears; it was difficult for me to speak.

"I'm incoherent, but I mean it, and my head doesn't ache," I managed to say. "You think I'm crazy, I dare say."

She assumed the prettiest of professional airs, which she must have caught from the admired nurse at the hospital.

"Crazy, oh no, not a bit. But you must be careful and not excite yourself. The brain is often the last thing wholly to recover from any great shock. If you only knew what a sensitive, complicated structure it was, you'd not be surprised, really you wouldn't. Haven't I learned a lot? It is naughty of you not to be well. I'm a bit fed up with sick men, especially ones with jumpy nerves; and the noise of the guns simply plays Old Harry with the nerves, you know. They say some simply can't stop trembling and shaking. They call it Shellitis. That must be jolly when you're dying to appear nice and brave. Oh, I'm full of it. I had no idea war was

so horrid. It is a pity, isn't it? But the great
thing, Sister Mary says, is not to let it get on your
nerves. That does *no* good. War's got to be, or
it wouldn't be, and there you are. Think how nice
it is you've done your bit, and don't worry. All your
troubles are past and gone, and you're going to settle
down comfortably with " (she put her head on one
side) " rather a nice little wife, eh? Now you do
feel better, don't you? Haven't I learned to talk
in a nice soothing way? Sister Mary says I've a
great knack, and turns me on to jumpy cases.
Funny, she, too, like you, has often said to me,
' You've a great fund of common sense, my dear.'
It was sweet of you to play up to me about the
young girl's dream of love. I know how brooding
on the war runs away with one. But you mustn't
brood any more. And then, Corinna Combe being
here. How is poor Corinna? These earnest people are always so depressing."

She prattled on, proud of the soothing skill on
which she had been complimented. I put in:

" Corinna hasn't depressed me at all."

" That's right. She does mean awfully well.
These peculiar people nearly always do. Have you
thought what you'll do? Now, I have been thinking, and I'm sure you ought to go into the Church.
I should love to live in a nice country parish, and my
experience at the hospital would come in very handy.
Oh, I've changed a lot. I've become far more serious. I don't want to rush about any more. Of
course I shall always want to look pretty, but that's
not wrong. Yes, I mean it. I'm quite serious.

I've not been converted or anything silly like that;
but after all this upheaval and dreadfulness, somehow a country vicarage does seem not at all the dull
stuffy place I used to think it, but quiet and peaceful
and comfy, and it would be so nice to feel you were
doing good and setting an example. Not that I'm
pious, but somehow the old gay round after . . .
well. . . . Besides, I'm sure it will be quite the
thing — the Church and all that. You see, we shall
all want to be good for ever such a long time after,
and we shall all be so poor we shall have to be. And
I'm sure you'd preach lovely sermons, and be immensely respected among all the county people, because you are so very obviously wounded, dear, aren't
you? They could never forget it, even if they
wanted to."

"Oh, Amy," I cried, "haven't you any feelings?
You prattle on as if nothing mattered much one way
or the other."

"Feelings! Of course I've got feelings.
Haven't I told you a whiff of war has changed my
point of view; that I want to settle down with you
and be good. If you mean it was horrid of me saying it was a good thing you were obviously wounded,
it is, and there's an end of it. It's not my fault that
people, even the nicest people, are inclined to forget;
and they won't be able to with you as you are.
There you stand, a constant reminder. And I'm not
set on your going into the Church. I merely throw
it out as a suggestion. I'm ready to listen to *your*
ideas, but *you* don't seem to have thought of the future at all."

"It's true, I haven't, but I can't possibly go into the Church."

"Well, don't, then. We'll think of something else. Only I think it's a pity, I do really. Before the war, I wouldn't have dreamed of your being a parson, but there'll be ever such a difference afterwards, you see if there isn't. It would have been best if you could have stopped in the Army; but you can't do that, so the next best thing is to be in the Church, the sister service. Think how splendid the Church has been all through the war. Every one will want to be joined up with the country, somehow. The Church of England! Think how patriotic it sounds, simply lovely. It sends a thrill right through me."

She repeated the words in a soft voice of ecstasy. "The Church of England! Oh, beautiful!" Then she continued in her soothing, practical voice:

"Believe me, now's the time. As soon as the war *is* over, there'll be a rush, and all the vacancies will be filled up before you can look round, and perhaps they'll take time in the trenches as doing for — you know, instead of other preparation. Being a curate might be a bit of a bore, but we've influence, and there are decent curacies even; and your disablement won't stand in your way, it will be an actual advantage. And it's not mercenary or horrid to think of that; it's simply common sense. And it's common sense you've always liked best in me, you wise old thing."

"I did. I know I did. But I meant what I said

just now. I honestly believe a girl's dream of love is worth more than all this waste of war."

"Oh yes. I see what you mean, of course, and it's sweet of you to put it like that. The possibility of one healthy baby is worth more than the fact of thousands of dead men. And when you say it quietly like that I'm quite ready to agree with you. I can't allow you, though, to excite yourself over the horrors of war and say horrible unpatriotic things, because that does *no* good, only makes you ill. Your nerves are still shaky, and so you think that a passing mood of depression is going to be your permanent frame of mind for ever and ever, Amen. That's a common trick the nerves play every one. You swing, don't you, from the rosiest of rosy dreams to the blackest of black thoughts. That's a regular symptom, you know. Life seems at one time a waltz on a perfect floor and at another a mere crawl to the grave. I've learnt a lot, and it's lucky for you I have, because if I took the sort of welcome you've given me seriously and the sort of things you've said, I shouldn't be nice to you, or anything. And as for marrying you . . . well! . . . Well, you've been blaming me for the one thing you most encouraged in me. And wasn't it you made me take up nursing? I'm glad you did, but still. . . . And you say I've no feeling."

She paused. To my dismay I saw the corners of her mouth trembling. "I'm awfully glad you are nursing," I said.

She took no notice.

" I've had rather a lonely, strange time. All these weeks among strange faces."

It wrung my heart the way she paused after each sentence: a child on the brink of tears.

" It's hard lines to come back and have to be treating you like any other invalid. You don't seem to see that. You talk of a girl's dream of love. You might love me a little, I should have thought."

The pauses grew longer as speech became more difficult to her. She had no little airs and graces; she was simply sad. I had felt a cad before; I felt an unutterable cad at that moment. She seemed to be drifting farther and farther away into the distance, whereas her sadness should have drawn her nearer to me. I was the sole cause of all her sadness, the wanton cause. Why ever hadn't I left her alone? I had merely tampered with her in my ignorance. I racked my brain to find comfort for her, and could find none.

" You've not kissed me yet, you know," I heard her small voice say. " And I'm very sad."

I couldn't speak. The silence was thick about me. I knew beforehand what her next words would be. I was right.

" Don't you love me any more? " came the faltering question.

" Amy," I cried, " you must forgive me. I've been knocked all to pieces. I didn't know what I was doing. It's my only excuse, and it's a poor one. We should be miserable together. It can't be. We don't love each other."

She turned on me, a mingling of anger and distress.

"Not love each other!" she cried. "That's hateful of you, shameful of you to say that, after — after . . ." Her voice broke, and she whispered: "Think how we've kissed each other."

"I know but . . . I may be crazy; but anyhow it's true, and I can't explain."

"One minute you want to kiss me, and the next you don't. I shall never trust a man again."

"Don't judge men by me! I'm not worth bothering about," I suggested.

"I know that, thank you," she snapped.

"I'm most awfully sorry. I can't tell you what a brute I feel."

"You might at least have written, I should have thought."

"I hoped . . . I didn't know . . . I mean ——"

"You needed the sight of me, I suppose, to be certain how much you disliked me."

"Oh, not that."

"Why not that, I should like to know?" she said, and began to abuse me.

I should not have minded paying any amount in suffering for what I had gained; but to make another person unhappy — and a person who looked such a darling as Amy — was a price beyond my reckoning. How unhappy she was I did not know. Her *amour propre* was hurt, and no doubt she may have felt it incumbent on her to play up a little to the broken-hearted part; but it was enough for me that she was unhappy, and unhappy through my despicable fault. She became to me more than ever a dear little creature, whom I had never taken the trouble to know;

with all manner of wonderful possibilities within her, as there were in every human being, especially every young human being; and these delicate possibilities might have been crushed by my clumsy selfishness.

I might have taken refuge behind the many ungentle, ungracious things she was saying, saying to myself, " Oh, well, a girl who can say this, or a girl who can say that, she can't feel much; or she deserves all she gets." Indeed, such thoughts did pass through my mind; and in their passage they brought home to me my grief, for the truth was sun-clear to me (and there was nothing to keep from me the glare of it) that these ungentle unworthy things were due to the mischief I had done her, and which, as it seemed to me, I had no power at all to undo. It was no excuse that I had not meant to be false, had not meant to play at love or to simulate holiness of the very existence of which I was ignorant.

Then she began to abuse herself, but that I would not have. I stopped her with words in confusion.

" It was my fault. All sorts of lovely things in you I didn't want through fear — no, not fear so much as ignorance really of what they stood for, or that was why I feared them. I wanted to use you for my own comfort, to have a pretty girl of my own. I didn't care for you. I was selfish, beastly selfish."

She broke in:

" That's exactly what appealed to me. You were so masterful; you were so strong, and all my nonsense you . . . oh, don't you see? I wanted really to be carried away, to be just a man's thing. I adored what you call your selfishness. That was why I was always being naughty and rude, because I loved you to manage me. And you always did the right thing. You are such an absolute gentleman. Sometimes I wanted you to be a little more . . . more natural. I·don't know, and I did try and upset you, but it was only in fun, to shock you, to see if you were a gentleman through and through and through; because a woman wants — oh, I love you to be a gentleman, but a woman wants. . . . well, she does, I'm sure, every woman does. . . . Oh, I don't understand what's happened. Why can't we begin again? What is it you want me to be? I'll be anything you wish. I'll adapt myself, I will really; and I know I can, because, look how quickly I got the hang of being a nurse. I know we shouldn't be miserable together."

" It's no good, darling. It can't be."

" Why do you say it's no good and it can't be, when you say it in a kinder voice than I've almost ever heard from you. I can feel you're fond of me, or you wouldn't talk like that."

" Yes, I'm fonder of you than I've ever been."

" Oh, I'm not pleading to be taken pity on or anything horrid, really I'm not. But it does seem stupid to want to break with a girl when you're fonder of her than you've ever been. And I've changed and you've changed. And I own it sounded like rubbish, sounded almost wicked, what you said about holiness and love and a girl's dream but couldn't you try and make me understand? It's quite true what I said about wanting to be good, and we could both be good together, not miserable."

I was deeply moved by the pathos of her entreaty,
and I accused myself of heartlessness in being able to
see anything funny in it.   But I couldn't help it, and
as this is a true record or nothing, I am bound to confess that I nearly burst out laughing.   Moreover,
at the moment that I saw the ridiculous side of her
position and mine, I realised how impossible it would
be ever to make Amy see with me.   And I began to
wonder whether there was anything much in it after
all.   This great change, what was it?   I remembered Corinna's words about Love's power working
through me — God's power, if you like; and it
seemed a strange irony that the first manifestation
of Love's power should be this hurting of a pretty
girl whom I had treated badly.   Didn't love mean
sacrifice?   Wouldn't it be magnificent to give her a
life-time's devotion as an atonement for the mischief
I had done?   Why not?   It would be quite easy to
hide from her the motive of sacrifice.   She need
never know; she might be quite happy; and at any
rate she would look smiling and pleased in less than
half a minute, and the sadness on her dear little face
was hard to endure.   A word only would do it, a
word so easily spoken, a word that would be so very
near the truth.   Why not say it?   Wouldn't it be
a really unselfish action, and shouldn't I be always
able, in bad future moments, to console myself with
the thought of my unselfishness and make it my life's
business to see that Amy was happy?   What could
be more in the spirit of Love than that?   The impulse was strong to open my arms to her and say
this word, and I didn't know what sealed my lips

and held my arms to my side. But my arms were held and my lips sealed, though at the moment I was definitely sure that a really high-minded fellow would have opened his arms and spoken.

I said to myself: "I have learned that Love is the only power; and my first action after this knowledge is to hurt the one person to whom I ought to be most tender and most considerate."

I blurted out: "I don't love you, Amy, and to live with you and have children, merely to soothe my conscience, would be to treat you even more basely than I have already treated you."

I listened to my own voice with hot shame, and what I said seemed the last word of caddishness.

I hoped that she would abuse me, as I deserved; tell me off like a fishwife in the only language that could meet the case of conduct like mine.

But she did not do so. She drew herself up with no sham dignity, and said without even disdain in her voice:

"Oh, very well. There's no more to be said, then."

She quietly looked at me, as though I were a creature to be pitied, as indeed I was.

"I hope you'll get on better in your next little affair. Only if I were you, I should be . . . but I won't give you any advice. You're not in love with Corinna by any chance? However, that's no business of mine, and I'm sure I wish you a better fate than that. I'm not ill-natured; and you always were such a perfect gentleman! My goodness, if any one had told me you could have behaved like this, I should have laughed. One lives and learns."

She was making towards the door. I thought she was going. So she was; but suddenly she rushed back, and was by my knees, sobbing:

"Oh, no, no, no. It can't be. Not like this. It's too humiliating for me. Don't let me go. I don't understand. I do care for you. I can't lose you. I never knew how much I cared. Never till now. I was pretending not to mind. Take me back. Forgive me. What have I done? Be kind to me, please; be kind to me."

I stroked her head. She wiped her eyes, looked up, and then, sitting back on her heels, she went on, misreading my dumbness:

"You *must* explain. Of course I wouldn't force myself on any man. But merely a mood . . . when you're not well, you know you're not. Not at all your *self*. I know I've been horrid in heaps of things. Cheeky and horrid and . . . but it wasn't really me; like this isn't really you. I hate modern ideas and all that, and I'd like to be like your mother. But you read things, and they seem clever and smart, and they go down in talking and you get in a muddle and try almost to be what you don't really *want* to be at all. But I've been going to church much oftener and liking it; and — don't laugh at me — I say my prayers regularly, like I used to do when I was a little girl, and I've been to a week-day service and enjoyed that. The same sort of thing has happened to you, hasn't it? And I feel you're sending away the horrid modern girl I was and never wanted to be — not the real me — when I have become much more the quiet home woman I always really wanted to be; that is the real me. We've changed together, if you'd only see it. Every one *has* changed. The war has made them change. Oh, do try me again; please give me another chance. It's not wrong to enjoy my being pretty and all that. No, I won't say things to shock you any more. They shock me too. I can't think why I say them. I pray to be a good girl; and — don't laugh at me, though it sounds silly — I pray that I mayn't want to know what no nice girl ought to want to know. Curiosity's at the root of it all. And if I only didn't know as much as I do, it would be ever so much easier. It's in the air now, and it wasn't when a good woman like your mother was a girl; so it's much more difficult for girls like me; and it's not my fault that it is in the air. I know I've played about with your feelings and been horrid, just to see what would happen, but I won't any more. I won't really. If you like, we'll never kiss at all until we're married, because I do believe now in the sacredness of marriage, that our bodies and all that are horrid until they are sanctified, and there is no way of sanctifying them without marriage. You see I do understand about holiness, and not just enjoying feelings for their own sake, which isn't nice a bit, and children, and how without a sacrament and worship and a service of some sort there can't be love. You too said there couldn't be love without worship, you know you did. So you see we really think alike, though I put it badly. I used to laugh about re-

ligion, I know, and usedn't to think it mattered, but
I do now.   It's plain as war.   I mean, just as war's
got to be, or it wouldn't be, so there it is, and it's
the same with the Church — if it weren't true, it
wouldn't be there, and we've got to let religion into
our lives.   That was my real reason for wanting
you to go into the Church; it was, indeed it was.
Only the other, the worldly reasons, are so much
easier to say, and they're true too."

Grief choked me while she was speaking; I did not
know how to be gentle enough with her.   All the
while something in me clamoured to say the kind
untruth; pointed out how easily I could always make
her believe I loved her, asked what prevented me
from taking her in my arms and petting back the
smiles to her sad little face, tearstained and earnest,
and with wisps of hair straggling over the forehead.
If my thoughts had stopped there, I believe the kind
untruth would have been spoken; but they hastened
away to dwell on her sweetness and devotion, and to
ask what more any man could desire than this little
bundle of delight.   So the comfort and ease which
the alluring picture promised, stripped the kind untruth of its glamour of unselfishness and silenced me
in time.   That vision silenced me, but it did not help
me in any way to feel less of a cad; it gave me no
immediate confidence even that I was right.   Right
or wrong, however, there remained one thing only
that I could say, and though I felt mean and cruel
beyond words of mine to describe, I said it; and the
fact that I was obliged to say it as gently and as
kindly as I possibly could added, for some reason

I do not know and never perhaps shall know, to my sense of meanness and cruelty.

"Amy, you darling, it's dear of you to talk like that to me, so frankly. I don't deserve it. Don't think I feel superior to you. I don't. I feel the most abominable cad, and a fool, too, because I don't know what has happened to me. All I know is this: that you can't make a thing holy from outside; it's got to be holy itself. And my love for you wasn't holy; it wasn't love at all. It was an ugly selfish thing, and all the ceremonies in the world couldn't give it what it lacked. That's what I mean by holiness: just our own human love. The Church doesn't sanctify us; we sanctify the Church. I mean it's an institution that men have made to remind them of what love should be, as a symbol of love's power. But it has come about that the institution has attracted all the holiness to itself and forgotten the holiness of what it celebrates. The holy base and fact of it all is that God is Love and Love is God. That's why I could never join the Church."

"I should have thought that's exactly why you ought to join the Church, because you've not forgotten or have found out or something. I'm sure all you say sounds beautiful, and is almost exactly the same as what I tried to say."

"Darling, it's the exact opposite."

"Well, even if you think it is, I don't think it is, and if I think it's the same, I don't see why we shouldn't be quite happy together and never quarrel at all."

"I'm stupid at putting things, or I could make

you see how it works out in daily life. Take a bald instance. If I loved some one, I shouldn't feel anything could make our love more sacred, not a service in church."

" Good Heavens! You don't mean to say you don't believe in marriage or God or anything. But that's wicked; that's all the modern stuff I thought you disliked in me. What do you mean by talking of holiness and love and worship and . . ." She stopped and looked at me in alarm.

" Jimmie, tell me, dear; of course I know you're not really crazy or anything like it; but it is all so twisted. Are you resting enough? You don't know how tricky the brain is, and what a shock like yours can leave behind it. Of course I can understand a man, or a girl for that matter, saying to himself, ' Oh, religion's all rubbish. I'm out for a good time here, and shall chance the next world, and I shan't marry till I must '; but what you say . . . well . . . holiness and worship and a good time, too, and well . . . I should rest, dear, as much as possible, and not worry your poor brain, thinking and thinking about things that have all been thought and settled ages ago. You'll only get into a hopeless muddle of a jumble."

I didn't mind in the least her misunderstanding me. I was too relieved to see that she was less unhappy, and friendlier.

" I told you at the beginning, I wasn't sure whether I was crazy or the world was crazy; one or the other it must be. I have a queer feeling, too, that no one hardly has ever lived before, and that I'm a baby with my eyes open in a new world. That's why I feel better than I have ever done, and that's why it's absurd to think of me marrying or being married. I'm a baby. Oh, let's laugh about it. It's much the best. I've got everything to learn. I'll go slow; you can take my word for it."

" Do be careful; that's all. You may be madder than you think, or cleverer or something."

" Not cleverer, anyhow. Be friends with the baby, will you? Do."

" I'll keep an eye on you. It's all right at the beginning, but you don't know where it may not lead to."

" No, I don't. That's part of the fun of it."

" I'm serious."

" So am I."

" And I'm awfully sad and disappointed too. I believe there's a scar on me somewhere."

" Don't let there be ! "

" Yes, there is; and I dare say you think you've turned me round your little finger nicely, and feel as proud as Punch inside."

" No, no. I've been dead sincere. That's true. Dead sincere. Honesty is a man's soul. Oh, Amy, I'm learning."

She looked at the ceiling and said casually, " The man's mad." Then she turned to me, smiling like the little brick she was, and said gaily, " I say, Punch has been wonderful during the war, hasn't it? "

And she left me to dress for dinner.

XIII

My talk with Amy did not leave me with any very
good opinion of myself. In many ways I had been
ignominiously worsted, but in one way I had gained
much more than freedom from an entanglement, for
I knew more about the strength of that, whatever
it might be, into contact with which I had been
brought. True, I had made a fool of myself, had
spoken like a cad, had been unable to prove I wasn't
crazy; yet I felt a renewal of confidence, and my
hope was established that the " happening " was real
and trustworthy, however childish and erratic my
behaviour under its influence might at first have been.
I felt a humility which was new to me because there
was in it no sense of humiliation, an inspiring humility which was so far from a genial acceptance of
the futility of effort that it released a little fund of
its own of desire and of energy, entrapped before
within me.

Amy could not have behaved better than she did.
She broke the news of our rupture to mother and
Doris that very evening, and she must have done
it very nicely, because mother was far less disappointed than I feared. Mother was helped no doubt
by her lack of belief in the break's finality, which I
gathered from her smile when she told me that Amy
had said, " We thought it better to remain only

friends." Her smile seemed to say that whatever *we* thought, nature might think otherwise.

Doris was indignant. "It's horrid of you both," she said. "One broken engagement so often leads to others, and it is such a bad example."

Amy was there, and she said in her demurest, most decisive manner: "The fact is, you know, we're really both too friendly to be anything more than friends. There's not enough romance, and we're both romantic."

I was obliged to look at Corinna, longing to know what was going on at the back of her mind. Whatever it was it remained there, for no trace of anything came to the surface as she gravely said:

"I believe every one is really."

At which Amy smiled her funny little worldly smile of one absolutely "in the know"; and I knew that if Amy lived to be a hundred she would always pity Corinna and people like Corinna. The Amys of the world always did. I wondered why, and whether Corinna noticed it. I meant to ask her about it, but I forgot as other more important things were always there, especially as Corinna's visit, which had already at my request been lengthened, was coming to an end.

I did not think I could be in love with her, because I had no feeling whatever that any time not spent alone with her was wasted. There was no nervous clamour to be alone with her, and I had no special desire to kiss her, except when I thought, "Should you like to kiss her?" when the immediate answer was, "Yes." I mean when I was alone with her I was happy talking or not talking; and the question whether I wanted to kiss her or not never occurred to my mind in her presence. Nor did I think much of her departure, which had been fixed for Thursday, though I knew she was going some way from home.

Yet I did not grow accustomed to the holiness which her presence breathed. It seemed somehow as natural and proper to her as fragrance to a rose; and it astonished me that I had been able to live so long and miss it. She had told me it was everywhere, and I believed her. But when I went for a walk, it was her counterpart only that I found, her poise in the trees, her sweetness in the flowers, her vigour in the line of the hills, her bigness in the sky, her swiftness in the wind and so on; but quite without end, for there was nothing I saw with any pleasure that did not instantly associate itself of its own accord with some quality of Corinna. Everything, if I may say so, took on her meaning, lived in her.

This was no pretty fancy, like that great lover's in the garden who chid the forward violet for stealing his love's breath, the lily, the marjoram and the roses for other thefts. I had not the wits to attempt such little exploits of the mind, nor had my mind much to do with it. I couldn't help it. It was almost as though an actual part of Corinna's spirit had come into me, when she drew me back in her arms to life, so impossible was it for me to see anything except in terms of her. Dr. Redman came on Tuesday, and I gave him as minute an account as I could of the climax of horror after my visit to Beach, and I learned that Corinna was coming to stay; of those awful moments while I waited in the passage and of how I came to *in* a sense of peace which had never left me for long.

Corinna's part in the miracle I treated as lightly as possible from motives of modesty. I ended up by saying:

"I've found a sort of pervading holiness, as though there were something I could tap for strength. It's all quite vague, but somehow I see a new meaning in — don't laugh — in woman. She's a link for a man between himself and nature and life. Does it sound nonsense?"

"Not entirely; she may be," he answered, and there was something whimsical in his voice.

"I mean more than that. Isn't she meant to be in the whole great arrangement of things?"

"Possibly; but by whom or what?" he asked brusquely.

"Ah, there you have me," I owned. "I suppose it's a question of feeling, not of argument. But religion and sex, somehow, their union . . ."

I lost myself, and he interrupted, pretending, awfully well, to be shocked:

"My dear James, no English gentleman likes to discuss either. We accept and follow. Think of your mother and sister; think of the Bishop of London, and pause, please, pause!"

"Don't rag!" I laughed.

"Youth's rashness!" he sighed, and continued with instant seriousness. "The more a man realises that Man also is a part of Nature, the more likely he is to get in touch with the great laws of life. Seen your — what do you call it? — familiar any more?"

"No, I haven't.   And I've hardly thought about it; more I mean, than one would about an interesting dream one remembered."

"That's rather ungrateful of you, isn't it?"

"To you?   You were interested, I know and wanted . . ."

"I've got all I want, thanks.   More than I hoped.".

"That puzzles me," I said, and it did.

"Never mind.   It doesn't matter."

"All right.   But let's go back.   About religion, I mean.   What you said — weeks ago — about religion; about finding oneself.   Do you remember? It made me angry at the time.   This holiness — isn't it — when you ask by whom or by what the arrangement's been made — isn't it this holiness that is the great cause — the first thing — God?   Or what is it?"

"The holiness?"

"Yes."

"All those words, my dear fellow — grace, holiness, faith, religion and so on, a whole crowd of them — they have lost their meaning for me.   They are coins that have been thumbed too thin for use. Oh, I speak for myself.   But the word 'God,' for instance, always calls up to my mind the image of a dear old gentleman with a white beard, surrounded by angels, warming his toes on the sun.   No, no.

I'm keen to discover the great laws of life, but in
their originator, if there is one — well, I'm content
to put him off to another chapter of existence.   I
find there's enough to occupy what power of work
and worship I possess, here and now, without too
much speculation.   The principle of life," he
brooded.   "The sea and the trees are especially
God to me, but whether it's in me or only in my love
for them, I couldn't say: probably in my love for
them, I should think.   After all, you can't get much
nearer than God is Love, the great co-operative force
that is coming to be seen as the main factor of evo-
lution beneath the tooth-and-claw theory.   Samuel
Butler hopped on to it; all poets always have.   The
creative   power.   I   have   it — symbiogenesis —
that's the scientific name for the text that God is
Love.   That form of life survives most strongly
which contributes most to the general welfare of the
life surrounding it.   Queer this law should be on all
sides coming to light, just as the tooth-and-claw theory should be having such a magnificent run for its
money, when millions of men are blowing each other
to pieces to see which are the fittest to survive.   The
Great Ironist must have something to amuse him
while he warms his toes by the sun.   Funniest of all
. . . but I'll spare you."

"No, do go on."

"I wouldn't think too much about the war, yet.
Follow up the other tack, this holiness you were talking to me about.   Much better for you."

"Things don't get on my nerves now.   I can face
them.   Or rather I'm beginning to be able to face

them.   There's all the difference.   I want you to
go on."

"I've forgotten now what I was going to say."

I prompted: "Funniest of all . . . The Great
Ironist. . . ."

"Oh yes!   I was talking to a brilliant man, a
young philosopher, about an inconclusive peace, as
he called it, *à propos* of peace terms (quite good,
sort of as-you-were terms) that Germany is said to
have offered.   He was very martial.   As I think
there's nothing more sacred than human life, I wasn't
martial.   I told him so, and he upped and said, like
a man inspired: 'There's only one thing more
sacred than life, and that is justice.'   I was entirely
speechless.   The man's no fool.   You'd have
thought that his love of justice would have made him
want to end the war at any price, because whatever
you may say for war, and there is a good deal to be
said, you know, it is the most flagrantly unjust business that has ever been conceived.   Millions too
many of the wrong people are slaughtered on every
side.   In this particular war, when every nation is
sure that it is fighting for the right against tyranny,
you get the elements of democracy in every country
killing each other wholesale, while the ruling classes
keep largely in the background (by comparison, I
mean) and gain strength and prestige.   You must
forgive my talking to a wounded soldier like this.
To a mere man of science war must always seem to
end in a pretty stalemate, though a triumphal march,
driving your enemy in front of you through his own
land, must be rather fun for a time, if you're suffi-

ciently without human feeling to be able to enjoy it.
I can understand journalists or preachers warming
to their daily or weekly work in Biblical prose, but
for men who are supposed to be thinkers — my
young philosopher for example — I should have
thought they would have wanted to put the military
machine out of action as soon as possible, and get to
business. Not they. Justice must be vindicated,
they clamour, and the rights of the smaller nations;
forgetful of their own record of forty wars in sixty
years; forgetful, too, that 'Britannia rules the
waves' is as offensive to a German ear as 'Deutschland, Deutschland über alles' is to their own; or that
Rudyard Kipling seems scarcely less military, and
vastly more popular, than the redoubtable Treit-
schke. No; I can by an effort of the imagination
understand a holy war, but a just war, a war to vin-
dicate the claims of justice — that my imagination
completely fails to grasp."

"But look here," I said, "mayn't a professor of
philosophy be patriotic?"

"Oh yes, yes, yes, yes, yes!" he said. "Only in
war's ferment I should have thought it might be
good for a country if one or two men kept their
heads. It's rather my young friend's job, I should
have thought, to point out that nothing much can
ever be settled by machine guns, even if it made him
a little unpopular for the moment, than to teach boys
how to kill, as he is doing."

"Can't he do both, though? Surely he can."

"It's difficult to go in two different directions at
the same time. The ultimate futility of dynamite

and machine guns would be a better subject for his
discourses than, say, military tactics, which he has
hastily crammed from textbooks which this war is
making obsolete.   Much of it he hates doing; and
the Christian streak in his character causes the unpleasantness to be a proof that he is doing right,
that, and the amount of fresh air he is obliged to
breathe.   Before the war I was talking to a military man.   No fire-eater by any means, but he
frankly thought that, human nature being what it is,
war was the making of a nation, which must run to
seed in peace.   I talked with him then as one might
with an amiable lunatic.   I said: 'At any rate we
shall never go into a great European war; we're a
sea-power, and you'll never get men to fight except
for hearth and home.'   He laughed, and with what
seemed to me incredible cynicism he said: 'Russia
and France have an alliance against Germany and
Austria.   Germany's only chance in the event of a
war is to attack.   She must attack France first, then
swing across to Russia, and she must attack France
through Belgium.   We shall come in, in defence of
a weaker nation.   You see if we don't have even
old Dr. Clifford preaching war sermons, and Free
Church parsons bursting themselves to enlist.'   By
Gad, he was about right.   Pity he and a few others
didn't know their job well enough to foresee what
trench warfare would mean.   It's the little fellows
at the top who have muddled things.   To my mind
democracy has never shown greater proof of its
rightness and never been in greater danger of its
life.   A war's the biggest of reactionary forces, es-

pecially if you win it.   Puts back the clock a good hundred years."

"I can't think politically or internationally, but what's happened to me I'm sure must have happened to scores of others."

"What's that?"

"Ah, now! That's just the point! What is it?" I laughed, "I can't exactly say.   But I feel as though everything had been done all through my education to turn me out a good little sheep, and by some freakish happenings I've discovered the way to become a man.   That's it, more clearly than I've been able to see it or say it before."

I saw a particular kind of twinkle in Dr. Redman's eye which made me blush and say:

"It's not simply that I'm in love with Miss Combe."

"Isn't it?" he asked awfully nicely.

"It may be that.   But honestly I don't think that it is.   Anyhow, it's far more than that.   Somehow, too, there's an odd connection between my grandfather and Corinna and my familiar in all this business.   Of course it was all on my nerves, and I fancied things.   I can't understand though why I was so positive that I was either going mad or going to die.   It got worse and worse, you know, until it burst."

"The nerves play queer tricks."

"Have you any medical explanation?"

"Of what?"

"Of my recovery."

"I could give you one, but this cutting up of things

is one of the chief mistakes we make. Moral and physical and spiritual and all the rest of it. Each one is interested in his special little bit of the truth, and hardly any one troubles to fit all the pieces together. Surely that's what artists and preachers ought to do, yet they don't; and the pieces remain disconnected, pigeon-holed, almost useless. Indeed, with all our technical terms we seem anxious to fence things off from each other. Oh, we are all so damned sophisticated. We want to start afresh."

A look of pain passed over his face such as I had never seen before. "All these young men in the prime of their manhood! For a man like me who is past his prime . . . to watch them marching out in their hundreds and their thousands. . . . They have hardly touched the cup of life. . . . Ninety men with fifty machine guns kept a French Army Corps at bay . . . dashing determined men fighting on their own soil for their own soil. Oh, the waste, the waste, the waste! "

I could not follow the trend of his thought. I was as surprised at the pain which marked his rugged face and under which his burly figure stooped as I had been at his enthusiasm for my grandfather. A passion of feeling had swept over him, and everything in me responded to it, even while my brain registered surprise. A voice spoke within me: "Once more you are in God's presence," and I felt a strange inrush of life, as I remembered Corinna's words: " I am sure it is everywhere."

Words came to my tongue spontaneously. I said with a literal thrill that tingled over my body:

" One thing I have learned: to know what a friend
may be."

There was a gentleness of understanding in his
eyes as he looked towards me and said curtly:

" And what's that? "

I was pleased and shy, and answered:

" Oh, I couldn't put it into words."

But a moment afterwards I stammered out:

" ' Where two or three are gathered together . . .'
The old coins seem newly minted for me. . . . I
mean . . . Love is God, and Jesus was the greatest
Lover, the very son of Love, and Love is Life; and
oh, I can't be articulate, but this our shared feeling
in Love's name, which is the opposite of the hate
feeling that is war. . . . In glimpses, in flashes, it
comes . . . a meaning. Anyhow, that's as near as
I can come to saying what a friend may mean. I feel
the truth of more than I can explain."

He smiled, amused, but not mocking, and announced:

" Thoreau says: ' The only way to speak the
truth is to speak lovingly.' Vauvenargues says:
' Les grandes pensées viennent du cœur.' Forgive
my accent. Both great men, great thinkers, and
neither what you might call in the fold. I get
peace of mind, refreshment, from being with your
mother."

He nodded and went out, pressing his hand on my
shoulder as he passed me; and by his method of
withdrawal he made me feel I was his friend. I
heard him go into mother's sitting-room.

Doris must have been waiting for him to go, for

she bounced into the room directly afterwards.   As
soon as ever she began to let out what had apparently been bottled up for some time inside her
(though her mind's bottling capacity was not great),
I realised that I took her for granted almost as completely as I took Roger, the terrier, and that I was
fond of her in the same sort of way.   Nor did I take
her engagement seriously; the thought of it seemed
funny merely, and of her marriage, incredible.   I
don't know if other brothers are the same in this.
At any rate, I thought, " I'll get to know Doris," as
one pulls down a book whose name and binding
have been so long familiar that one feels one has
read it, discovers that one hasn't, and decides to
begin.

In this spirit I listened to Doris, inveighing against
the stupid old war which kept her " darling boy "
from her, " just when we might be having such lovely
times together.   And it's no good talking — being
engaged is being engaged, and it's a waste of time
that can't come again, being away from each other
now."

And again she insisted that I was a horrid old
thing to have broken off my engagement, because
these things always ran in threes, and she couldn't
help having " sort of fears " that something might
happen between her and Jack, and that she couldn't
bear anything odious of that kind to happen.   Of
course she wasn't really nervous about Jack's safety
(he was a motor expert and in the transport) because he was practically out of the danger zone except when he had to see a car that had broken down

near the firing line; and the nearest a shell had ever burst to him was fifty yards; but she could not help being nervous about broken engagements running in threes, like the fall of wickets, and ever so many things, and I *must* say something to comfort her and tell her she was silly or something.

So I told her that mine had never been a proper engagement, because Amy had wanted time to think it over. Amy had been previous in telling mother, that was all. And who had been naughty enough to worm the news out of mother? I called her a darling little goose, and kissed her, and said it was horrid bad luck about the war and never seeing Jack. At which she asked me: " I say, do you think it's true it makes a man of . . . of a man? "

I couldn't help smiling at her sudden earnestness.

" They all say so," I answered, hedging.

" Well, do you know what? " She spoke defiantly. " I think it's silly rubbish, whoever says it. I'm sure he'd be much more of a man being with me, and working to make a home. So there! "

" You stick to your opinion, then, for all it's worth."

She looked at me doubtfully, uncertain whether I was teasing her or not; so I hugged her as best I could and added warmly: " I think it's worth a jolly good lot."

She answered my hug and said: " Oh, Jimmie, I do love him! It seems ages since I saw him. My eyes ache to see him. Of course when he's here I quarrel with him and tease him and have all sorts of fun; but when he goes away, he does seem to take a great bit of me with him. Don't think it silly of me to talk like that."

" I don't think it is silly at all," I answered manfully, for as she spoke I wondered whether I should feel " like that " when Corinna went away. My talks with Doris and Dr. Redman had stirred my heart to anxiety. I remembered that eleven fifteen was the time of her train's departure, and that till then there was one day and a negligible number of hours, which were slowly slipping by.

I dreaded finding that I was simply and sensibly in love with Corinna in the ordinary way. That would somehow diminish by explanation the wonder of what had happened. Supposing, too, that I asked her to marry me as I should be obliged to do, and that she said " No "— how she would know her own mind on such a point ! — the wonder would be turned indubitably to a very usual misery, and misery would be the end of it all. I could imagine nothing else, and that word of the wise, illusion — or were they only the crafty-wise ? — troubled my mind.

Doris announced that I was getting more and more and more of a darling; and her high spirits tumbled away her little treasure of gloom, because she, the dear kid, did treasure any little store of gloom; for it was unusual to her then, and made her feel important.

She twirled off in a dance, waving her arms and chanting:

" Oh ! When the stupid old war *is* over, and he *does* come back for good, oh, what a lovely beano, beano, beano we will have ! "

She hugged herself with a little squeal of delight and Maudallened, as she called it, out of the room.

I was supposed to rest, so I lay down flat on the couch and shut my eyes.   A new idea instantly came to me: that the man who had received so much from a woman, as I had received from Corinna and who was not in love with her, must surely be a contemptible fellow.   It was not a restful idea.   I began to wonder if I knew at all what this " being in love " really meant.   Wasn't it due precisely to the fact that Corinna made no appeal to the lower side of my nature that she had been able to introduce this pervading holiness to me?   The antagonism between the spirit and the flesh must be a real thing, or it could not have gained such sway over the minds of men.   I must in ignorance have bumped into what Dr. Redman called one of the great laws of life.   Yet I was puzzled by the memory of much that Corinna had said, especially of the words, " Love will always be to me a glad deliberate thing."

I swerved again.   I knew no other method of approach to a woman than the curious mixture of solemnity and jocose artfulness, of slyness and a rather ominous silence, which had marked my amatory adventures in the past; and the thought of such behaviour with Corinna was inconceivable.   Fancy " taking liberties " with Corinna!

A riot started in me, as I lay with closed eyes on the couch.   One faction assumed superiority and declared its gladness that I loved Corinna as a child loves its mother, that no baseness entered into my love for her; while the other faction clamoured and shouted against its exclusion, until the cold superior was shouted down, and then, having cleared the ground by its clamour remained sulky, ashamed and dumb.

In the lull the thought came: " I can't let Corinna see what kind of a beast lurks in me "; and I began to dread lest it might break loose in her presence.

" Ass to worry!   Ass to worry!   Let things take their course," I cried out to myself as wisely as you might cry out to a boy, first learning to swim, that quietly does it.   His struggles continue, and so did mine, though I knew that they were absurd.   Moreover they were made more frantic for me by my suddenly remembering my exclamation to Amy: "Honesty is a man's soul.   Oh, Amy, I'm learning!"   And I tried, without success, to mock the memory away by adding, " Oh, Amy, I am! "

Then all the fine words I had spoken to Amy about the sacredness of love came grinning in upon me, and seemed ridiculous.   But what amazed me was that the sacredness which ought to have vanished like a touched bubble before this ridicule, induced by bald visions of physical fact, did not vanish, but remained as substantial as the couch on which I lay.   Sacredness and obscenity jostled in my mind, to its confusion, and neither would yield an inch   Only in a kingdom of heaven, surely, could this lion and this lamb be at peace.   And I gained some time by wondering which was lion and which was lamb, and which I wanted devoured.

Then my reason, backed by authority, pointed to

the necessity of a definite choice between the two; even while something else in me wished vaguely but with determination that the two should be reconciled. Parallel lines do not meet, my reason asserted; but the wish spread until, facing every physical fact of love, it calmly required me to believe that one was impossible without the other. Accordingly I tried to floor this wish, as it unrolled itself, with a sneer: " You might as well deny the fact that there's a higher and a lower side to every man's nature."

But the sneer was foiled by the senseless conundrum:

" And which is which? "

What is man, then? A spirit or an animal? And quite patly came the answer: a man only ceases to be an animal when he obeys certain human conventions, and, not pairing like the beasts of the field, goes to church before celebrating his nuptials. That was as unanswerable as a sledge-hammer.

Then what had I meant by faltering out to Dr. Redman that woman was meant to be the link for a man between himself and nature and life? And what on God's earth had I meant by declaring to Amy with so much conviction that if I loved a woman nothing could make my love more sacred? No wonder the poor child thought that I was spoofing her. I floundered in the muddle.

I had told Corinna that I was a baby. The full extent of my babyishness then dawned upon me. My ignorance seemed unexampled and complete.

If there was anything but folly and obstinacy in my wish why was there a general consent to silence

about the physical facts of love; silence so general
and so pervading that there were no words but obscene words with which I could think of it, let alone
speak of it, to another?   Certainly all through my
life that side of my nature had been expressed only
in what was bawdy or unpleasant; and one of the
most boring things about my service was that I had
hardly a moment's peace from bawdy talk.   A little,
of course, I liked as much as any man, but it must be
at the right moment and from the right person,
whereas bawdy was the main topic in camp.   All
roads led to Rome; it was an obsession.

I wasn't ashamed of myself.   I was simply puzzled.   There was the sacredness which I worshipped
in Corinna; there was the bawdy which I liked at
times and disliked at others, and to which general
consent had relegated the actualities of love.   My
wish persisted that these irreconcilables should be
united; and it persisted, though my mind grew dizzy
at the depth of the chasm which divided them.   And
all the while each seemed, by some mysterious process, to have the power of making the other more
real.

"It is damned strange," I said to myself, "that
now I come to think of it I've never talked seriously
about this to any one, and I've never read a serious
book about it.   Yet I've always been curious about
it, and thought my curiosity rather nasty.   About
bawdy and what can be bought I know as much as
most men.   About love I know nothing whatever, or
how a decent man approaches a decent woman.   It
stands to reason there must be a difference other than

saying to one, " Will you marry me? " and to the other, " All right; I'll come."

I saw no clue. The irreconcilables stared at me. The only comfort to be found was in the thought that I couldn't be in love with Corinna or I shouldn't be thinking in that way. But the comfort was slight. I knew that I should feel lost and alone when she was gone, and I asked myself why she should trouble to write to me every day or at all.

More I wanted from her, more, all the keenlier for the vagueness of what that more actually meant.

" I must matter to her in her life," I cried. I could not bear the thought of her going away and perhaps forgetting me.

Again the thought came to me: " Honesty is a man's soul," and no smallest doubt of its truth came with it. Only I realised something new: that to be honest is not always as easy as copybooks and moral teachers suggest, and that in this case, for instance, I was too ignorant about myself and Corinna and everything else, for that matter, to be able to be honest. " I'll be as honest as I know how to be," I very humbly thought; and the resolution remained strong in spite of the little rider my reason was quick to add: " And in your fumbling attempts at honesty you'll probably give a totally false impression."

Yet (believe it or no, I can only state the fact) I was unaware of what I stood to lose or gain, and I could not see how this trend of thought fitted in at all with what had happened to me; it seemed a side issue merely, freakish and unimportant, for all its interest. It amazes me now that I could have been so blind. My blindness, I think, was caused by my intense desire for things to remain as they were between me and Corinna; any change appeared to me as necessarily a change for the worse, and the obvious change of falling in love with her the certain worst. That was why I gave such a welcome to any sort of proof that this worst change had not occurred. Whether other men have the same gift of self-deception that I possessed, I cannot say, but I am inclined to think that they may have.

I emerged from my rest in no very tranquil frame of mind. "To think is one thing; to act is another," I said to myself cheerfully. "I don't know which I'm silliest at. Plump at it, my little friend. To be yourself you'll have to be the most egregious ass that ever chewed a thistle. Thank God, I've had the sense to own to her that I am an utter baby. That's one step, anyhow, in the right direction."

And I wondered if a man had ever attained the blissful state when he no longer thought one thing at one moment and its blank opposite at the next.

The only apparent result of my riotous rest was the creation of the dread lest I should be no longer in touch with the holiness I worshipped in Corinna. Why should a child like to pull his snowdrop to bits? Should I have pressed and dried and cherished it? Snowdrop indeed! My genius for footling seemed limitless. Snowdrop! She came upon me refreshing as a mountain wind when a burst of sunshine has turned its anger to a laugh. Stuffiness scattered at her approach; all sickly fancies and nasty little desires fled.

  " Never again will I forget." I glowed in righteousness. " Nor ever again wish to drag her down to my level. Fancy a man wanting to paw a creature of glory like Corinna ! "

I was so exalted that the chit-chat and homeliness of tea-table triviality could not lower my mood of exaltation. I floated in the air. Never before had I felt so sensitive to majesty.

  " She is supreme," I thought. " She has caught the secret of the wind and the sunshine. She is health and life and beauty. They stream from her presence. The world takes on new meaning because I've seen her."

And visions of the world's beauty gleamed within my mind, stored there by memory for this moment when they might receive their proper tribute of worship, until this moment withheld.

  " Within me, within me ! It's all within me," sang my heart. The stars shone there and the moon; the sea was stretched out before me, lapping against the shore; night passed and the dawn came, and with the rising sun the ripples and the wet sand took on the light and laughed and danced. The change was from one beauty to another, and I could appreciate it. I, the little man who had through Corinna's power passed from gloom to what I felt of the ecstasy of joy and worship. Love for man, colour for the earth. And oh ! swift as the wind is the mind of man !

Rivers I saw, and their remembered beauty took

on significance as the sea and wet sand took on the colour and the light. I stood on a hill-top on a showery day in April and felt the jolly rain-drops spank against my cheek — a gay little battery of them — and watched a black cloud sweep across the sky and light come pouring along the valley, and colour, colour, colour everywhere shining from the wet earth, from the washed wet air, from the trees and hedges and grass-blades, drenched in jewel-drops of brightness. "Within me, within me! It's all within me," sang my heart.

I went to my temple among the pines, up the hill, its slope clad in aisles of pine-trees, with their smell of health, dark and quiet, listening to the wind's sad song in their branches. Over the soft earth I passed among their purple trunks; through aisles of them rising straightway from the curling bracken and the sprawling brambles; and my footsteps made no sound over the springy path, a mattress of pine-needles and cool earth, as I entered the place — my temple — where eleven giant pine-trees and two beeches had space for growth and had grown to their full stature. The temple waited for me, for I brought what only that part of Nature herself which is man can bring — I brought the spirit of worship which I had caught from Corinna and which made me at one with the age and austerity of the trees. "Within me, within me!" sang my heart. "It's all within me."

And the moors. They came to life with their rolling stretches of heather; now in hushed greyness, the emblem of all sadness; now in weeping, drifting mist and rain; now in a buffeting great laughing wind, with shoots of sunshine and white clouds racing across the sky — what place comparable with moors for feeling the sky — and a wicked touch of ice in the wind and no dust as it swept over miles of clean moorland and blew through you as you leaned against it and shouted to your friend near by, as on board a ship, to make him hear through the wind's jubilance.

I saw all one walk I had taken on such a day, how we skirted a sweep of the shore by mighty cliffs and struck inland by heaps from disused mines, down a steep gully through which babbled a stream, and up either steep side of the gully trees thickly grew, with here and there a peeping primrose.   Up and up we climbed from the warm bottom, up and up we climbed out of cultivation on to the moor again and into the wind that laughed and buffeted.   We followed the track, mere wheelruts in the heather, with moor on rolling moor as far as the eye could see — a world of moor, with little birds that fluttered from bush to bush of heather (such heather!), and every now and then a grouse that fled our coming with a startled shout, swerved down at a distance among the heather and sat quacking on like a fat duck a little longer always than we expected.   We saw hares. We heard the cry of the curlews.   Then through all the gates — seven of them, is it, or is it eight? — that shut off the peace of Harwood Dale from the bleak moorland, tucked away in its rich seclusion under a towering heather-covered hill, a thick black line against the horizon, and falls shorn off like a cliff by the sea, into miles and more miles of wilder moorland. The hill looks one sheer steep slope to its top, but as we climbed it from the wooded dale, left the woods below and climbed on, we came to a little grass-clad, unexpected plateau, not visible from the valley, where sheep grazed and hawthorns grew and a line of birches, the straggling advance-guard of the larchwood. "What's that?" my friend called, pointing to a dip by the birches. "Daffodils!" I shouted. "Wild daffodils!" They were. A yellow sheet of them, hundreds and hundreds, tight and short and undisturbed, flung out and flowering. Such a find! We lay among them, and then up and up the hill again, steepest towards the top, and on the top a level flatness, as though the hill had been sliced to its shape by some Titan's sword, and beneath and around were moors and moors, and above, the sky, and lying in the warm heather the wind rushed over us.

"Within me, within me. It's all within me," sang my heart. All I had ever seen of beauty in the world flowed through my mind in swift visions, and I seemed to be enjoying it all for the first time, as though the memory had been storing itself with the substance that needed God's touch to kindle it to life.

You smile and say I exaggerate? I frown and answer that you have never loved. That is what happened to me. That is what happens when a breath of love blows ever so gently upon a little human creature; it makes him one with the stars, one with the sky and earth and wind and sea, and with the flowers and trees on the earth; one with Nature, the great mother of us all, trees and weeds, men, flowers and grasshoppers. For Love is God. What else did Jesus say, Jesus your Church's one foundation?

I felt one with nature and all life during those moments of quiet enchantment while my lips moved to the usual chit-chat and ate and drank the usual tea —not at all in a dream, mind you, or gazing at Corinna. I was careful to appear a little more on the spot than usual to hide my state, which was too real to need parade and too intimate to bear it.

I was unaccustomed to the heights, however. I could breathe there for an instant in vision; I could not live there. When tea was cleared and I was alone with Corinna, I was conscious of nothing else but delight in the glow that came from her, like that from the sky at sunset. I did not want to look at her. It was not a question of eyes or nose or bearing. To be alone with her was enough.

At last I turned to where she stood, looking into the fire, and she turned and smiled and sighed. Then she pulled the tuffet near me and sat down on it.

"Oh, James," she said, "I am so lonely and unhappy," and she put her arms on my knees and her face on her arms.

Her action was dear and natural. She wanted a little kindness from a friend. But I sat stupefied, at first with surprise, soon with fear and confusion. Not surprise at her action, or at her grief or at her confession of grief to me; but surprise at myself, for just at the very moment when for the first time in our friendship she who had given me so much honoured me by asking for gentleness, the beast in me leapt to life. I wanted to stroke her head and comfort her, be gentle with her as though she were my hurt little sister. I could not comfort her or be gentle. In my accursed ignorance shame and desire laid hot hands on me, and I saw my power of gentleness leaving me when I would have given my life for its possession. A sneer usurped its place with mockery. "Now, be honest! Be honest! You know you want to. Put the one hand you have got under her chin, bend back her head and have her lips. She can't get away. What's it matter whether she likes it or no. Besides, all girls like it. What's purity? Faugh! You're merely afraid. What else did she come there for? Now's your chance. Take it. Be a man. Be a man and take it!"

I knew that to kiss her in that spirit was an outrage, that the wish was a blasphemy; but the wish grew, and as it grew my strength of resistance diminished.

"What right has she to play on my feelings?" I said to myself. "It's her own lookout. I'm a man."

She sat up and looked at me. Astonishment came over her face. "Whatever is the matter?" she asked.

"Matter! Oh, nothing!" I said harshly. "I'm just damnably in love with you. That's all."

Her cheeks flushed with anger and resentment. She sprang to her feet. " Why do you speak to me like that? "

I didn't expect her to be angry; I expected her to be sympathetic.

" I don't know," I answered doggedly.

" But it's stupid," she exclaimed, and the words came quivering out of her mouth.

" Good Lord! I know that. It's worse than stupid. The folly of it! All this illusion, this prettiness, this . . . it might be excusable in a boy. . . . Being tricked along. It's utterly unfair. Oh, don't think I imagine you meant to lead me on. It's no one's fault. We can't help how we're made. I perfectly understand all you wanted was a little gentleness. Do you think I wouldn't . . . what's life? . . . to have been able to give you what you asked? Well, I couldn't; that's all. I'm a man — a beast, if you like. It doesn't much matter what you call me."

" You're talking rubbish. There's nothing beastly in being in love with a person; but when you're in love with a person, you can behave in a beastly way."

" No doubt you are right. It's not a thing you can argue about. A man's lured on by pretty dreams till he bumps into reality, and there's an end of it."

" Yes, if a man's a fool," she rapped out, " there is an end of it."

I laughed morosely:

" And you should have heard the beautiful things I said the other day to poor little Amy. No wonder she thought me mad. Perhaps I am."

" Mad! You're not. You're only thickly, thickly self-satisfied. You talk of reality! Haven't our times together been real? "

" I'm too bitterly ashamed and miserable to mind anything you say. I wish to God you'd hit me. I dare say it's all my fault, but that doesn't make it any the less damnable."

She was walking up and down the room, enraged.

" If only you wouldn't be so pompous about it! Rolling in your shame and misery and all the rest of it."

" If only you'd be a little kind! "

" I'm too angry to be kind. Not angry with you so much as . . . . These stupidities, they infuriate me."

" I'm not worth it."

Up and down the room Corinna paced.

" It's what you stand for. This senseless division! These water-tight compartments! " She stopped and stretched her arms wide apart, shaking each hand in turn. " These kicking scales! Here an angel and lovely dreams, here a beast and reality."

She tossed her arms up and began again her fierce pacings, as she flung out with contempt:

" Oh yes, and then of course, illusion. Cold-hearted deadness, or the consolation of religion or any old shelter where you can be snug and safe and think no more. And a man's lost, or a woman's lost. And the wretch creeps a vampire among men — how does it go? — infecting all with his own hideous ill. Oh, it sickens me. I can't bear it. The same lie, the same lie, spreading, spreading, spreading its energy-sapping evil of complacence. And such is life, they say, and shake their woolly heads, when it's not life or anything but their own stupidity and fear and half-heartedness."

She became inarticulate with rage. I put in:

"You needn't be unjust to me, anyhow. I can't help the facts of human nature."

"That's it," she stormed. "The old senseless catchwords! Trot them out! Human nature! Human nature! As though you knew anything about human nature. You don't even take the trouble to learn. Your own experiences mean nothing. Your dreams are human nature; your beastliness, as you call it, is human nature; and it's human nature too that's got the power to weld the two into harmony, and that's a man. It's all human nature; and God is the most human thing in nature. Oh, it's not your fault. You've just been to a public school and the 'Varsity, and been turned out into a good little puppet, and it's only your dearness and good-nature that's made you see all the good everywhere and be content. It's a shame. Don't you see that your dreams are as real as the little physical feeling you call being in love which made you horrid to me when you wanted to be kind? Why, supposing I did respond to you in that way, you'd only be frightened. As it is, you're more frightened than anything else."

"You know a lot about me," I said, feeling like a slapped schoolboy and speaking like one.

"Of course I do.   What's a woman for, except to complete a man's knowledge of himself?   A sort of toy, I suppose, you think, eh?   Thank you!   And even as a toy you'd be able to get nothing out of her.   It's pathetic.   You think you're in love with me.   You don't know the beginnings of what love means yet.   The first little touch of desire. . . . Oh, I've no patience with it.   And you, too, you, with the possibilities in you of being a great lover. Never for me, alas!   I'm about two hundred years older than you are.   Get it out of your head that you're in love with me, or you'll be building up a wretched little hut of misery in your mind to live in all your life.   I won't have it.   You're my friend. I care for you.   You've got to be free and fine, as you were meant to be.   Do you know what poetry is?"

"Yes.   No.   I like . . . I like some . . . all right," I stammered, feeble against the rushing tempest of her.

"I'll tell you.   Poetry redeems from decay the visitations of the divinity in man.   It strips the veil of familiarity from the world and lays bare the naked and sleeping beauty which is the spirit of its forms.   And listen, listen.   It's Shelley. . . .   It purges from our inward sight the film of familiarity which obscures the wonder of our being . . . the wonder, do you hear, of our being.   It compels us to feel that which we perceive and to imagine that which we know.   Imagine that which we know.

That's what you've got to do. You need a lot of poetry."

She suddenly stopped and stood quite still, erect, staring in front of her. " So do we all," she added in a low voice, and without looking at me she walked swiftly to the door.

" Corinna," I cried. " Don't you go away."

She came right back to me.

" Yes, I must go. Her voice had entirely changed. " I'm getting rude and excited. We'll have a long talk — not now, dear — and face things out. Two things you must keep in your thoughts uppermost: that I'm immensely fond of you, and that I'm more fond of you now, after this. Don't forget. Your honesty and you are such a dear. Yes, I'll say it. Why not? I'll be your sister. You wait and see what a sister. Do let me. Such a sister you shall have, my dear. You see if we don't make our friendship into a lovely life-giving reality, in spite of all the rubbish that's ever been talked."

I couldn't speak, or no doubt I should have added to the heap. Such a sister! She gave me such a kiss. I have spoken of her holiness before; I knew more closely what it meant then.

XIV

" THE wonder of our being. . . ." The words
sounded on in my mind and recalled what Dr. Redman had said months before: that he who realises
the mystery of all things in life is not likely to be
made ill by one manifestation of it. I understood
what he meant. It explained the dwindling concern
about my visitant. I was interested in him, certainly; but I was far more interested in mysteries
nearer at hand, of this world rather than of the world
of dream, or from whatever world it was he came.
One mystery seemed to belong to a state of sickness,
the other to a state of health, and promised deeper
health; to it, moreover, was added the excitement of
a clue, on the thread of which my fingers were closing.

I was awake to the wonder of our being; ready to
learn, that is to say. And the greatest wonder was
that my blunt stupid confession and Corinna's outburst of anger did not scatter the holiness but increased it. Nor was it less of a fact for its mystery.
It was as real as the smell of an onion. To some,
perhaps, it may not be a mystery, just as some may
know why an onion smells rank and a tulip faintly
delicious.

Two things were clear about this holiness, this
state of health with its large promise of an ever-
widening prospect: one was that self-satisfaction, for

which Dr. Redman and Corinna chid me, slew it; the
other was that honesty, into whatever depths of silli-
ness or turpitude it might seem to point, always
encouraged it to thrive. Self-satisfaction slammed
down like an iron shutter, and left you, impenetrable,
alone with your stagnant little self; honesty threw
open the windows.

But to think with me was still to worry, and I could
not worry. I rejoiced too deeply in the knowledge
that a great beauty which I thought had passed from
my life had become more intimately mine. The
tumult of gladness crushed the small voice piping
that a rejected suitor ought not to be glad. Not to
be glad? I was glad. Isn't a little boy glad who
has sighed for the moon and been given an electric
torch?

I shall never forget the talk I had with Corinna
next morning. It sweetened every recess of my being. I emerged from the chrysalis a whole man.
Much must have happened in the mind of Paul of
Tarsus (I've never liked him) before the heavens
opened and he heard the great voice of God. I have
tried to recount the happenings in mine. In my earliest stirrings I had dreaded some kind of conversion,
lest I might be forced into some box of the devout.
Conversion, after all, awaited me, though not of the
kind I had imagined, the only kind I had been able to
imagine — not a shutting off, but an opening out
from vagueness and shadows and dread and an obscure sense of sin, to light and fulness and comple-
tion. Oh, I may stumble by the way, but I know the
direction now. I know the light is there. I have

seen what I can never forget, what no man could forget when the knowledge blazed upon him as it blazed upon me.   I know what to pray for.   I know what I want to attain.   I know that freedom lies within a man, and that freedom is in the gift of Love.

Spring loosening the earth from the hold of winter; rain on a parched land; sunshine bursting the veils of mist; to every token of health and vigour, beauty, growth and life her coming gave intention.

Corinna talked with me that morning.   She said many wonderful things to me, but a greater wonder than anything spoken lay in my own developed consciousness of the holiness of her presence.   Corinna's power was her womanliness — her grace, her charm, her quality; and she was honest as a spring wind. Yet there was nothing blunt or manly about her honesty.   A difference exists, though I cannot define it, between a woman's honesty and a man's, just as there is a difference between a boy's running and a girl's.

I was a little fearful of the talk, although I looked forward to it with nearly all my heart.   I had to brace myself to hear the whiplash crack with the thought of how much good a sting or two would do me, and of how much I deserved it.   But no whiplash cracked.   She was pleased and shy when she came into my room, and talked of other things, putting me more and more at my ease, leading me up (or opening me out) to what she wanted to say. We talked of her passion for dancing, and she told me about the pioneer work of Diana Watts, and how the dance might be a rite in which the body was offered in perfect condition, stretched and naked to

the sunshine. "So linked up with the brain," she
cried. "All spirit, all spirit, so alive and sensitive
and strong." I told her of my grandfather and of
my familiar, and I read her some extracts from the
packed note-books, about which she was enthusiastic.
I told her of Dr. Redman, and of how angry he had
made me; of my flirtation with the Church of England; and when the subject she had come to discuss
with me no longer overshadowed us, she took my
hand and smiled and said:

"I am so sorry I was rude to you yesterday and
rough and excited."

"Oh, don't be sorry!" I exclaimed. "What else
could you possibly have been? Besides, all you said
was true, except perhaps . . . I expect I was more
frightened of you than anything else, not so much of
you as of . . . of . . . well, my own ignorance, and
the feeling that the end had come of a lovely thing."

"It is the beginning, you know, really."

"What's so queer is that when I'm talking with
people like Amy or Doris I feel I'm somehow a sea-
soned man of the world, knowing all there is to be
known, with a sort of prestige in simply being a man
at all. It's taken gloriously for granted that a man
knows this and a man knows that — what, exactly,
I haven't the ghost of a notion — and one plays up
to it instinctively. It's very funny. But when I'm
talking with you, I feel like a child talking with its
mother, quite ignorant and longing to learn, and
rather naughty. Yet you're far more of a woman
than all that lot. Not that I don't like Doris and
Amy: I do. I'm awfully fond of them both, but

somehow they seem fantastic and unreal. You're substantial. You're real. You're solid. You're bread to a starving man. They are more like some sort of delicate puff."

I spoke with enthusiasm. Corinna laughed.

" I don't know that I like to be called anything so dull as bread."

I laughed, too, and declared that she knew what I meant.

" What made me most angry was that I could not give you more. I might if I were different. But I'm cold and reserved. . . ."

I interrupted with a hoot at her calling herself cold. She went on: " It's no use forcing things. One can't go against one's nature, even if one isn't very pleased with one's nature. Why should I hold back when I'm so fond of you? It isn't even holding back. There's nothing to hold back. It would be unfair on you to pretend."

" Oh, don't talk about giving me more, when you have given me so much. It's my stupidity. But don't you think by the queer circumstances of our friendship — by your loving me back to life in your arms as you did — we have somehow reached a stage of intimacy that few lovers reach in the usual way, that for us it would be going back? It's only this moment flashed upon me."

" There's truth in that, dear; but be careful. It's so dangerous to . . . to speak of the usual way or to admit any scoff at the lovely facts of nature. How can I put it? Oh, I should hate you to stop. I should hate you to feel that what I give you is all a

woman can give.   No, let me go on.   I want to
free you, so that you may become the lover you
were meant to be.   I want you never to forget that
our friendship, our love, however beautiful it is, and
however it may grow in beauty, is almost nothing
compared with : . . . compared with the full great
music.   To forget that would be to build our friendship on a lie."

"I'd rather sit quietly and talk with you than be
the lover of the most beautiful woman in the world."

"Oh, at the moment, you darling; but you speak
in ignorance.   I don't want to tie you up in a cold
barren dream."

"Warm, life-giving dream, you mean," I interposed.

"It's bad of you," she laughed, "to confuse me."

"I won't have even you belittle our friendship."

"I'm not, I'm not.   It's precious to me, and for
its own sake especially you must let me go on, and
you must understand.   I will have nothing false between us.   And the falsest, commonest, easiest thing
is to deny what should be finest in your nature.   Denial leads to misuse, always and always and always.
I want you to surmount it, not to deny it.   Face
facts and surmount it by knowledge and control.   I
should hate you to be content with me, almost as
much as I should hate you to be caught out by some
pretty little puss."

"The last's unlikely now, I think.   The first —
well, I do see what you mean, but I don't like it."

"But you must like it; only so, can we get all there
is to be got out of our friendship.   And you can't

have any idea yet how much that is. There are, quite roughly speaking, three distinct kinds of love, for a moment to limit and label. There's our love; there's love with mutual passion in it; there's love with the desire for new life in it."

" Our love has given me new life," I interrupted a little resentfully.

She waved her hand to silence my interruption.

" All three may find expression with one person, though they almost never do. Usually . . ." She began to pace up and down the room. " Usually . . ." She was obviously fighting to find words; she flung up her hands in a characteristic gesture. " Oh, I'm not clear enough in my own mind. The conditions of life are so disgusting, and come swamping in. Every care is taken in all our customs to kill love, to make love impossible by degrading the body. There is no fusion of body and spirit. Without love there can be no fusion. Ignorance and shame are fostered. Our customs are suitable for monkeys, not for men and women. The most life-giving, health-giving, energy-releasing thing in our nature is dragged in the mud, sterilised, despised, abused. Oh, to be free of custom's evil taint! The conditions of life will remain horrible so long as men fetter and revile God's power in them. Sex is God's power, though the word has become sticky. It's the flower of a man's or a woman's nature. Fetter and revile it and it uses man and becomes what it is now, loathsome; but give it its true value and beauty, and man can use it, and it becomes what it is meant to be and will be, and even now sometimes is, the sweetener of life, the creating power. We misuse our nature; we degrade our bodies, and breed in consequence on every side the germs of hatred and envy and greed and sloth, and all the passive, miserable, inactive things that find their only expression in destroying, in war. It's no good to blame the nation that strikes first; this taint, this evil, this denial of life is everywhere, is in our selves. The evil grows acute until at last it breaks out in the awful calamity, in the monstrous unreason, of war, and the passion for service which is the deepest instinct in human nature, the very love spirit, is caught hold of and used, not for fruition, but for destruction. That is the last and most terrible blasphemy against life, the culmination of all our misuse. Oh yes, now is the great parting of the ways. One way or the other every one of us must go. Forward, with effort towards love and life and freedom; or backwards, drifting, towards indifference, hatred and destruction. For the forward-goers the word is to clean the dirt and sentiment and shame that chokes our bodies and stifles our spirits from love's influence."

She stopped and stretched her arms out, almost in supplication:

"Oh, I have a vision of an army of lovers, men and women, in such condition! Brave, young-hearted and gallant; gay, fastidious, laughter-loving; known by the spring in their step, the life in their eyes. . . ."

She leaned forward to me almost in anger.

"They say visions are Utopian and silly. Why not have visions? Nothing could be more silly and

more hellish than trench warfare.   They say human
nature is human nature.   But it's human nature, too,
to have visions, and to live up to them; and it's human nature, too, to long for a finer kind of existence,
and it was a human being wrote:

> " ' Of naught but earth can earth make us partaker,
>   But knowledge makes a king most like his Maker.'

And though it may be a dream for all the world, for
us it is no dream.   We, you and I, can start it now in
our lives, living it, and it's that, this kinship of vision,
which is the body and soul of friendship.   We, you
and I, can spread love's influence through our lives;
let our lives be conductors of Love's power to earth.
In human love lies the religion we are seeking, in
human love, with its union of body and spirit, with
its glad discipline, with its ceremony of delight which
lifts the whole fabric of a man's or a woman's nature,
and frees that passion for service into its right direction, to create life, not to destroy it, to leave this
earth — such a setting for our days! — not more
desolate, but actually more beautiful, for our brief
presence on it.   Love is the creative spirit; nothing
good in art or life can be done without love.   This
is the great parting of the ways.   There must be no
more hovering and faltering, no more drifting and
doubt and fear."

She seemed to soar as she spoke, to be poised over
me, quivering in the air.   I cried out with tears in
my voice:

"We will.   I swear we will build our friendship
into a lovely thing.   I have no doubt, no fear.   They

will intrude, but the memory of you will scatter them."

She seemed to droop and shrink before me; Corinna small and trembling and fragile, hid her face in her hands.

"It's so pathetic. A little creature like me. To think this, to feel this, to know this. In all this sea of waste and misery. Why can't one drift and sink quietly? This faith, this love, this hope, this knowledge! Why is it? How can one bear the anguish of remaining sensitive? What's it all for? You and me, touched by the faintest gleam of love's sun . . . what might be only a mockery. . . . Yet we know, don't we?"

"Yes, we do," I said, shaken by the change in her.

"How can we stand against all the blasphemy of hatred and indifference! How can we breathe in all this smother of ignorance and coldness! How can we live!"

She asked no question. The words and the way she said them put my mind in sudden darkness, as though she had blown the light out of a lantern.

"I don't know," I said.

She did not speak; she sat, crumpled under a weight that crushed her. She lay at the foot of a mountain of grief, far beyond my reach. I did not know before of such grief's existence, or that a human being had such daring of endurance. For at last she slowly raised her head and said in a clear low voice without a falter in it, so simply:

"I'll tell you why."

I waited. But still she did not move; she did not

speak, and I felt that she was summoning up all her reserve of strength, as she repeated in the same low clear voice as before, so simply:

"I'll tell you."

Then she rose. I knew her rising was an act of courage, though I did not know why, and she walked slowly to the window, and humbly, reverently, like a priestess before the shrine in which the holiest of holies was kept, she pulled the curtain right back, and said, still drooping, still frail and little, still crushed, said with the directness of a shy, obedient child:

"Because we have all the beauty of the world to help us."

She caught hold of the black handle of the window, and I thought for a moment that she was going to faint. Her hand showed me how tightly she was holding. She stood looking out for some time. My worship for her seemed to pass out and beyond her to the sky and clouds, the treetops and distant hills on which she was looking. Then she rearranged the curtain as it usually hung, and came back to me.

"That's why," she said. "We can and must. And that's why one sometimes feels lonely and tired and sad. You know now."

The simplicity with which she spoke was like a caress, or rather like a sacrament which gave me the freedom of her heart, the right of entry. I knew then what all lovers seek in the last intimacy of love. The physical facts of love took on the naked and sleeping beauty which is the spirit of their forms.

The veil of familiarity was torn aside. I was at the heart of life.

I took her hand and said:

"One day I'll make you know how much you've given me."

She kissed my hand.

I made no effort to stop the tears that rolled down my cheek. I said:

"Only my life can show it."

"We little human beings," she said, "how we do live by each other!" and she wiped my eyes with her handkerchief.

I looked at the clock on the mantelpiece. It was half-past twelve. I hated to think of time.

"Do read to me," I said. "I want to hear your voice. Anything."

She went out and fetched a book, full of extracts in her own writing.

"My book of common prayer," she said. "Oh, look here," and she showed me a line, which she read —"'Everything that lives is holy'"— putting such wealth of meaning into the word "lives." "And in exact proportion as they do live," she added. I settled down to listen, and she said:

"I don't know that I want to read to you much."

"Please don't waste time."

She said I mustn't dragoon her, and began to read. She had been reading scarcely a minute when the door opened abruptly, and I turned to see Doris standing in the doorway with a letter in her hand. My anger at the interruption vanished at the sight of her. Her face was white and pinched. .

She walked into the middle of the room, leaving the door wide open, not looking at Corinna or at me.

"I'm sorry to be a nuisance," she said in a shrill voice which did not belong to her, "but, Jimmie, I must come in. Do you know what? He's been killed. Read this."

"I'll go, dear," Corinna whispered, and went.

I read the letter, which was from Jack's mother. I wished with all my heart that Doris would cry.

I found nothing better to say than "How did the letter come?"

"By car," she answered. "It's such a surprise. I thought he was quite safe. You see, there's a relic — all that's been found of him — a button. Is there anything left to bury after a shell has hit a man?"

I was dumb with horror. She went on in the same terrible shrill voice:

"I thought he was quite safe. Why have I never realised about the war — not till this moment? Am I a fool? I do now. All his letters were joky except for lover bits. As if it were merely a nuisance his having to be away from me. What does the Latin mean exactly?"

She pointed to the letter. I read the words aloud: "Sed miles; sed pro patria," and said: "But a soldier; but for his country."

She gave a shuddering sigh that brought colour to her cheeks. She stiffened her back. Young and lovely and defiant she looked, yet bruised, like a boy who has been unjustly beaten.

"Why have they done it?" she cried. "Those Germans!"

Hatred spoke in her voice. All her young un-reasoning love was turned to unreasoning hate.

"Have you always thought me callous?" she asked sharply.

"I was thankful that some of the horror of it missed you."

She gave a hard little laugh.

"Well, it's got me now."

"Oh, Doris!" I cried as though I were trying to call her back from some dark place.

"I see now it's a holy war," she declared.

"Darling, one's such a poor comfort. I'm so sorry."

"I need no comfort, Jimmie."

"Don't shut me out!"

"I need no comfort, Jimmie. It's as clear as day. I know what to do."

"What?"

"Help make shells."

She smiled.

"Couldn't you . . . couldn't you do hospital work?"

"What! Be a nurse like Amy? Oh, I wish a girl could really fight."

"Not if you'd . . . Doris, I've killed a man."

She did not heed the shame in my voice. Her eyes glowed.

"That's something!" she said eagerly. "A young man? Do you think he was a lover?"

My heart cried out in agony: Little sister, what have they done to you? But I was silent. I could not by any word of mine assail her one comfort of revenge.

"They want girls in munition factories. I shall learn quickly. I shall be miserable until I start work — to help make shells."

She looked at me, and drew herself up.

"You'll see. A girl's got pluck too. No crying for me!"

And she rushed out of the room.

She left me, stunned with grief. It seemed years since Corinna had been with me. At last I looked up and out of the window, and again I saw Corinna standing by the window, and again I heard her voice say —"I'll tell you. Because we have all the beauty of the world to help us."

And a flame of sorrow burnt the truth of Corinna into my heart.

EPILOGUE

FRIENDS, that is my book. Please read it in the spirit in which it is written, and bear with its faults. Especially forgive me if I have seemed at any place to have stepped aside from the simple telling of my story and to have preached at you. Friends, believe me, it is not at you that I have preached, but at myself, to convince myself, do you see, for I am still weak in love's service, and war and hatred still scream on every side.

All night I have been writing in a farmhouse in Cornwall. Dawn is approaching. The boles of the great trees outside darken to shapes against the withdrawing night, as though they clung to the departing darkness. The old white-washed wall takes to itself the whiteness of the oncoming light. The farm buildings begin to stand out. A pig grunts sleepily. A heifer begins to call angrily. A cow sniffs up the freshness. Between the noises of the awakening day the quietness of the departing night is quieter. Perceptibly the darkness withdraws. Leaves of trees, twigs on bushes, become visible. I can see the colour of a rose by the whitewashed wall. Quick little twitterings come and go and gather sound. The birds are waking. Here and there, too, quick little flutterings. A cock flaps his wings three times and crows with startling lustiness; a

distant cock answers.   Three times each they utter
their ludicrous loud salutation of the day, and the
solemnity upon which their noise breaks becomes
more potent and mysterious.   Bats flicker in the twi-
light.   A horse rattles his halter in a near stable.
Expectation grows.   And then at last, gently,
rustling through the leaves of all the trees, it comes,
the first breath of dawn.   Day has begun, a new
day.   The sun has risen.

Ah, friends, that I might share the beauty with
you!   It overcomes me.   I put my face in my arms
and pray.   This is my prayer:

" O Powers of Peace and Beauty, Love and Life,
pour through me with your influence.   Use the passion for service which lies in the heart of me and of
every one of us.   Help me to kill in myself self-
satisfaction, greed, sloth, indifference, fear, and the
other satellites of hatred and destruction which will
keep me from the kingdom of man on this earth,
which is the kingdom of love.   Make me worthy to
be used in your service, and use me.   I have been
a feeble soldier of death; with your help I want to
become a good soldier of life.   I want to be a man.
Kindle my intelligence that I may grow worthy of
manhood on this wonderful earth.   O Powers of
Peace and Beauty, Love and Life, keep me free,
keep me sensitive to your influence, keep me a lover."

THE END

PRINTED IN THE UNITED STATES OF AMERICA

THE following pages contain advertisements of a few
of the Macmillan novels.

Changing Winds

By ST. JOHN G. ERVINE

Author of "Mrs. Martin's Man," "Alice and a Family," etc.

One of the most popular stories of recent times was St. John G. Ervine's "Mrs. Martin's Man." With its publication a short time ago, a new novelist of distinct power and originality was heralded. Since that book Mr. Ervine has issued "Alice and a Family," a tale strikingly different in idea and treatment and yet not a bit less masterly, and one or two volumes of plays, all of which have gone to establish him firmly in modern letters. His new book has been awaited with more than average interest. It is entitled "Changing Winds" and is as admirable a piece of work both in its character drawing and in theme as anything its author has yet done.

THE MACMILLAN COMPANY
Publishers   64-66 Fifth Avenue   New York

Regiment of Women

By CLEMENCE DANE

This is a story of a clash of wills. How Alwynne Durrand, a sweet-natured, optimistic young girl, comes under the sway of Clare Hartill, clever, attractive, unprincipled, wholly selfish, and how in the end the spell is broken by a man,—this is the author's theme and as she handles it, it is a tremendous theme. Seldom has there been so outstanding a character in fiction as in Miss Hartill. She dominates the entire story, and though the reader cannot like her, nevertheless he will be fascinated by her, much as Alwynne is. And in addition to Miss Hartill there are other clearly drawn people in the book; Alwynne, who is all that a heroine should be; Roger, who saves Alwynne from the unhappiness towards which she seems to be moving, the Elsbeth, Alwynne's aunt, who more than once crosses swords with Clare. The tale is full of incident and variety and cannot but be welcomed by the reader who appreciates a story in which real people move and act.

THE MACMILLAN COMPANY

Publishers   64-66 Fifth Avenue   New York

Mr. Britling Sees It Through

H. G. WELLS' NEW NOVEL

NOW OVER 100,000.

" A powerful, strong story. Has wonderful pages . . . gems of emotional literature. . . . Nothing could express the whole, momentous situation in England and in the United States in so few words and such convincing tone. . . . For clear thinking and strong feeling, the finest picture of the crises in the Anglo-Saxon world that has yet been produced." — *Philadelphia Public Ledger*.

" Not only Mr. Wells' best book, but the best book so far published concerning the war." — *Chicago Tribune*.

" The most thoughtfully and carefully worked-out book Mr. Wells has given us for many a year. . . . A veritable cross-section of contemporary English life . . . admirable, full of color and utterly convincing." — *New York Times*.

" A war epic. . . . To read it is to grasp, as perhaps never before, the state of affairs among those to whom war is the actual order of the day. Impressive, true, tender, . . . infinitely moving and potent." — *Chicago Tribune*.

" For the first time we have a novel which touches the life of the last two years without impertinence. This is a really remarkable event, and Mr. Wells' book is a proud achievement. . . . The free sincerity of this book, with its unfailing distinction of tone, is beautiful . . . a creation with which we have as yet seen, in this country at least, nothing whatever to compare." — *London Times*. $1.50

THE MACMILLAN COMPANY
Publishers   64-66 Fifth Avenue   New York

EDEN PHILLPOTTS' NEW NOVEL

$1.50

" As long as we have such novels as *The Green Alleys* and such novelists as Mr. Phillpotts, we need have no fears for the future of English fiction.   Mr. Phillpotts' latest novel is a representative example of him at his best, of his skill as a literary creator and of his ability as an interpreter of life." — *Boston Transcript.*

" *The Green Alleys* is the best of all, as good a story as Mr. Phillpotts has written." — *New York Globe.*

" A drama of fascinating interest, lightened by touches of delicious comedy . . . one of the best of the many remarkable books from the pen of this clever author." — *Boston Globe.*

" Mr. Phillpotts has the gift of conveying atmosphere in a remarkable degree . . . a finely artistic piece of work." — *Philadelphia Public Ledger.*

" Strongly individualized characters, each the vessel of some human drama, crowd the pages, . . . revealed by a thousand delicate and subtle lines of portrayal." — *New York Times.*

THE MACMILLAN COMPANY
Publishers   64-66 Fifth Avenue   New York

The Turtles of Tasman

By JACK LONDON

Author of "The Valley of the Moon," "Star Rover,"
"Scarlet Plague," etc., etc.

Cloth, 12mo, $1.25

Mr. London was past-master of the short-story form of literature. Few writers were gifted. with his brilliant imagination, and still fewer were so well grounded in the technique of the art. For years he stood pre-eminent in this field both in power of theme and facility of expression. The present collection of stories is gripping, varied, and unusual, and will captivate the reader from cover to cover.

"Jack London is at his best — that peculiar best which is inimitable. . . . Nothing is more important to note, however, than the soundness of the psychology of all these stories. They are made out of the deep fibre of humanity. By command over such material does Jack London hold his place in our literature. By command over the knack of clearly flowing, acid-biting English that often takes rich colour."—*Boston Transcript*.

"Few collections of short stories from the pen of this author show a greater versatility of thought and literary style than 'The Turtles of Tasman.'"—*Boston Daily Advertiser*.

"One can get eight first-class tales in one book by one of the best writers of the present era."—*Boston Globe*.

THE MACMILLAN COMPANY.

Publishers   64-66 Fifth Avenue   New York

Lightning Source UK Ltd.
Milton Keynes UK
UKHW02n2033090418
320773UK00004B/13/P